Property Valuation Techniques

By the same authors

Property Investment (D. Isaac and J. O'Leary)
Property Valuation Principles (D. Isaac and J. O'Leary)
Property Development: Appraisal and Finance (D. Isaac, J. O'Leary and
   M. Daley)
Property Finance (D. Isaac)
Urban Economics: A Global Perspective (P.N. Balchin, D. Isaac and J. Chen)

Property Valuation Techniques

3rd edition

David Isaac

Professor of Real Estate Management, School of Architecture, Design and Construction, University of Greenwich, UK

John O'Leary

Senior Lecturer, School of Architecture, Design and Construction, University of Greenwich, UK

palgrave
macmillan

First published 2013 by
PALGRAVE MACMILLAN

Palgrave Macmillan in the UK is an imprint of Macmillan Publishers Limited, registered in England, company number 785998, of Houndmills, Basingstoke, Hampshire RG21 6XS.

Palgrave Macmillan in the US is a division of St Martin's Press LLC, 175 Fifth Avenue, New York, NY 10010.

Palgrave Macmillan is the global academic imprint of the above companies and has companies and representatives throughout the world.

Palgrave and Macmillan are registered trademarks in the United States, the United Kingdom, Europe and other countries

ISBN: 978–1–137–30241–0 paperback

This book is printed on paper suitable for recycling and made from fully managed and sustained forest sources. Logging, pulping and manufacturing processes are expected to conform to the environmental regulations of the country of origin.

A catalogue record for this book is available from the British Library.

A catalog record for this book is available from the Library of Congress.

To John and Rebecca Pelling for their valued advice
and support given to our School over the years.

Contents

Preface to the Third Edition

First published in 1991, this book is now in its third edition, but the focus remains upon exploring selected property valuation techniques. In common with earlier editions, this edition has been written with different readerships in mind. For the student, it extends the basic texts to explore valuation techniques at a level commensurate with the second and third year undergraduate levels and it also provides a basis for postgraduate work. For the practitioner, the book is not intended to be too theoretical but seeks to show the application of different techniques in contexts which are likely to be encountered in practice. Finally, it is useful for professionals who are not valuers but who may require some familiarity with the vocabulary, principles and application of the valuation toolkit. After all, property valuation and analysis is not the exclusive domain of valuation professionals, it is shared with other stakeholders who may be asset managers, property developers, landholders, accountants and corporate clients with property investments.

One of the objectives of the book is to demystify valuation techniques and in that spirit each chapter sets out the aims and key terms which will be encountered in the chapter. Worked examples have been included and tips are provided on how to structure the appraisals in Excel® spreadsheets. Self-assessed questions have been included at the end of topic-based chapters and the counterpart model answers can be found towards the back of the book.

Terry Steley who was joint author of the first two editions of this book has now retired and he has been replaced in this edition by John O'Leary. Our thanks of course go to Terry for his earlier contributions, which have made the task of updating for this edition far easier than it might otherwise have been.

David Isaac and John O'Leary
School of Architecture, Design and Construction
University of Greenwich
March 2013

Acknowledgements

The authors wish to thank the team at Palgrave led by Helen Bugler for their advice and support in bringing this third edition into production. The authors would like to thank Ann Edmondson for her diligent work at the production stage.

Thanks go to Steven Ball for taking the time to read and make helpful suggestions on a draft of Chapter 11 which discusses residential leaseholds.

The authors and publishers wish to thank the following for permission to use copyright material:

RICS for enabling reproduction of valuation definitions which appear in the 2012 edition of the Red Book whose formal title is: *RICS Valuation – Professional Standards* (Coventry: Royal Institution of Chartered Surveyors).

1

Introduction

Aims

This introductory chapter provides key definitions and concepts which will surface at various points throughout the book. Some over-arching principles are aired, such as how taxation is treated in a valuation context and how to convert annual in arrears property income into quarterly in advance. The chapter will also identify and explain the most commonly used valuation formulas.

Key terms

>> **Valuation** – the process of estimating the market value (or market rent) of a property in advance of a sale (or letting).
>> **Analysis** – the sometimes in-depth process which leads to the estimation of the investment value or worth of a property to a specific entity.

1.1 Introduction

Because of the risks and the large sums of money involved, there will probably always be a need for valuation expertise in the closely related fields of property development and property investment. High standards are quite rightly expected of the registered valuers who undertake this work by both the professional body (the Royal Institution of Chartered Surveyors or RICS) and clients to whom a duty of care is owed. Valuers are expected to act with integrity and to show sound judgement when they use the valuation toolkit, large parts of which are explored in this book. The valuations which emerge are expected to be robust and defensible, and this is no easy task given that the property market is said to be imperfect and in a constant state of flux.

Valuers are expected to liaise with clients so that there is clarity around the basis of valuation, in order that *market value* is identified prior to a sale or *market rent* is determined in anticipation of a letting or that *investment value* is calculated to reflect the worth of an asset to a client. This chapter provides the full definitions and discusses the context in which they are applied. A synopsis for the book is also set out and a few preliminary issues will be broached, such as why taxation is customarily left to one side when valuations are undertaken. The chapter will round up with a summary of the most commonly used valuation formulas.

1.2 An overview of the material

The chapters in the book focus upon selected aspects of the valuation toolkit which valuers use in practice. Some parts of the toolkit lend themselves to the evaluation of existing property investments such as shops, offices and industrial units while other parts of the toolkit are used to evaluate property development. There are also parts of the toolkit which are used for statutory valuations where legislation requires a value to be placed on specific property rights. Statutory valuations are often undertaken to determine the compensation payable where property rights are to be acquired compulsorily. There are examples of all of these types of valuation in the book.

Because valuation is more of an art than a science, valuers have been given the headroom by their professional body, the RICS, to exercise judgement on which part of the toolkit should be used in the particular circumstances encountered. The RICS does however issue guidance notes on a variety of valuation issues. In that spirit, the tone of the chapters in this book is explorative and thought-provoking rather than prescriptive.

To begin the exploration of the valuation toolkit, Chapter 2 examines the traditional valuation method which began its evolution long before the advent of pocket calculators and personal computers. Traditional property valuation has similarities with mercantile capitalism where invested capital is expected to earn a rate of return commensurate with the risks involved. Because some of the jargon is historically derived and not particularly easy to grasp, the chapter (and all others up to Chapter 14) contains definitions of key terms, worked examples and five self-assessed questions at the end. When exploring Chapter 2, readers might like to sustain a healthy degree of scepticism, as the traditional method of valuation has attracted criticisms that it is a 'dark art' which relies a little too heavily on the judgement of a valuer.

Chapter 3 provides a contrast to the traditional valuation approach by exploring the so called *modern method* of valuation. The method relies heavily on discounted cash flows (DCFs) in which costs and income are explicitly laid out over time, bringing a degree of transparency to the valuation process. However, despite the apparent sophistication of DCF, there is still a requirement for judgement on the part of a valuer to fine-tune the variables.

Chapter 4 deals with interest rates which surface in one form or another in virtually all valuation techniques but where they are often referred to as a *yield* which reflects a percentage rate of return. The chapter provides a working vocabulary of the different types of yields encountered in property.

Chapter 5 is set in the context of high value commercial properties where the purchasers are often corporate property investors such as pension funds or insurance companies. These purchasers adopt medium- to long-term perspectives on their property acquisitions and the chapter explores how investment performance is assessed using what is known as the equated yield. This involves trying to assess the rate of rental growth needed to meet financial expectations and whether such a rate of growth is realistic.

Chapter 6 focuses on how to identify the capital value of reversionary properties. Whether it is a shop, office or factory, what characterises a reversionary property is that it will soon be subject to a rent review or re-letting which will alter the financial picture. Chapter 6 explores the hardcore method of valuation, which has evolved to try to pin down the capital value of reversionary properties.

Chapter 7 acknowledges that investors have choices in terms of the types of assets that they invest in, and these could, for example, be antiques, works of art, company shares, government gilts or property. In each case the anticipated returns need to be compared with the risks involved. The chapter explores one way that investors can make this comparison by using a common benchmark, which for property is known as the equivalent yield.

Chapter 8 examines situations where landlords have granted rent-free periods to tenants as an inducement for them to commit to a lease. In other circumstances tenants might have paid a premium to secure a lease. Whether it is the landlord offering an incentive or a tenant paying a premium, the true rental value for a property is obscured and the chapter explores a way of identifying the true picture, which is called the equivalent rent.

Chapter 9 considers the trend towards valuing on a quarterly in advance basis as opposed to the traditional approach to valuing annually in arrears. Chapter 10 considers situations where commercial properties have become over-rented because the market has fallen since the lease was originally signed. Chapter 11 examines leasehold residential property, where the extension of a lease or the purchase of the freehold has become an option for many leaseholders. The valuation challenge in that context is to calculate the compensation due to the landlord whose property interests are acquired.

Chapter 12 explores development valuations where land is purchased to enable housing or commercial property to be developed. Chapter 13 examines the apparently simple concept of risk as it applies in a property context. Chapter 14 considers different options for funding property development which in some cases leads to the formation of a partnership between the funder, developer and landowner.

Chapter 15 is the final chapter and it looks at some current issues where not all the answers are known. One of these agendas is trying to place a value on what has become known as the green premium. This is an elusive concept but it is thought to represent the additional value that a market will pay for a green building, i.e. one which has attracted a recognised sustainability certificate. In some situations green buildings are fast becoming the norm and we may soon have a 'brown discount', i.e. the non-green or standard buildings are worth comparatively less than their energy efficient green counterparts.

1.3 The Red Book, key definitions and responsibilities

If accurate and consistent valuations are to be generated from the use of the valuation toolkit then there is a need for commonly agreed and precise definitions, as well as clarification of the qualities and responsibilities of valuers. This is where the RICS plays a central role by setting those standards through the Red Book whose formal title is the *RICS Valuation – Professional Standards* (2012).

The Red Book (RICS, 2012: 17) requires that valuers are appropriately qualified to undertake valuation work and in this respect they must possess academic and professional qualifications which demonstrate technical competence. In addition, valuers must be members of a relevant professional body (which for most will mean the RICS) as this demonstrates a commitment to ethical standards. Valuers must possess relevant practical experience in the particular locality and sector of the property market where the work is to be undertaken. Valuers must in addition comply with relevant regulations which govern the right to practise as a valuer and which in the UK means that valuers must register with the RICS. Assuming that a valuer meets these criteria, the Red Book allows the valuer to judge which valuation techniques should be used in any particular set of circumstances.

Regarding the basis for a valuation, the Red Book defines four potential bases. The most common is *market value* where an interest in a property is to be sold in the open market. The definition of market value has gradually evolved across a number of editions of the Red Book to arrive at the following.

> The estimated amount for which an asset or liability should exchange on the valuation date between a willing buyer and a willing seller in an arm's length transaction after proper marketing and where the parties had each acted knowledgeably, prudently and without compulsion. (RICS, 2012: 30)

Because the definition of market value is based upon the premise of a capital sale, the Red Book (RICS, 2012: 31) provides a counterpart definition of *market rent* where a property is to be leased. The only change to the definition above is that for market rent the words leased, lease, lessee and lessor replace references to an exchange, buyer and seller.

Whether it is *market value* or *market rent* the valuation is a best estimate in advance of a sale or lease in an uncomplicated open market situation, where there has been adequate time to expose the property (freehold or leasehold) to the widest possible range of potential purchasers or lessees. The parties are assumed to be acting without compulsion and are not connected in any way. To work within the remit of this idealised model of the perfect property transaction, a valuer will need to possess knowledge of specific property markets. The valuer will also need to be aware of recent comparable sales or letting data so that it can be interpreted against the specific characteristics of the property being valued. Even given a busy market which has produced plenty of data, a valuer will probably still have to make a few assumptions to overcome information gaps. It is not surprising therefore that, given the need to pull off this kind of juggling act, the valuation process is said to be more of an art than a science.

The Red Book goes on to define another key basis for a valuation, which is *investment value* (RICS, 2012: 32):

> Investment value is the value of an asset to the owner or a prospective owner for individual investment or operational objectives.

The *International Valuation Standards Framework* which is integrated into the Red Book explains (in its paragraph 38) that investment value is *entity specific* and relates to the benefits of owning an asset. Investment value could coincide with market value but not necessarily so, because the market may place a higher value on an asset than its owner (creating a motivation to sell the asset) or the owner might value the asset higher than the market (in which case there is an incentive to retain the asset).

An estimation of investment value does not require the prospect of a sale as it is an evaluation of the *worth* of the asset to the owner, normally based upon its investment performance. This type of valuation work is more closely associated with analysis which may take place against the backdrop of the performance of a representative peer group of properties. A proxy for the representative group is usually taken to be an index which provides a performance benchmark such as the Investment Property Databank (IPD) index. This type of work might be undertaken, for example, in the context of a review of a mixed-asset investment portfolio, where particular properties might play an important role in diversification and risk reduction.

The worth of an asset to a particular owner (or prospective owner) might therefore extend beyond the assessment of financial performance (which might be very average) and into the degree of diversification that the asset may bring to a portfolio or even to the extent that an asset may be unique, presenting difficulties of finding something with similar performance characteristics.

The Red Book goes on to provide two definitions of *fair value* which may arise in unusual situations. There may (for example) be a transfer of a property between parties who are in some way connected and where a power relationship may exist between them. Either the market has been locked out of the transaction or there is a degree of compulsion upon one of the parties. The concept of fair value applies in specialised circumstances which are not going to surface anywhere in this book; the concept is mentioned here for completeness, so that readers are aware that there are four recognised bases upon which a valuation could rest.

The Red Book therefore provides important definitions and it sets standards and fosters ethical practice, things that are helpful and necessary to the work of a valuer. Despite the constructive framework set by the Red Book, the work of a valuer will always remain to some extent problematic because the operating context of the property market is known for its fluctuations and imperfections.

The following section does not rehearse all of these imperfections but it does serve as a reminder that, despite the availability of a commonly agreed set of standards and a valuation toolkit, trying to determine value within the property market will always come with a degree of risk. This is particularly true during periods of market correction, which is a euphemism for market falls. During those times, the sense of grievance experienced by some property owners who may have lost large sums of money (at least in nominal accountancy terms) may lead to a search for scapegoats. Sometimes that can result in legal action against valuers on the grounds that their valuations have been negligent. There are of course defences against such actions. However this illustrates that valuation practice does pose some risks for which professional indemnity insurance is required.

1.4 The imperfect property market

The property market is said to be imperfect because there is seldom perfect information on market transactions, in contrast to stock exchanges where share prices are constantly updated to reflect market activity. Despite improvements in the recording of property transactions by Land Registry and through residential and commercial property web sites, there can still be commercial sensitivities around what is actually divulged by parties to a deal. It also takes time for data arising from transactions to appear on these web sites, although networking between agents can sometimes reduce this problem.

There can be lean periods in the market in some locations for some types of property leading to a paucity of reliable sales or lettings data and requiring valuers to use great ingenuity when trying to value a property. Properties may be similar but never identical and this makes them difficult to value even when there is a wealth of market data.

Although it is possible to buy and sell shares in property companies fairly rapidly, the purchase or disposal of properties of any scale cannot be transacted at anything like the same pace. The marketing and conveyancing process can take several months and it can be problematic, with no certainty of a successful conclusion until contracts are finally exchanged. In addition there is the lotting problem which relates to high value properties where there is effectively a diminishing pool of potential purchasers in the market as the value increases. This is to some extent alleviated by the increasingly global nature of property markets and it is not unusual for example to find that major London properties are owned by international investors.

Participants in the property market also face barriers to entry such as relatively high transaction costs and a price threshold which excludes many from direct participation. For these reasons the property market is said to illiquid and pre-disposes itself to medium- to long-term commitment.

1.5 Taxation and property valuation

Property valuations are normally undertaken on a gross of tax basis, because tax liability depends on the status of the recipient and this might not always be known. The property market comprises a wide variety of participants, each of whom will have a specific tax status and thus nothing is gained when valuing for sale on the open market by deducting tax at an assumed rate. Analysis of sales in the market is therefore normally conducted on the same gross of tax basis.

In actuality, rental income may be subject to income or corporation tax, dependent upon the tax status of the entity. However by treating the income from property on a gross basis it is then put on the same standing as, for example, investment in government stock or company shares where income is paid gross of tax. Incomes from investments such as company stock, securities or different types of property can then be capitalised using the appropriate Years' Purchase (YP) to reflect the investment's security. Even if tax were to be deducted at the standard rate from investment income, the relative position of each investment would not change, and this is another reason why tax is not normally deducted from rent before it is capitalised in property valuation.

There might however arise situations where a tax adjusted valuation is required and, as the following examples illustrate, the conversion process is relatively straightforward.

In situations where the interest from an investment is paid net of tax, the rate of interest can easily be grossed up should that be required for comparative purposes. For example a building society quoting an investment rate of 6 per cent net equivalent of 8 per cent gross for tax payers at 25 per cent would have made the calculation:

Gross interest rate	0.08
Tax @ 25% × gross interest rate =	0.02
Net interest rate	0.06

If two investments needed to be compared, but one was quoted at a yield of 10 per cent gross of tax, with the other at 8 per cent net of tax, the yields could be put on the same basis, where a tax rate of 25 per cent is assumed for illustrative purposes:

Gross of tax yield	10.00	
Net tax factor @ 25%	0.75	(1 − tax rate)
Net of tax yield	7.5%	

This shows that the net yield quoted will give a higher return. Alternatively, the net of tax yield can be converted to gross to confirm that the net of tax yield provides the better return:

Net of tax yield	8.00	
Gross tax factor @ 25%	1.333	(1/ (1 − tax rate))
Gross of tax yield	10.67% (rounded to two decimal places)	

If a situation arose where a net of tax initial yield needed to be identified then a simple adjustment to the rental income can be made. In this illustration a commercial investment property is assumed to be producing an annual income of £100,000, and the market values this type of asset at a 10 per cent all risks yield.

Gross valuation

Annual rent passing	£100,000
YP @ 10% gross	10
Capital value:	£1,000,000

True net valuation

Annual rent passing	£100,000
Less tax @ 40%	£40,000
Net income:	£60,000
YP @ 6% net	16.67
Capital value	£1,000,000

The capitalisation rate used in the net of tax calculation is the gross rate less the tax on that rate; that is, 10 per cent less 4 per cent (derived from 40% of 10%). The net rate is therefore the gross rate multiplied by $1 - t$. In order to gross-up a net rate then the multiplier becomes: $1/(1 - t)$.

Taxation can have implications for Annual Sinking Funds (ASFs) which are sometimes established in a property context so that money regularly invested in an account will compound over time to replace the original outlay on an asset. ASFs might also be established to provide a pool of money to meet the costs of major repairs which some types of property may require on a periodic basis.

ASFs are usually designed to replace the original capital only, but it is possible to take inflation into account by using the Amount of £1 compound interest formula to factor in an allowance for inflation. For example, a group of leaseholders may have enfranchised their block of flats but their building surveyor advises them that the flat roof which is of basic board and felt construction will at best have 10 years remaining before it will need to be entirely replaced.

One approach to this dilemma is to obtain current quotes for the work and then to apply an average inflation rate over 10 years to provide an estimate of the scale of expenditure that will then be needed. That figure can be used to condition the scale of annual contributions needed to meet that future commitment. Assuming that the current estimates for the work are for £100,000 and that inflation has averaged 2.8 per cent over the last 10 years, the calculation becomes $((1 + 0.028)^{10}) \times £100,000 = £131,805$ which could be rounded up to £132,000 for practical purposes.

Establishing an ASF to meet the future cost of £132,000 in the above scenario would be prudent estate management, enabling the gradual compounding of monies collected alongside the annual service charge to meet the estimated financial commitment. This would overcome the 'ouch' factor when flat owners are presented with their portion of what are sometimes considerable repairs bills. The ASF in this example therefore has to compound into £132,000 in ten years' time as the roof of the block of flats is essentially a wasting asset which needs to be replaced.

The concept of an ASF has potential application to wider categories of wasting assets, whether they are physical or legally derived entities. ASFs were traditionally embedded in dual rate valuations of leasehold interests, so that the ASF compounded over the remaining term of a lease to replace the initial expenditure made on purchasing the lease. However there is now general agreement (see for example Baum *et al.*, 2011: 276–7) that this practice has become obsolete. Valuers now effectively devalue a lease relative to its freehold equivalent by either using the YP single rate method with adjusted capitalisation rate or a DCF for the remaining term of the lease with an appropriate discount rate. Either way, the limited life lease is valued in contrast to the freehold equivalent which, because it is owned in perpetuity, will normally be worth considerably more.

Although the establishment of a sinking fund may have become obsolete in the context of valuing leasehold interests, it may still have applicability for the replacement of wasting physical assets such as the deteriorating roof on the block of flats discussed above. In those circumstances a reliable, low-risk investment account is required which, to overcome any uncertainty, would probably be a fixed rate savings account.

Given that reliability is the priority for a sinking fund, it is unlikely that the rate of interest would be particularly attractive and for the sake of this example it is assumed to be 5 per cent. The interest earned in such an account would normally be subject to income tax, which exerts a drag on the rate at which monies in the account will compound. To deal with that reality, the rate of interest should be 'netted down' to identify the effective rate as discussed earlier. Thus if the interest rate for the account was 5 per cent and the tax rate was 40 per cent, the net effective rate would be 3 per cent:

Account rate of interest:	5%
Netting down adjustment $(1-t)$ with tax @ 40%	0.6
Net effective rate:	3%

The net of tax interest rate can then be used in the ASF formula below to calculate the annual investment required to meet the estimated cost of replacing the roof in 10 years' time:

$$ASF = \frac{i}{A-1}$$

$$= \frac{0.03}{\left((1+0.03)^{10}\right)-1} = \frac{0.03}{0.3439}$$

Annual investment $= 0.0872 \times £132,000 = £11,510$

The Amount of £1 per annum formula below (see also the end of the chapter) can be used as a check to see if an annual payment of £11,510 would be sufficient to compound into £132,000 over 10 years at the net of tax interest rate of 3 per cent.

$$\text{Amount of £1 per annum} = \frac{A-1}{i}$$

$$= \frac{(1+0.03)^{10}-1}{0.03}$$

$$= \frac{0.3439}{0.03}$$

Fund after 10 years $= 11.4633 \times 11,510 = £131,943$

The difference of £51 is inconsequential at that scale of investment and is due to the combination of rounding in the ASF and then Amount of £1 per annum calculations. The point is that the collective annual investment by the flat owners of £11,510 would be sufficient to deal with the need for a new roof in 10 years' time. Assuming that there were say 30 flat owners in the block, they would each be faced with an annual bill for this item of £384. However, not to take on that obligation would expose each of the residents to one thirtieth of the capital cost in 10 years' time, which would be around £4,400 each and would be an unpleasant surprise for some.

1.6 Converting to quarterly in advance rental payments

Although this topic is considered in more depth in Chapter 9 it is raised here because it is becoming more mainstream and the conversion principles involved could be applied to other chapters in the book where there are income producing property scenarios.

Conventional valuation approaches rest upon the assumption that the rent on investment properties is received annually in arrears. In reality this is a fiction because the rents for commercial properties are usually paid quarterly in advance although in some cases the lease stipulates monthly in advance payments, which is common practice for leased residential property. The very gradual acceptance that reality should replace fiction in valuation work requires an adjustment to valuation calculations but not the fundamental approach. The conversion process can be taken in a step by step process. To begin with, a change from payment in arrears to payment in advance will increase the Years' Purchase (YP) as shown in the following calculation.

YP in arrears ($n - 1$ period) $+ 1 =$ YP in advance (n periods)

For example assume that the YP multiplier is required to calculate the value of an income for 10 years on an in advance basis. The valuer could use the conventional in arrears YP formula (shown towards the end of this chapter) to identify the YP for 9 years and then add 1 to find the YP for 10 years in advance as follows.

(YP in arrears for 9 years @ 10%) $+ 1 =$ YP in advance for 10 years @ 10%

$$5.759 + 1 = 6.759$$

For quarterly payments in advance over 10 years the conversion is:

(YP in arrears for 39 quarters @ 2.41%) $+ 1 =$ YP in advance for 40 quarters @ 2.41%

$$25.102 + 1 = 26.102$$

Recent editions of Parry's Tables (Davidson, 2013) provide the multiplier for the relevant number of periods, which can be annually, quarterly or monthly so long as the interest rate is calibrated to be consistent with the periods used. In the above example 2.41 per cent is the quarterly rate which, when compounded, will produce an annual rate of 10 per cent as the following calculation shows.

Given an annual interest rate of 10 per cent, £1 will compound to £1.10 over one year. The compound interest formula, which is known as the *Amount of £1* (see also towards the end of this chapter) and is $(1 + i)^n$, would apply in this situation. In this case, the interest rate, i, is 10 per cent (or 0.1 in decimalised form) and the number of years, n, is 1, so the sum of £1 is multiplied by $(1 + 0.1)^1$. On a quarterly basis, the same answer will be provided by $n = 4$ and $i = 0.0241$, thus $(1 + 0.0241)^4 = 1.1$ (rounded up).

The quarterly interest rate can be found by transposing it as the unknown variable x in the following way.

$$(1 + 0.1)^1 = (1 + x)^4$$

$$x = (1.1)^{1/4} - 1 = 0.241 \text{ (rounded)} = 2.41\%$$

1.7 Valuation formulas and tables

The valuation calculations which will appear at various points in the book rely in one way or another on compounding or discounting factors and their associated formulas. For example, in investment situations the challenge is to evaluate the present value of the right to receive an income stream over a period of time. The task in that setting is therefore to convert the value of a future income stream into an equivalent present capital sum. The formulas and their counterpart tables such as *Parry's Tables* (Davidson, 2013) provide a convenient way to convert present and future sums and to provide equivalence between capital sums and income streams. The tables deal with the process of compounding and discounting across time and so, for instance, the Amount of £1 table will add compound interest to an initial sum to produce a future capital sum.

A summary of the most often used concepts with their associated formulas is set out below. The names given to these formulas are historic and, from todays's perspective, the terminology is not particularly user friendly. Thus the concept of *Years' Purchase*, which will surface below, would probably have been called 'rent multiplier' if it had been invented more recently. Unfortunately this is just one of those situations where cumbersome terminology goes with the territory.

Amount of £1

The formula for the Amount of £1 is: $(1 + i)^n$ which is also known as the compound interest formula, and provides the building block for the suite of valuation formulas. The formula enables the convenient calculation of the amount into which that £1 will compound over n years at an annual interest rate of i. It thus compounds up from a present capital sum to a future capital sum.

Present Value (PV) of £1

The present value (*PV*) of £1 gives the sum which needs to be invested at the interest rate i to accumulate to £1 in n years. The PV of £1 is the process of the Amount of £1 in reverse, as it discounts a future capital sum to a present capital sum. The formula is: $1/A$.

Amount of £1 per annum

This is the amount to which £1 invested annually will accumulate in n years. It is thus compounding an income stream into a future capital sum and the formula is $(A - 1)/i$.

Annual sinking fund (ASF) to produce £1

This is the amount which needs to be invested annually to accumulate to £1 in n years at an interest rate of i. It thus discounts back and converts a future capital sum into an equivalent income stream. An example of the use of the ASF was discussed earlier in the chapter where the formula was used to identify the annual sum which would need to be invested in an interest bearing account so that it compounded up to meet the cost of replacing the roof on a block of flats. The formula is: $i/(A - 1)$, which is the inverse of the formula for the Amount of £1 per annum above, because the two concepts are in fact the reverse of each other.

Annuity £1 will purchase

This is the income stream that will be generated over n years by an original investment of £1. The income produced will be consumed as part capital and part interest on capital. Assuming the rates of consumption are the same, a single rate approach gives an equation $i/(1 - PV)$. If the rates differ, then the formula $(i + s)$ needs to be used, where s is the annual sinking fund formula above at a different interest rate from i. This is essentially the way a mortgage is calculated by a building society which provides the initial capital sum and expects repayments of equal amounts throughout the loan period (assuming fixed rate interest), to cover interest and capital (that is, the sinking fund).

Years' Purchase in Perpetuity (YP in perp.)

The Years' Purchase in Perpetuity or YP in perp., as it is commonly known, is a multiplier applied to the net annual rent from an investment property to identify its capital value. The term 'in perpetuity' is appended because the technique is used to value the freeholds of investment properties which have been let at a market rent and where the income is assumed to continue into the future without interruption.

The YP in perp. multiplier is found from: $1/i$ where i is the all risks or initial yield. This is an interest rate derived from market comparison and fine-tuned by a valuer to reflect the perception of that market of the potential of an investment property. Thus where an asset appears to have growth prospects the investment community is likely to bid up the capital value relative to its current rental income and this will drive down the initial yield. The investment community may therefore accept a 5 per cent initial yield on a particular type of property asset because it is felt that there will be capital and rental growth in the future. By accepting 5 per cent initially, investors are showing a willingness to pay up to twenty times the current net annual income to purchase the asset. In that situation the YP in perp. multiplier is $1/A$.

The Years' Purchase in perpetuity deferred by n years is given by: $1/i((1 + i)^n)$.

PV of £1 per annum (or Years' Purchase for n years)

The present value of £1 per annum is confusingly also known as the *Years' Purchase (YP)* for *n* years, but, whichever term is preferred, it is the present value of the right to receive £1 per annum for *n* years. The income is therefore for a specific period, which might be the remaining term of a lease, in contrast to the YP in perpetuity where the income is assumed to continue into the future without limit.

The future income for the specific period of time is discounted back to the present value and it is the opposite of the annuity calculation. Thus the formula for the PV of £1 per annum or YP for *n* years is: $(1 - PV)/i$. There is a hybrid of this formula known as the 'dual rate' version whose formula is: $1/(i + s)$, where *s* represents an annual sinking fund. The dual rate YP formula was historically used to value leases which had no terminal value, so that the sinking fund compounded to replace the original capital spent on purchasing the lease. However, as discussed earlier in this chapter, the dual rate method has become obsolete in practice, although sinking funds are still used in other contexts. Readers are therefore more likely to encounter the more straightforward YP 'single rate' as set out above.

Summary table

Option	Cash Flow		Formula
	Now	*Future*	
Amount of £1 (A)	Capital Sum	Capital Sum	$A = (1+i)^n$
	Compounding →		
PV of £1 (PV)	Capital Sum	Capital Sum	$PV = \dfrac{1}{A}$
	← *Discounting*		
Amount of £1 per annum	Income	Capital Sum	$\dfrac{A-1}{i}$
	Compounding →		
Annual Sinking Fund (ASF) to produce £1	Income	Capital Sum	$ASF = \dfrac{i}{A-1}$
	← *Discounting*		
Annuity £1 will purchase	Capital Sum	Capital Sum	$\dfrac{i}{1-PV}$
	Compounding →		
Years' Purchase in Perpetuity (YP in perp.)	Capital Sum	Income	$\dfrac{1}{i}$
	← *Discounting*		
YP in perp. deferred by *n* years @ $i\%$	Capital Sum	Income	$\dfrac{1}{i((1+i)^n)}$
	← *Discounting*		
PV of £1 per annum (Years' Purchase: *YP*)	Capital Sum	Capital Sum	$YP = \dfrac{1-PV}{i}$
	← *Discounting*		

1.8 Summary

This introductory chapter has begun to explore some of the vocabulary, definitions and concepts applicable to property valuation techniques. A synopsis of the book was set out, with signposting to chapters where particular valuation techniques are discussed. Some preliminary issues were explored both to provide a platform for the chapters which follow and to act as *warm up* exercises for the reader. Preliminary topics included the way taxation is normally treated in a valuation context and how annually in arrears valuations can be converted to a quarterly in advance basis if required. Key RICS definitions such as *market value*, *market rent* and *investment value* were provided and the core qualities expected of valuers explained.

The chapter discussed how, while the mathematics and rationale for each technique in the valuation toolkit can be learnt, the application of these techniques to any given set of circumstances requires judgement and experience and for that reason valuation is said to be more of an art than a science.

The chapter rounded up by summarising the most commonly used valuation formulas and related terminology because these items will surface at various points throughout the book. Although some readers will be familiar with this toolkit, others may be less aware or confident regarding the context in which these formulas are used and thus some initial guidance was provided. For example it was explained that while Annual Sinking Funds are no longer used in the context of dual rate leasehold valuations, they may still have a role to play in property, such as to build up funds to pay for major repairs where physical assets are gradually deteriorating.

References

Baum, A., Mackmin, D. and Nunnington, N. (2011) *The Income Approach to Property Valuation*, 6th edn (Oxford: EG Books).

Davidson, A. (2013) *Parry's Valuation and Investment Tables*, 13th edn (London: Estates Gazette).

RICS (2012) *RICS Valuation – Professional Standards* (Coventry: Royal Institution of Chartered Surveyors).

The Traditional Method of Investment Valuation

Aims

This chapter summarises the traditional investment method of valuation in which the concept of yield plays a key role. The chapter provides a baseline from which more elaborate techniques can be explored in subsequent chapters. For some readers this will be relatively new territory, while for others the chapter will play a role in consolidating or refreshing existing knowledge.

Key terms

>> **Present Value of £1 Per Annum** – also confusingly referred to as the *Years' Purchase* which is commonly abbreviated in calculations to YP for *n* years, is the present value of an income for a specific length of time at a given interest rate. Its counterpart, which applies to freehold property let at the market rent which is assumed to continue unchanged for the foreseeable future, is the YP in Perpetuity whose formal title is the *Present Value of £1 Per Annum in Perpetuity*.

>> **Initial yield** – reflects in percentage terms the annual return to an investor in the form of rental income when a property is first purchased relative to the capital value paid for the property. For reversionary properties, where a lot of the capital value is tied up in a future reversion to market rent, the initial yield may be very low in contrast to the yield on a similar investment property which had recently been let at the market rent and valued into perpetuity.

>> **All risks yield** – will coincide with the initial yield when there is no reversionary scenario. The all risks yield will reflect the efforts of a valuer to hone the yield for a specific property using the benchmark of market information which provides the tone for yields on particular property classes. The valuer is implicitly reflecting in the chosen 'all risk yield' the trade-off between the various risks to the investment and its potential to achieve capital and rental growth. This calls for expertise and judgement and there is some scepticism that this artistic fine-tuning can really portray the interplay of risks and potential embodied in any particular investment property.

>> **Reversionary properties** – are those whose current rental income is likely to change in the foreseeable future to align more closely with the prevailing market rent. This realignment could take place because of an impending rent review, lease renewal or re-letting. The anticipated future rental income does not have the same risk characteristics as the rent passing and so, in the traditional valuation process, the valuer normally adjusts the yield on the term income to reflect what is normally a lower risk relative to the reversionary income.

2.1 Introduction

The intention of this chapter is to summarise the traditional method of valuing investment properties. Without this foundation it will be difficult for readers to make very much progress with the valuation techniques which are discussed in the following chapters. Inevitably some will find this chapter elementary, while others may find it useful for refreshing or consolidating existing knowledge in this field. If at the conclusion of the chapter some readers still find that their understanding of the techniques remains fragile, then an introductory property valuation text, such as Armatys *et al.* (2009), Blackledge (2009) or Isaac and O'Leary (2012), is recommended before trying to make further headway in this book.

2.2 Basic principles

Most investors seek to obtain a return on their invested money either as an annual income or a capital gain or a combination of both. Property investments, whether they are office developments, shops, industrial units or buy-to-let dwellings, offer the prospect of a rental income and potential capital growth. The investment method of valuation is traditionally concerned with establishing a capital value for such properties relative to a known income which is either passing on a property or is likely to do so (and so is referred to as the *estimated rental value* or ERV).

Where an investor is faced with the potential acquisition of a fixed price asset upon which a minimum rate of return is required, the income required from the asset can readily be calculated from:

$$\text{Income} = \text{Capital} \times \frac{i}{100}$$

where i represents the investor's required rate of return.

For example, if a house can be acquired for £240,000 as an investment property and the investor's required rate of return is 8 per cent, the annual income arising from letting the house will need to be:

$$\text{Income} = £240{,}000 \times \frac{8}{100} = £19{,}200$$

In this situation, the capital value of the property is a known variable because it may represent the minimum that the vendor will accept in order to sell the property. The purchaser/investor therefore needs to establish whether an income of £19,200 could realistically be achieved given the characteristics of the property and its location. However, for most investment properties the annual rental income is known, because it is either the rent passing under a lease or it can be estimated to a fair degree of certainty from the letting of comparable properties. In this situation it is the capital sum which needs to be calculated by adapting the formula so that the capital value becomes the subject:

$$\text{Capital value} = \text{Annual income} \times \frac{100}{i}$$

Inserting the numerical values produces:

$$\text{Capital value} = £19{,}200 \times \frac{100}{8} = £240{,}000$$

The conversion of an annual income into a capital sum is known as 'capitalising'. However it is essential that the income to be capitalised is 'net', that is, clear of any expenses incurred by the investment, and so the formula needs further modification to make it explicit on this issue.

$$\text{Capital value} = \text{Net income} \times \frac{100}{i}$$

For given rates of return where the income is assumed to continue in perpetuity, $100/i$ will be constant:

Rate of return	$100/i$
5%	20
6%	16.67
7%	14.29
8%	12.5
9%	11.11
10%	10
11%	9.09
12%	8.33

The formal name given to this constant is the *Present Value of £1 Per Annum in Perpetuity* but property valuers tend to use the more convenient form which is *Years' Purchase*, abbreviated to YP in perp. The capitalisation formula can therefore be further refined to:

Capital value = Net income × YP in perp.

The YP in perp. calculated by using $100/i$ only applies where the annual income is assumed to be receivable in perpetuity, and this usually pertains where a freehold property has recently been let or is about to be let at the market rent. As was noted above, this is sometimes referred to as the ERV and, just to add to the confusion, it is also sometimes called the 'rack rent'. The latter expression is based upon an analogy in which the rent has been stretched to its maximum possible extent on a rack.

For incomes to be received over finite periods, the 'in perpetuity' appendage is removed and the YP formula adjusted to reflect the specific number of years applicable in the circumstances. The YP formula for n years, given in Chapter 1, generates constants which are also contained in valuation tables such as *Parry's Valuation and Investment Tables* (Davidson, 2013).

In an age when hand-held micro-computers and smartphones predominate, it is perhaps surprising that the rather bulky investment tables, which were first published in 1913, still have a role to play. This may be because not all students and practitioners are equally confident when using algebraic formulas and, even where that fluency does exist, the tables can still play a useful role as a reference source for checking purposes.

At this point it is worth re-capping on the basic principles which have emerged from the discussion so far and which have revealed that there are ordinarily three variables in a traditional investment calculation. The variables are the net rent, the capital value and the yield. The yield either represents the investor's required rate of return or more normally is market derived. However, in either case it is usually converted into a YP multiplier for calculation purposes. Ordinarily, two of the variables are known – usually the net rental income and the yield – so the derived variable is the capital value.

Even when a property is not let or may be in the process of development, a suitably qualified valuer will normally be able to ascertain the estimated rental value (ERV) by analysing comparable properties where a market rent has been agreed or is already passing under a lease. The valuer will also be able to investigate transactions in the property investment market to identify the yield applicable to the particular property.

Later in this chapter a fourth variable will be considered – the time dimension. This is simply because most commercial investment properties will be subject to periodic rent reviews and ultimately the expiry of a lease when, in both cases, the annual rental income is very likely to change.

2.3 The yield as a reflection of the risks

The yield attributable to a particular property investment will reflect the investor's view of the risks likely to be encountered. Where the risk is perceived to be high, then a rational investor would normally expect a high yield to compensate for accepting the above-average risks. In contrast, a low yield might be accepted where the risks were perceived to be low.

The traditional property investment method of valuation adopts a single yield to reflect the unique combination of risks posed to a particular property asset, and this is known as the 'all risks yield'. There is therefore a relationship between the risks presented by the particular property asset and the calibration of the yield. There is also a pre-existing property investment market in which other investors have made purchases that reveal their perception of risk relative to return. The pattern of transactions in the market sets a tone for yields for different property asset classes in different localities and this pattern inevitably influences the honing process that takes place when a yield is being fixed for a particular investment property (or tranche of income generated by a particular property).

Given that the yields for investment properties are largely driven by market behaviour, it is for individual investors to weigh up whether a given yield represents a satisfactory trade-off between risk and return, given the attributes of the particular property investment. A prudent investor would therefore carry out some form of analysis to assess the risks. Key issues which would normally arise in that process include income security, the potential for capital growth, the transfer costs associated with the asset, their own liquidity and tax situation.

Prudent property investors might well start by considering whether there was security of income, and this would typically involve some investigation of the ability of the tenant to meet the rental obligations arising under a lease. Where the tenant is a corporate entity and a high-value commercial lease is involved, there would normally be some investigation into the corporate credit rating of the proposed tenant before lease terms were agreed. Even for more straightforward residential lettings, residential managing agents acting for landlords are likely to seek verification of income and will normally conduct credit checks on prospective tenants to provide some reassurance that rental obligations can be met.

Consideration of income security is not just about whether the rent will be paid on time, it also concerns the security of income in real terms – whether the purchasing power of the income will be maintained. For a commercial property, a prudent investor would therefore consider the frequency of rent reviews under the lease and whether there were realistic prospects for growth in the rental income, enabling it to at least stay abreast of inflation.

As well as considering the income side of the equation, a prudent investor would consider whether there was potential for capital growth so that the invested capital was not eroded by the effects of inflation. Because the capital value is related to the income, there will be a degree of real security where there is potential for rental growth. A careful investor would also try to gauge whether the particular property asset was prone to depreciation and obsolescence, which could perhaps be triggered by the development of new and more sustainable stock.

Prudent investors would also consider the transfer costs of acquiring and disposing or property assets, which for a major investment property can be considerable when stamp duty, survey fees, agency and legal fees are combined. Although these are not risks in the strictest sense but costs, investors will typically want to keep these costs to a minimum. They will therefore be sensitive to any unknowns which could cause these costs to escalate or which might require specialist insurance policies to be taken out.

Prudent investors will also consider liquidity as they may have to restructure investment portfolios by converting particular assets into cash for re-investment elsewhere. Careful investors will also take advice on the tax implications arising from annual income and capital gains when property investments are bought and sold. The outcome of that advice will of course vary from investor to investor, as each will have a unique tax position.

The discussion above identified some of the risks involved in property investment which investors have to compare with the potential returns. There are other risks, which will be considered in Chapter 13, but the key point at this stage is that there is no easy or formulaic approach which will circumvent the need for the evaluation of risk in each case. There will always be a need for judgements to be made on how the unique bundle of risks translates into yield calibration. It is not surprising therefore that, for high-value transactions, established property investors and the banks and financial institutions lending money in these situations will tend to rely heavily on valuation surveyors to assist in the analysis and decision-making process.

There is a degree of scepticism regarding traditional investment valuation techniques. This is primarily because the calibration of the yield by a valuer can appear arbitrary, given that it is supposed to 'implicitly' reflect the unique combination of risks posed to the investment. The defence is said to be that valuation is an art and not a science and that the valuer should be trusted to exercise judgement and experience when selecting an appropriate yield for a particular property. However, in an age when there are legitimate expectations that decision-making should be objective and transparent, it is not surprising that black-box methods like this come under scrutiny.

2.4 The traditional term and reversion approach

To illustrate some of the conundrums discussed above and to allow readers to form their own judgements on the efficacy or otherwise of using traditional valuation methods, Example 2.1 considers the use of two yields in a traditional term and reversion valuation which seeks to identify the capital value of a hypothetical investment property.

Example 2.1

A valuer has been asked to value the freehold of a shop in a secondary location which has been let at a net rent of £30,000 per annum. The lease has four years remaining during which time there is no provision for a rent review. Following an analysis of market data arising from transactions on comparable premises, the valuer estimates that current market rent for this property is £45,000 per annum and that a reversionary yield of 8 per cent is appropriate. The valuation would take the following format.

Term		
Net annual rent received	£30,000	
YP 4 years @ 7%	3.3872	
		£101,616

Term (from previous page)		£101,616
Reversion		
Net annual market rent	£45,000	
YP in perp. def. 4 years @ 8%*	9.1879	
	£413,456	
		£515,072

* The formula for the deferred YP in perp. is given in the summary table on p. 13.

The estimated capital value would probably be rounded down in this case to £515,000. Although the calculation looks beguilingly simple it does rest upon a number of assumptions which warrant some discussion. The first assumption is that the annual rent which will apply in four years' time will be the same as the current market rent. One interpretation of that assumption is that the valuer has 'played it safe' by using known data rather than indulging in a forecast of what the rent might be in the future. This assumption has probably led to a conservative valuation, as there is a fair chance that the current market rent of £45,000 will be higher in four years. However the valuer might argue that the capitalisation rate for that income of 8 per cent has both reflected its growth potential and the risks. For example, one of the risks is that the income could freeze or reduce or evaporate entirely because this shop is in a secondary location and economic volatility has adversely affected the UK high street in recent years.

There may be some justification for using data which is known rather than speculating on the future rent. This ostensibly conservative approach might therefore play an important role in preventing the purchaser from being over-exposed to financial risk. If the market rent does strengthen over the four-year period this will amount to a bonus upon what the purchaser expected.

The valuation reflects an assumption that during the term the income is more secure because the lessee is enjoying an annual 'profit rent' of £15,000 arising from the difference between market rent of £45,000 and the £30,000 actually being paid. This is a sizeable profit rent and it suggests that the tenant is less likely to default on rent payments. The valuer has therefore adjusted the yield downwards for this income to reflect a degree of added security. The amount of reduction is dependent on the subjective view of the valuer and this can typically range from 0.5 to 1.5 per cent. In this case, the profit rent of £15,000 is considerable relative to the rent actually passing and thus the valuer decides that a 1 per cent adjustment to the term yield is justified.

2.5 The leasehold dimension

Example 2.1 included a £15,000 profit rent enjoyed by the retail tenant and this is an asset which can be capitalised and traded as a leasehold interest in the market. However, this type of commercial leasehold interest is typically a less attractive investment than a freehold equivalent because the freeholder's consent is required for any proposed alteration to the property or disposal by assignment or sub-letting. It is also common practice for lease terms to place responsibility for all repairs and insurance on the leaseholder. For these reasons, the leasehold yield will normally be increased by 0.5 to 1 per cent over the freehold yield.

Leasehold interests are also wasting assets and therefore an allowance is made in the calculation for an annual sinking fund (ASF) to replace the capital originally invested when the lease expires. The ASF account must be virtually riskless and, given that stipulation, the rates of interest earned are quite low, comparable with a high-street savings account. An allowance for tax also has to be made because the interest earned in an ASF account is taxed annually and is not normally deductible for income tax purposes. The annual amount to be contributed to the ASF must therefore be grossed up by the rate of tax paid by the investor, enabling the account to compound sufficiently to replace the initial capital by the end of the lease. To encompass these requirements, leasehold investments are valued by using what is known as the *YP dual rate adjusted for tax*, in which the first interest rate is the yield and the second interest rate is that earned in the sinking fund. In Example 2.2 the respective interest rates are 9 and 3 per cent.

Example 2.2

The valuation of the leasehold interest in Example 2.1 would be as follows.

Net annual market rental value	£45,000	
Net annual rent paid	£30,000	
Profit rent therefore		£15,000
YP 4 years @ 9% and 3% (tax 40%)	2.0476	
Estimated capital value therefore:		£30,714

The calculation has been worked in reverse below to demonstrate that, by paying £30,714 for a four-year leasehold interest, an investor would receive a 9 per cent return while simultaneously contributing to a sinking fund earning 3 per cent per annum. After allowing for tax he would recover the initial capital invested.

Profit rent	£15,000	
Less annual sinking fund		
Capital to be replaced	£30,714	
ASF 4 years @ 3%	0.239027	
Annual sum payable		£7,341
Gross tax factor @ 40% × $1/(1-t) =$	1.6667	
Annual allowance for ASF therefore		£12,236
Remaining income (profit rent less ASF allowance)		£2,764
Return on capital therefore	$\dfrac{£2,765}{£30,714} = 9.00\%$	

The tax rate of 40 per cent used in Example 2.2 is arbitrary and chosen for illustrative purposes. If this type of valuation was specifically requested by a client then the tax rate would be selected to reflect the client's tax status and whether this would have any bearing on the standard rate of taxation on investment accounts applicable at the time.

In practice, ASFs are seldom actually set up to run in parallel with leasehold investments and authors such as Chan and Harker (2012) are not the first to suggest that the dual rate method may in fact be defunct. They report that the method has long been abandoned by valuers in the USA and Canada and that, in a rapidly globalising property market in which valuation practice is progressively being harmonised, it may be time for valuers in the UK to follow suit. If there is a lingering defence of the dual rate method it might lie in the role played by the allowance made for an ASF, as this de-calibrates the capital value of a leasehold interest relative to its freehold counterpart. However as Chan and Harker (2012) point out, the same result could be achieved using the single rate method by adjusting the capitalisation rate upwards to reflect the reduced attractiveness of the leasehold interest.

2.6 The initial yield, running yield and equivalent yield

In Example 2.1, the investor paid £515,072 for the freehold of a tenanted property producing an annual rental income of £30,000. The investor's initial yield is therefore £30,000/£515,072 which equals 5.82 per cent and is markedly lower than the 8 per cent yield used to capitalise the reversionary income in the calculation and the 7 per cent yield used to capitalise the term income. However, the increase in capital value which occurs as the reversion moves closer has not yet been considered. This shows in the valuation after one year.

Term
Net rent received	£30,000	
YP 3 years @ 7%	2.6243	
		£78,729

Reversion
Net market rent	£45,000	
YP in perp. def. 3 years @ 8%	9.9229	
		£446,531
		£525,260

Thus one year later there has been an increase in the capital value of £10,188 (the result of £525,260 minus £515,072) which, if it is added to the income of £30,000, gives a notional total income for that year of £40,188. The yield then becomes £40,188/£515,072, which is 7.80 per cent. This is an example of calculating the *running yield*. It could be done for each year that the investment is held, with the constant remaining the original capital invested while the variables are the year, the current rental income and the revised capital value each year.

The running yield is useful in providing a picture of how things stand at any point in time. However the *equivalent yield*, which is the weighted average annual rate of return being earned over the holding period relative to the capital invested, might be of more interest to the investor. The equivalent yield, which is explored in more depth in Chapter 7, is also known as the *Internal Rate of Return* whose calculation is explained in Chapter 3. However, at this point in the discussion it is sufficient to state that the equivalent yield in Example 2.1 has been calculated by iteration to be 7.87 per cent rounded to two decimal places. This is intuitively correct given that the figure must lie somewhere between 7 per cent (used to capitalise the term income) and 8 per cent (used to capitalise the reversion). Because most of the asset's value is in the reversion it will tend to pull the equivalent yield towards 8 per cent and away from 7 per cent.

As was noted earlier, a 7.87 per cent return to the investor is based upon the conservative approach taken in the calculation whereby the reversionary rent in four years' time was calibrated against the current market rent. If the investor has chosen wisely and the economy performs well (there is an element of luck in this) then it is likely that there will be some rental growth over the four-year period. In all probability there will therefore be both an uplift in the annual income and capital value on reversion. Thus 7.87 per cent might be seen as a minimum or cautious expectation. If, for example, the market rent for this type of property grew at an average rate of 3 per cent per annum over the intervening four years, then the investor's yield would increase to 10.76 per cent.

2.7 Summary

The traditional investment method of valuation capitalises the net annual income from a property by using a yield to reflect all of the perceived risks. The yield can be induced if the particular investor requires a minimum rate of return. However because the vast majority of transactions take place in the open market, the yield normally used is that which arises from the interplay of supply and demand for the particular type of property asset.

The valuer's job is perhaps a little easier when valuing new developments or properties which have recently been let at the market rent, enabling the income to be capitalised in perpetuity using the YP in perpetuity as a multiplier. However this convenience evaporates when a valuation is required on a property which has reached an intermediate point between rent reviews or when there is some time to go before a lease expires or is renewed. In these reversionary situations it is more likely that the rent currently passing does not correspond to the market rent which could be achieved on the property. The valuer then has the task of making a defensible adjustment to the yield to reflect the differential risks posed to the term income (which is usually more certain) and the reversionary income (which is usually less certain). There is no mechanism or formula which can be used to engineer these yield adjustments and it requires judgement on the part of the valuer, underlining the fact that that this type of valuation is more of an art than a science.

Regarding the reversionary rental income which might arise several years after the date of the valuation, the practice is to benchmark it against the current market rent rather than trying to forecast what that rent might turn out to be. This type of assumption and the artistic adjustment to yields, has not surprisingly led to a degree of scepticism about this form of valuation. Although the yield selected might imply rental and capital growth, there is little additional information to support the implication.

If there is a defence of this type of traditional technique, it is that it may be more prudent to use known market data than to speculate on what market rents might become. To include rental forecasts in this type of valuation would probably lead to over-inflated capital values and which would place investors at greater risk. By comparison, it would be hazardous to try to predict the value of shares in a FTSE 100 company in several years' time, as that might also leave investors nursing unrealistic growth expectations.

Valuers might also defend the traditional approach as an established practice which, in the hands of experienced practitioners, has enabled assets to be valued using a consistent methodology. Such an approach, in theory, should enable assets to be ascribed realistic values relative to one another and this in turn generates a degree of predictability and stability within sub-sectors of the property market.

The chapter also identified a number of different yields because it is a little simplistic to rely upon one piece of information such as the initial yield arising from a transaction. The other types of yield which have some importance for the investor are the running yield and the equivalent yield. The latter is also known as the Internal Rate of Return, and it will be explored further in Chapter 3.

Chapter 2 confirmed that leasehold interests are conventionally valued using a yield related to the freehold yield and not from analysis of sales of leasehold investments. Annual sinking funds (ASFs) with an allowance for tax are factored into these valuations although ironically ASFs are rarely set up in practice. The point of making an allowance for an ASF and for tax on instalments is to produce a more credible capital value for a wasting asset in contrast to the more durable and valuable freehold equivalent.

References

Armatys, J., Askham, P. and Green, M. (2009) *Principles of Valuation* (London: EG Books).

Blackledge, M. (2009) *Introducing Property Valuation* (Abingdon: Routledge).

Chan, N. and Harker, N. (2012) 'Dual rate taxed valuation: a more rational approach', *Journal of Property Investment and Finance*, 30 (2), pp. 105–14.

Davidson, A. (2013) *Parry's Valuation and Investment Tables*, 13th edn (London: Estates Gazette).

Isaac, D. and O'Leary, J. (2012) *Property Valuation Principles*, 2nd edn (Basingstoke: Palgrave Macmillan).

Self-assessment questions

1   Provide simple definitions of the following types of yield:

  • the initial yield,
  • the running yield,
  • the reversionary yield; and
  • the equivalent yield.

2   Outline the basic principles underpinning the traditional approach to valuing a leasehold interest, the value of which arises out of a profit rent.

3   Outline the key criticisms which are levelled at the traditional method of valuing reversionary investment properties.

4   What are the defences for using the traditional investment method of valuation?

5   Using the traditional term and reversion valuation technique and making any necessary assumptions, value the freehold interest in a prime high-street shop which is located in a prosperous town centre. The shop is currently let to an established national retailer on an annual net rent of £50,000 although the current net market rent for the property is estimated to be £62,000. The lease has three years remaining and upon expiry it will probably be renewed for the benefit of the existing retailer. The freeholds for similar rack rented properties in the high street are changing hands in the investment market to reflect an all risks yield of 7 per cent.

Outline answers can be found towards the back of the book.

Discounted Cash Flow

Aims

This chapter introduces cash flows and in particular discounted cash flows (DCFs). Using worked examples, the chapter will illustrate how this technique is used generally in a business context before identifying applications to property. The discussion will explain the vocabulary which accompanies DCFs and includes the Net Present Value and the Internal Rate of Return.

Key terms

>> **Discounted cash flow (DCF)** – a technique which discounts future cash flows to the present date.

>> **Net present value (NPV)** – the net value, which may positive or negative, arising from a DCF appraisal of a project.

>> **Internal rate of return (IRR)** – the discount rate at which the NPV equals zero.

3.1 Introduction

Cash flows are an established part of business practice and of course the concept also applies at the micro level to an individual's or a household's budget. It is an unfortunate fact that most small businesses fail because they cannot generate sufficient cash flow to survive. Essentially the creditors and financial backers of such firms reach a point where they are no longer persuaded that the future promise of income will overcome current debts. Cash flows are not, however, just instruments for deciding when a business is no longer viable. They can play a more constructive role in identifying company and project viability – how much the company might reasonably be paid for an investment property – and they may provide the evidence which justifies prudent borrowing to enable firms to expand and projects to progress. Cash flows are therefore versatile tools which can be used to support decision-making in a wide variety of contexts. This chapter will begin by looking at simple period by period cash flows before moving on to consider discounted cash flows (DCFs) and the roles that this appraisal technique can play in a property context.

3.2 The cash flow concept

Financial analysts and surveyors working in business and property contexts have used cash flows to appraise business ventures, developments and investments for many years. Cash flow analysis provides an important overview of the income and expenditure arising from a project. Most ventures will involve initial costs commensurate with the scale of the undertaking. Where the outlay is modest, a cash flow analysis is probably not warranted. However, where the acquisition is a major property investment there is justification for some form of cash flow analysis.

In whatever context a cash flow analysis is felt to be justified, the principle underpinning the technique remains constant: the present and future costs and incomes must be identified and positioned in the cash flow time line with as much realism as possible. A degree of rigour should be applied to estimating the scale of future costs and incomes to overcome the tendency for costs to be under-estimated and incomes to be over-estimated, which can lead to financial difficulties at a later stage.

Example 3.1

An asset can be purchased for £10,000 and it is estimated that it will produce £2,000 income per quarter for one year, at the end of which the asset will be sold for £5,000. A simple cash flow for this investment would appear as follows.

Quarter	0	1	2	3	4
Income	0	2,000	2,000	2,000	2,000
Sale					5,000
Expenditure	−10,000				
Net income	−10,000	2,000	2,000	2,000	7,000
Cumulative balance	−10,000	−8,000	−6,000	−4,000	3,000

Although Example 3.1 is very simple, it does establish a number of basic conventions regarding cash flows. It can be seen that the base period is numbered 0 to reflect the present moment when the expenditure is to be made but there is as yet no income from the asset. The acquisition of the investment requires expenditure by the investor and, because it is a debit, it is recorded as a negative sum. The cash flow also generates an outcome, which in this case suggests that the purchase of the asset would generate a net profit of £3,000. Of course if the outcome had been negative a loss would have arisen.

The basic cash flow format can be enhanced to increase the degree of realism. For example, interest charges would normally be incorporated to reflect borrowing (or the cost of capital) and further subtleties can be included to represent the effects of inflation, the anticipated growth in income, tax liability and the estimated depreciation of the asset.

Example 3.2

If the £10,000 used to pay for the asset in Example 3.1 had been borrowed at a 5 per cent rate of interest payable at the end of each quarter, the analysis would appear as follows.

Quarter	0	1	2	3	4
Income	0	2,000	2,000	2,000	2,000
Sale					5,000
Expenditure: capital	−10,000				
interest		−500	−425	−346	−264
Net income	−10,000	1,500	1,575	1,654	6,736
Cumulative balance	−10,000	−8,500	−6,925	−5,271	1,465

The net profit has now been reduced to £1,465 by the total amount of interest paid of £1,535.

Cash flow analysis assists decision-making on whether or not to proceed with a particular project. However, more frequently a choice has to be made between alternative projects. If the time basis is the same for the alternatives, the simple cash flow analysis in Example 3.2 can be used to select which investment to make.

Example 3.3

Consider an alternative asset costing £30,000 and generating £7,000 per quarter income with an end disposal value of £20,000. Using a quarterly interest rate of 5 per cent, the cash flow would look as follows.

Quarter	0	1	2	3	4
Income	0	7,000	7,000	7,000	7,000
Sale					20,000
Expenditure: capital	−30,000				
interest		−1,500	−1,225	−936	−633
Net income	−30,000	5,500	5,775	6,064	26,367
Cumulative balance	−30,000	−24,500	−18,725	−12,661	13,706

This shows a net profit of £13,706 and there is no need for a highly skilled analyst to confirm that a return of £13,706 on £30,000 outlay is preferable to £1,465 on £10,000.

3.3 Discounted cash flow

Comparison is not as simple when the alternatives being considered have varying costs and incomes over several years. One technique used to overcome this difficulty is 'discounting' which brings all future revenue and expenditure to present day values using a given rate of interest which is the 'discount rate'. The use of discounting transforms an ordinary cash flow into a Discounted Cash Flow (DCF).

DCF is a technique used by analysts to assess the overall profitability of a project. It is also used by property appraisers, largely because the financial institutions which invest significant sums in property have not always been entirely convinced by the traditional valuation methods. The DCF approach can accommodate variations in income and expenditure over a project's time horizon at whatever frequency is required, i.e. yearly, quarterly or monthly.

A DCF explicitly takes into account the 'time value' of money by discounting to present value. A single sum of money which is expected to be receivable at a future date – the *Present Value of £1* – can be looked up in *Parry's Tables* (Davidson, 2013) or calculated using the PV formula:

$$PV = \frac{1}{(1+i)^n}$$

If the same amount is being received for a series of years, then the *Present Value of £1 per Annum* can be used. This is more familiarly known as the *Years' Purchase* (YP). The YP is simply the sum of a series of individual present values.

For example, the present value of an annual income of £10,000 receivable for four years and discounted at 8 per cent could be calculated step by step as follows.

PV of £1 in 1 year @ 8%:   0.9259 × £10,000 =   £9,259
PV of £1 in 2 years @ 8%:   0.8573 × £10,000 =   £8,573
PV of £1 in 3 years @ 8%:   0.7938 × £10,000 =   £7,938
PV of £1 in 4 years @ 8%:   0.7350 × £10,000 =   £7,350

Total Present Value = £33,120

Alternatively the answer could be found by consulting the Years' Purchase tables in *Parry's Tables* (Davidson, 2013) for four years at 8 per cent to identify the constant 3.3121 which, when multiplied by the income of £10,000, produces £33,121 (the difference of £1 arises because of rounding). Alternatively the same result could be obtained by using the YP formula:

$$YP = \frac{1 - \left(\dfrac{1}{(1+i)^n}\right)}{i}$$

For those who prefer to use Microsoft Excel® for their calculation work, the value of £10,000 could be inserted into a column of four cells in a worksheet (A1 to A4 say) and the NPV (Net Present Value) function invoked in cell A5 to produce the same result. The formula could also be typed directly into cell A5 and for this example it would appear as:

=NPV(8%,A1:A4)

It could be argued that DCF is just a re-branding of the traditional investment method of valuation which estimates the present value of future periodic incomes. Figure 3.1 shows this comparison diagrammatically for the simple freehold valuation in Example 2.1. Both the traditional method and DCF produce the same net present value of £515,072 in that example. However, the important difference lies in the thought processes involved in using each technique, particularly the rate of interest used. A DCF approach is also a little more flexible because it can more easily accommodate irregular patterns of costs and income across the project time horizon.

When deciding upon the discount rate to use in a DCF, the appraiser has at least four choices:

1 Adopt the rate which has to be paid for borrowing capital to fund the project.
2 Adopt the rate which could be earned if the capital were to be invested elsewhere, sometimes referred to as the opportunity cost of capital.
3 Adopt the weighted average cost of capital (WACC) which is a composite of **1** and **2** and would reflect the balance between debt and equity used on a particular project. Thus if 80 per cent of a project's funding had to be borrowed at 10 per cent interest and 20 per cent of the funding was equity which could have been invested elsewhere to earn 2 per cent interest, then the WACC for the project would be: (80% × 10%) + (20% × 2%) = 8.4%.

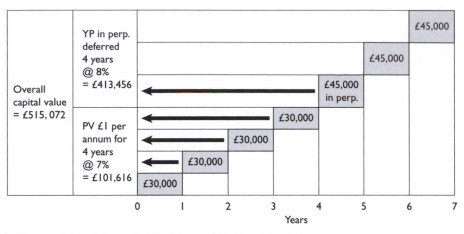

YP in perp. deferred 4 years @ 8% = 9.1879 x £45,000 = £413,456
PV £1 per annum for 4 years @ 7% = 3.3872 x £30,000 = £101,616
Overall capital value = £413,456 + £101,616 = £515,072

Figure 3.1 The present value of future annual incomes

4 Adopt the rate of return which the investor requires to compensate for the risks involved, the loss of immediate consumption and inflation, called the *target rate*.

In investment and development appraisal it is often the target rate which is used because it is a product of corporate policy. The target rate will normally reflect a comfortable margin above what could be earned from relatively safe forms of investment such as government stock.

Example 3.4

DCF and its resolution using Excel®

An asset can be purchased for £200,000 and will generate the following estimated incomes: year 1, £30,000; year 2, £50,000; year 3, £60,000; year 4, £30,000; year 5, £65,000; year 6, £57,500 and year 7, £30,000. In year 4, maintenance costs of £10,000 will arise, and at the end of year 7 the asset will be disposed of for £15,000, so the combined income that year will be £45,000. If the investor's target rate is 10 per cent then the DCF will be calculated as shown in Figure 3.2. The Excel® alphanumeric column and row cell references are shaded in grey.

The DCF format lends itself to calculations in Excel®. Cells can contain formulas which are linked to calculate, in this example, the net cash flow, the PV of £1 @ 10 per cent for each of seven years and the DCF values. Excel®'s SUM function can also be invoked to calculate the NPV arising from the sum of values in column F. For example, year 1 on the left hand side of the DCF occupies cell A4 in the worksheet and 10 per cent has been positioned discretely, i.e. separately from text to enable calculation, in

	A	B	C	D	E	F
1					10%	
2	Year	Expenditure £	Income £	Net Cash Flow £	PV of £1 @ 10%	DCF
3	0	200,000		−200,000	1	−200,000
4	1		30,000	30,000	0.9091	27,273
5	2		50,000	50,000	0.8264	41,320
6	3		60,000	60,000	0.7513	45,078
7	4	10,000	30,000	20,000	0.6830	13,660
8	5		65,000	65,000	0.6209	40,359
9	6		57,500	57,500	0.5645	32,459
10	7		45,000	45,000	0.5132	23,094
11				Net present value £ =		23,243

Figure 3.2

cell E1; the PV of £1 @ 10 per cent in year 1, which is shown in cell E4, is the result of an Excel® formula in that cell:

=1/((1+E$1)^A4)

The dollar sign ($) inserted between E and 1 in the formula creates an absolute cell reference. The formula in cell E4 can then be dragged down column E so that the values for the PV of £1 @ 10% in all years are simultaneously calculated. Rows and columns of cells can be grouped for formatting, so that values can be rounded up as required. In this example, currency values have been rounded up to the nearest pound while column E, which contains the PV of £1 @ 10% values, has been rounded up to four decimal places for presentational purposes.

Using Excel® for this type of exercise has a number of benefits, including transparency for auditing purposes, convenient editing and consistent presentation. Excel® is also very versatile and there are often several different ways to accomplish the same objective.

In Example 3.4, Excel®'s NPV function could be invoked at an earlier point to calculate the NPV arising from the Net Cash Flow shown in column D. The proviso is that the NPV formula would need to be edited to take account of the fact that it defaults to 'in arrears'. Thus, in Example 3.4, Excel®'s NPV function would discount the £200,000 which appears in year 0 to represent a current payment, as if it were a payment made in one year's time. In that scenario the result would be -£181,820 and all subsequent income and expenditure in the cash flow would also be set back one year. The overall effect would be to distort the outcome. To overcome this problem, the first value in year 0 is initially ignored when using the NPV function but then added back at the end of the formula string. Thus, in Example 3.4 the NPV function formula would generate the correct result of £23,243 if it were tweaked so that it appeared in cell F11 (and displayed in the formula bar) as:

=NPV(10%,D4:D10)+D3

3.4 Interpreting the Net Present Value (NPV)

The examples so far confirm that the NPV can be thought of as the result from a DCF. However, even among those who can use Excel® fluently and have grasped the mathematics and construction of a DCF, there sometimes remains a misunderstanding of what the NPV actually signifies. In Example 3.4 the positive NPV confirms that the purchase of the asset would meet the investor's target rate of return plus a surplus on top of £23,243. Essentially the investor would get back all of the £200,000 initially invested plus the equivalent of a 10 per cent per annum return over seven years on that investment, plus a bonus of £23,243. Therefore the significance of the NPV is that it reveals how easily the investment has met or has failed to meet the investor's target rate of return. In this case, a positive NPV of £23,243 suggests that it has met and exceeded the target rate relatively easily.

If the NPV had been just £5 or £1 or even zero, the investment would still be meeting the investor's target rate and it would therefore be paying back all of the initial capital plus the equivalent of a 10 per cent per annum return. However in those scenarios, the investment would only just be achieving the 10 per cent rate with little or no margin to spare.

The target rate of return is sometimes referred to as the 'hurdle rate', which creates the analogy with a hurdle set at a particular height over which the investment is expected to jump. An NPV of £23,243 in Example 3.4 signifies that the investment has cleared the hurdle with room to spare and it is therefore earning something in excess of 10 per cent per annum. The formula for the precise percentage will be explored below.

If, however, the NPV had been negative then the hurdle rate would not have been cleared and thus 10 per cent per annum would not be earned. If the NPV was only marginally negative, it does not mean that the investment would lose money, but it does mean that the investment would not earn 10 per cent. It might, for example, earn something in the vicinity of 9 or 8 per cent. However if the NPV was a large negative sum, then it would signify that the investment was nowhere near earning the investor's expected rate of return. Even in that scenario (and depending on the figures) the investment might still be paying back the initial capital but earning a very low annual rate of return. Of course, there also comes a point at which a very large negative NPV means that there is no prospect of even a small return and instead the initial capital is being eroded, thus signifying a real loss.

Although a DCF approach is useful for establishing whether individual projects meet an investor's target rate of return, it can also play a useful comparative role where competing projects are under consideration. DCF can identify which projects achieve the investor's target rate and which of those earns the largest surplus beyond that threshold. To use the hurdle analogy, DCF identifies the investment which clears the bar by the largest margin.

Example 3.5

An alternative asset to that considered in Example 3.4 will cost £218,000 and it is expected to produce the following incomes: year 1, £25,000; year 2, £30,000; year 3, £47,000; year 4, £50,000; year 5, £65,000; year 6, £60,000 and year 7, £45,000. No maintenance costs will be incurred and there will be no terminal value. The investor's target rate of 10 per cent remains unchanged and the DCF would appear as follows.

Year	Expenditure £	Income £	Net Cash Flow £	PV £1 @ 10%	DCF
0	218,000		−218,000	1	−218,000
1		25,000	25,000	0.9091	22,728
2		30,000	30,000	0.8264	24,792
3		47,000	47,000	0.7513	35,311
4		50,000	50,000	0.6830	34,150
5		65,000	65,000	0.6209	40,359
6		60,000	60,000	0.5645	33,870
7		45,000	45,000	0.5132	23,094
			Net present value £ =		−3,696

The DCF produces a negative NPV suggesting that the investor's target rate would not be met by this investment opportunity. To use the alternative expression, the hurdle rate has not been achieved. However at −£3,696 the magnitude of the underperformance does not suggest that the initial capital is threatened. While this investment would not earn 10 per cent, it would achieve a lesser (although as yet unspecified) rate of return. However in a two-horse race, and without knowing all of the competing investments' characteristics, most rational investors would choose the first investment, because it both meets the target rate and comes with a cushion of £23,243 to protect its viability from unforeseen risks.

The DCF examples considered so far have produced an outcome in the form of a NPV which indicates whether the target rate would or would not be achieved. However the NPV does not reveal the precise rate of return expected to be earned by each investment. The NPV for the first investment opportunity suggests that it would earn something above 10 per cent per annum, while the NPV for the second investment suggests that it would earn a rate of return somewhere below 10 per cent. To identify the precise rate of return in this type of situation, the Internal Rate of Return (IRR) needs to be calculated.

3.5 The Internal Rate of Return (IRR)

An important piece of information for analysts, valuers and investors is the actual return on capital to be obtained from an investment. This is the Internal Rate of Return (IRR) arising from the interplay of income and expenditure and it is also the discount rate at which the NPV is zero.

To illustrate how the IRR is found, the investment opportunity in Example 3.5 has been chosen. That investment was assessed against a target rate of 10 per cent and was found to have an NPV of −£3,696. In thin investment markets, such marginal underperformance might be looked at again to establish what the investment would actually earn, i.e. to calculate the IRR. The first step would be to trial the same variables at a lower target rate to try to establish the level above which the investment was performing and which would produce a positive NPV. The calculation of the IRR by formula requires the selection of two discount rates, one generating a positive NPV and the other a negative NPV, and then interpolating between the two.

Example 3.6

The NPV for a trial target rate of 8 per cent would be calculated as follows.

Year	Expenditure £	Income £	Net Cash Flow £	PV £1 @ 8%	DCF
0	218,000		−218,000	1	−218,000
1		25,000	25,000	0.9259	23,148
2		30,000	30,000	0.8573	25,719
3		47,000	47,000	0.7938	37,309
4		50,000	50,000	0.7350	36,750
5		65,000	65,000	0.6806	44,239
6		60,000	60,000	0.6302	37,812
7		45,000	45,000	0.5835	26,258
			Net present value £ =		13,235

Given that the NPV at the target rate of 8 per cent is positive at £13,235 but was negative at a target rate of 10 per cent, then the IRR must lie somewhere between 8 and 10 per cent. The precise rate is a product of linear interpolation and can be calculated using the formula:

$$IRR = R_1 + \left[(R_2 - R_1) \times \frac{\text{NPV @ } R_1}{\text{NPV @ } R_1 - \text{NPV @ } R_2}\right]$$

where: R_1 = lower target rate of 8 per cent.
NPV @ R_1 = NPV at the lower target rate = £13,235.
R_2 = higher target rate of 10 per cent.
NPV @ R_2 = NPV at the higher target rate = −£3,696

Inserting the numerical values produces:

$$IRR = 8\% + \left[(10\% - 8\%) \times \frac{13,235}{13,235 - -3,696}\right] = 9.56\%$$

Excel®'s IRR function produces a similar but more accurate result of 9.54 per cent (rounded up). The calculations in Example 3.6 produced a less accurate result because rounding has been undertaken at various stages for presentational purposes. The IRR function may be invoked or typed directly into a cell so that the formula would appear as follows, where cells D3 to D10 contain the Net Cash Flow figures in the DCF.

=IRR(D3:D10,9%)

The 9 per cent in the formula represents an initial estimate to enable Excel® to start the iteration. To prove that the IRR is correct it could be re-inserted into the DCF format where a NPV which is zero or very close to zero should result. Thus, in Example 3.7 the cash flow has been discounted at 9.54 per cent giving an NPV of £36. Although the NPV is not exactly zero, given the intermediate rounding in the cash flow and the scale of the investment the result of £36 provides sufficient confirmation that the investment's IRR is 9.54 per cent.

Example 3.7

Year	Expenditure £	Income £	Net Cash Flow £	PV £1 @ 9.54%	DCF
0	218,000		−218,000	1	−218,000
1		25,000	25,000	0.9129	22,823
2		30,000	30,000	0.8334	25,002
3		47,000	47,000	0.7608	35,758
4		50,000	50,000	0.6946	34,730
5		65,000	65,000	0.63419	41,217
6		60,000	60,000	0.5788	34,728
7		45,000	45,000	0.5284	23,778
				Net present value £ =	36

3.6 IRR and investment analysis

The IRR has been introduced in this chapter primarily because it will re-surface in a property appraisal context in later chapters. However before exploring the property dimension, the IRR should also be seen as a method for comparing the rates of return achievable on different investment media. For example if the IRR on what is traditionally considered to be a safe investment such as government bonds (familiarly known as gilts) was say 4 per cent then the IRR on a riskier prospect such as an investment property would ordinarily need to be greater than 4 per cent. How much that gap would need to be is largely a matter of perception of the added risk based upon the characteristics of the particular property and the investor's attitudes towards accepting additional risk. The context is provided by base rates and prevailing market conditions in which rates of return across an array of investments will vary.

An underlying principle which will surface at various points in this book is that investing in property will ordinarily be a riskier undertaking than investing in government gilts. For example, earlier in this chapter an investment opportunity costing £218,000 was identified and, although it was a wasting asset with no terminal value, its income over seven years generated an IRR of 9.54 per cent. Suppose that this was a tangible investment with certain risks, so a rational investor would naturally be curious to know the rate of return obtainable on a virtually riskless alternative in the form of government gilts. If the IRR on matched government gilts – those which also have seven years to run until maturity – was similar to 9.54 per cent, then a rational investor would choose the lower risk option for a similar rate of return.

The following illustration explores how to calculate the IRR for an alternative investment opportunity, such as a 4.5 per cent Treasury gilt which was issued four years ago and will be redeemed in seven years' time. Assume that these bonds are trading on the market at £121.30 against a face value of £100. In the background, the Bank of England Base Rate has been 0.5 per cent for some time and this sets the tone of expectation around rates of return on safe investments such as gilts, premium bonds and high street savings accounts.

Purchase Price	£121.30
Interest only yield	3.71%
Gross redemption yield	1.32%

The interest only yield of 3.71 per cent takes no account of the receipt of £100 in seven years' time and is simply the annual premium paid on the gilt, which is £4.50 (given that this is 4.5 per cent stock) divided by the £121.30 market price at which the gilts are currently trading. When the £100 payable on maturity is brought into the cash flow and discounted, the true yield can be calculated as in Table 3.1.

The IRR of 1.32 per cent can also be referred to as the Redemption Yield, because the return of capital has been taken into account. More correctly, it is the Gross Redemption Yield because the expenses incurred in acquisition and disposal have not been included.

Table 3.1

Cash flow	Multiplier at R_1 (1%)	PV	Multiplier at R_2 (3%)	PV
−£121.30	1	−£121.30	1	−£121.30
£4.50	YP 7 years: 6.7282	£30.28	YP 7 years: 6.2303	£28.04
£100.00	PV £1 in 7 years: 0.9327	£93.27	PV £1 in 7 years: 0.8131	£81.31
	NPV @ R_1 =	£2.25	NPV @ R_2 =	−£11.95

$$IRR = R_1 + \left[(R_2 - R_1) \times \frac{\text{NPV @ } R_1}{\text{NPV @ } R_1 - \text{NPV @ } R_2} \right]$$

$$= 1\% + \left[(3\% - 1\%) \times \frac{2.25}{2.25 - -11.95} \right] = 1.32\%$$

If a virtually riskless investment was only generating 1.32 per cent and annual inflation was higher than that, most prudent investors would be searching the market to try to obtain a higher rate of return. Thus the investment opportunity which had an IRR of 9.54 per cent begins to look much more interesting as there is a significant yield gap between it and the government gilts. However, before making a commitment the investor would need to know more about the characteristics and risk profile of the investment opportunity and indeed rates of return obtainable on its peer group of investments. The topic of risk has a number of dimensions and will be explored properly in Chapter 13.

3.7 DCF and property applications

This chapter has so far discussed DCF appraisal of generic projects to enable the basic principles and vocabulary to be explored. Given the concerns of this book, it is perhaps obvious that DCF has a number of applications in property, some of which will surface later in this chapter and in other chapters. At this juncture it is worth briefly considering the two principal applications of DCF in property, which are to appraise property investments and developments.

Perhaps the most common use of DCF in property relates to commercial property investments, which come in all shapes and sizes and may, for example, be tenanted offices, shops, retail warehouses, industrial units or leisure properties. There is also a specialised buy-to-let residential investment sector, which is popular among smaller investors and where DCF is not commonly used for appraisal purposes.

Mainstream corporate property investors such as pension funds, insurance companies and Real Estate Investment Trusts (REITs) will tend to acquire and hold income-producing commercial properties for a number of years with the objective of achieving some combination of capital and rental growth. Surveyors acting for these corporate property investors will be very familiar with DCF modelling, perhaps using corporate software packages to assess the worth of particular properties within portfolios. In recognition of the volume of work undertaken in this field, the RICS (2010) has issued guidance to its members on the principles and standards expected when DCF is used to assess commercial property investments.

Example 3.8 illustrates how DCF can be used to model the acquisition of the freehold of a large recently completed business unit which has been let and is producing a net annual income of £300,000. The property investment is assumed to be acquired for a price inclusive of purchase costs which reflects an initial yield of 7 per cent. The property is assumed to be held for five years up to the first rent review, when the rent is increased to £365,000. That figure is capitalised at an exit yield of 8 per cent to produce the disposal value which is added to the final year's income of £300,000 to bring the overall income to £4,862,500 in the final year. The property investor expects a minimum return of 8 per cent on this type of property investment and it appears from the resulting NPV that the expectation has been met.

Example 3.8

Year	Expenditure £	Income £	Net cash flow £	PV £1 @ 8%	DCF
0	4,285,714	0	−4,285,714	1	−4,285,714
1		300,000	300,000	0.9259	277,770
2		300,000	300,000	0.8573	257,190
3		300,000	300,000	0.7938	238,140
4		300,000	300,000	0.7350	220,500
5		4,862,500	4,862,500	0.6806	3,309,418
			Net Present Value £ =		17,304

Chapter 9 will explain that a quarterly in advance approach would normally be taken in such assessments. However at this stage, a conventional annual in arrears approach has been adopted. Readers who wish to considerer further examples of DCF appraisals of property investments could consult Wiggins (2000) or Shapiro *et al.* (2012).

Because this type of modelling exercise is forward looking, it necessarily involves forecasts or assumptions about the reviewed rent and exit yield. Those forecasted figures would normally arise from some interpretation of past trends, but there is no guarantee that those values would actually arise. Chapter 13 will examine how in such circumstances there is a role for some form of probability modelling.

DCF can also be used to appraise property developments, although developments tend to have shorter time horizons than investments and are more commonly appraised using the residual valuation technique linked to period by period cash flows. These would normally be structured on a monthly or quarterly basis with interest accumulating each period, as explained in Chapter 12. However DCF remains a potential, although perhaps secondary, method for assessing the viability of development, as Example 3.9 illustrates.

In Example 3.9 a site could be acquired for £1.4 million inclusive of purchase costs and then developed, let and disposed of over a three-year period. The costs arising from construction, ancillaries, contingencies, and professional, letting and legal fees have been parcelled up and inserted into the DCF, which has been structured on a quarterly basis. The bulk of the costs are consumed between the fourth and eighth quarters when construction activity is expected to peak. Costs then trail off in the last four quarters when construction has been completed but there is likely to be a void period during which rates have to be paid, followed by letting and disposal fees to reflect a capital sale in the last quarter. The asset is expected to have a gross development value (GDV) of £5 million at that stage.

Example 3.9

Quarter	Expenditure £	Income £	Net cash flow £	PV £1 @ 4.66%	DCF
0	1,400,000	0	−1,400,000	1	−1,400,000
1	150,000	0	−150,000	0.9555	−143,325
2	175,000	0	−175,000	0.9129	−159,758
3	175,000	0	−175,000	0.8723	−152,653
4	200,000	0	−200,000	0.8334	−166,680
5	225,000	0	−225,000	0.7963	−179,168
6	300,000	0	−300,000	0.7609	−228,270
7	325,000	0	−325,000	0.7270	−236,275
8	300,000	0	−300,000	0.6946	−208,380
9	30,000	0	−30,000	0.6637	−19,911
10	30,000	0	−30,000	0.6342	−19,026
11	30,000	0	−30,000	0.6059	−18,177
12	60,000	5,000,000	4,940,000	0.5789	2,859,766
			Net Present Value £ =		−71,857

In Example 3.9, the quarterly discount rate of 4.66 per cent derives from an annual rate of 20 per cent. This is a significantly higher discount rate than might be adopted for standing investments in order to compensate for the additional risks involved in a speculative development. The discount rate also includes the developer's cost of capital, much of which is traditionally borrowed to fund development.

The conversion of an annual interest rate into its quarterly equivalent is explained in Chapter 9, but in summary it can be calculated by using the formula: $((1 + i)^n) - 1$, where i is the annual interest rate and n is the fraction of a year, in this case, 0.25 to reflect quarterly periods. When applied to the scenario the formula produces: $(1.2^{0.25}) - 1 = 0.0466$ (rounded) which is 4.66 per cent. The corresponding Excel® formula string is:

=(1.2^0.25)-1.

Once the quarterly interest rate is known it can be discounted in relation to the particular quarter. For example, the discount rate applicable to the fifth quarter is derived from: $1/(1 + i)^n$ in which i is the quarterly rate of 4.66 per cent and $n = 5$. The calculation therefore becomes: $1/1.0466^5 = 0.7963$ rounded up to four decimal places.

The negative NPV suggests that the development is not viable. However, a developer might be in a position to reduce costs or to reduce the offer on the land by around £72,000 or some combination of both to balance the equation. If neither were possible, the IRR could be calculated to see how close it was to 20 per cent and whether that rate could still be acceptable to the developer.

It is also possible to structure the DCF differently, so that it shows an explicit profit in the last quarter. That figure would appear in the expenditure column because, although it is a return to the developer and not an expense in the usual sense, it is a sum which is extracted from the scheme's cash flow and must therefore be accounted for as if it were a payment. The profit might, for example, be benchmarked at 15 per cent of the scheme's GDV and so in this example would be £750,000. If that approach were taken, then the 20 per cent discount rate would need to be reduced significantly so that it only reflected the cost of capital and not a return for risk.

3.8 Incremental analysis

The examples considered so far illustrate that DCF can be used to assess whether a project or property investment is able to meet or exceed a target rate of return as signified by the NPV or IRR which arises from the analysis. DCF can also be used to assess whether additional expenditure to enlarge a project can be justified relative to the added value that may be achieved. It is obvious that additional costs will be incurred by adding floors to a multi-storey development. That additional expenditure will only make sense if the additional value added to the development covers those costs plus the developer's minimum rate of return.

The relationship is seldom linear because the additional costs to enlarge a scheme seldom transfer on a *pro rata* basis to the added value of the project. Put simply, the addition of an extra 10 per cent of costs to enlarge a project or improve its quality does not necessarily translate into an extra 10 per cent of value.

In the case of adding extra floors to an office tower, there will obviously be additional construction costs plus expenditure on enhancing the foundations and installing or increasing the capacity of lifts, pumps and other services. On the higher floors, the services will consume an increasing proportion of the floorspace so that the net lettable area progressively reduces. In essence, the value-added effect declines with additional height, a phenomenon known to economists as diminishing marginal returns. Ultimately a cut-off point is reached at which additional expenditure is no longer justified because any value added is insufficient to cover additional costs. Superimposing the specific timeline of a project can make it difficult to determine exactly where that cut-off point lies. A form of DCF called incremental analysis can help to bring clarity to this type of situation, as Example 3.10 will demonstrate.

Example 3.10

A developer is considering whether to commit to a significant office development which will require the expenditure of £14 million to acquire the site and construct the building, inclusive of all ancillary costs and fees. The developer then plans to let the building and retain it for 5 years until the first rent review when it will be sold to property investors. The developer's market research suggests that, when let, the building could be expected to produce a net annual income of £1,115,000. The reviewed rent at the end of the holding period is expected to reflect growth at 4 per cent per annum and the capital sale is expected to reflect a yield of 7 per cent. Given the risks involved, the developer has set the project a minimum target rate of return of 12 per cent and has assembled the figures in DCF format as follows.

Year	Expenditure £	Income £	Net cash flow £	PV £1 @ 12%	DCF
0	6,000,000	0	−6,000,000	1	−6,000,000
1	8,000,000	0	−8,000,000	0.8929	−7,143,200
2		1,115,000	1,115,000	0.7972	888,878
3		1,115,000	1,115,000	0.7118	793,657
4		1,115,000	1,115,000	0.6355	708,583
5		1,115,000	1,115,000	0.5674	632,651
6		20,494,543	20,494,543	0.5066	10,382,535
				Net Present Value £=	263,104
				IRR=	12.46%

The NPV and IRR in Example 3.10 show that the project does meet the developer's target rate of return. Enquiries of the local authority reveal that there would no objection to an enlargement of the scheme. On the assumption that formal planning consent could be obtained, the developer has factored in the additional £3 million of costs as well as the added value that enlarging the scheme would bring. The revised figures are shown in the DCF below.

Year	Expenditure £	Income £	Net cash flow £	PV £1 @ 12%	DCF
0	7,000,000	0	−7,000,000	1	−7,000,000
1	10,000,000	0	−10,000,000	0.8929	−8,929,000
2		1,300,000	1,300,000	0.7972	1,036,360
3		1,300,000	1,300,000	0.7118	925,340
4		1,300,000	1,300,000	0.6355	826,150
5		1,300,000	1,300,000	0.5674	737,620
6		23,894,986	23,894,986	0.5066	12,105,200
			Net Present Value £=		− 298,330
			IRR=		11.57%

Although there is added value in the enlarged scheme, the burden of additional costs has pushed the scheme marginally below the developer's target rate of return. This in itself might not cause the developer to abandon the revised plans, because the margin of under-performance is slight. The incremental analysis below can bring clarity to this type of situation by isolating the additional costs and the added value of moving from the original to the enlarged scheme. The IRR of 6.86 per cent is the return for taking that action, which incurs an additional expenditure of £3 million.

Year	Expenditure £	Income £	Net cash flow £	PV £1 @ 12%	DCF
0	1,000,000	0	−1,000,000	1	−1,000,000
1	2,000,000	0	−2,000,000	0.8929	−1,785,800
2		185,000	185,000	0.7972	147,182
3		185,000	185,000	0.7118	131,683
4		185,000	185,000	0.6355	117,568
5		185,000	185,000	0.5674	104,969
6		3,400,443	3,400,443	0.5066	1,722,664
			Net Present Value £=		−561,434
			IRR=		6.86%

In a context where there were less risky alternative investment options which could provide a 7 per cent return or better, there would need to be some special reason why the developer would switch to the enlarged scheme. Additionally, if the developer's cost of capital was 7 per cent or above (subsumed within the overall target rate of return of 12 per cent) then moving to the revised scheme would not be prudent, because the additional investment of £3 million would effectively be losing money.

Although in Example 3.10 there does not seem to be a good reason for pursuing the enlarged scheme, it does not follow that incremental analysis will always reach that conclusion. This type of analysis, which treats the parent scheme and the potential extension to it as if they were two different projects, will identify what each part of an overall project is earning. It may be that the project extension might earn a marginally lower rate of return than the parent, but that lower rate might still exceed the developer's or investor's minimum expectation and in that scenario there would be a motive for pursuing the expanded scheme. In fact there might be several other options worth exploring on this basis. Although Example 3.10 has focused upon an original and then potentially extended scheme, the analysis could be applied to alternative stand-alone projects.

3.9 Summary

The principle underpinning DCF is that a target rate of return is set by the investor or appraiser to see if a project, which probably requires significant up-front investment, can match or exceed the rate of return desired. DCFs are normally structured on an annual basis where projects will be undertaken or investments held over a number of years. However quarterly or monthly periods can also be used for DCFs, so long as the annual discount rate is adjusted to reflect quarters or months.

DCF can assist decision-making where there is only limited investment capital but where there are competing investment opportunities. The result of a DCF appraisal is the Net Present Value (NPV) which, if it is positive, indicates that the investment has been able to match or exceed the target rate (sometimes referred to as the hurdle rate). By doing so, the investment promises to pay back all of the initial capital invested and to achieve an annual rate of return on that investment equivalent to the target rate. The scale of a positive NPV signifies how easily the target rate was achieved or, if the NPV is negative, then the general scale of underperformance.

There is often a misunderstanding of what the NPV actually signifies. It is not in itself the profit from the undertaking, but it is something which can be added to the profit if the NPV is positive. Thus an NPV of just £5 on a £3 million investment over 8 years discounted at 15 per cent does not mean that only £5 profit has been made. It means that £5 can be added to the annual return of 15 per cent, although of course at that scale of investment it makes no material difference. The sum of £5 does, however, mean that the investment has barely scraped over the bar, suggesting that more investigation of the risks would be justified.

The NPV is usually presented as a monetary sum and it does not reveal the overall rate of return from an investment. Thus if an NPV were −£50,000 on a £4 million investment discounted at 10 per cent over 6 years, it is probable that the investment is still earning a rate of return, albeit at something less than 10 per cent. Similarly if the NPV were +£50,000 the investment would be earning a rate of return above 10 per cent. In this situation the IRR is calculated by formula or by using the IRR function in Excel® to identify the precise rate of return. The IRR is useful for comparing the performance of investment opportunities within and across asset classes. The analysis can be extended to compare the relative performance of a core project with an extended one in what is termed incremental analysis. Whatever the context, it would be expected that higher IRRs are commensurate with more risk and lower IRRs with virtually risk-free investments.

References

Davidson, A. (2013) *Parry's Valuation and Investment Tables*, 13th edn (London: Estates Gazette).

RICS (2010) *Discounted Cash Flow for Commercial Property Investments* (Coventry: Royal Institution of Chartered Surveyors).

Shapiro, E., Mackmin, D. and Sams, G. (2012) *Modern Methods of Valuation*, 11th edn (London: Estates Gazette)

Wiggins, K. (2000) *Discounted Cash Flow: The Principles and the Practice* (Reading: College of Estate Management).

Self-assessment questions

1 A numerate friend has become interested in buy-to-let residential investment and has carried out a DCF appraisal which models the purchase and letting of a house over a 10-year period before final disposal. It appears to you that a credible discount rate of 11 per cent has been used to reflect the risks and the cost of capital involved. The underpinning assumptions and data also look robust. However your friend has decided to abandon the idea as the NPV is only £10,000 and feels that this is insufficient profit for all the effort over 10 years. Advise your friend.

2 A colleague wants to convert a DCF for a development project which has been modelled on an annual basis over 3 years and in which a discount rate of 22 per cent has been used to reflect the risks and cost of capital. Your colleague feels that a quarterly rate of 5.5 per cent should be used in the conversion and that an allowance for a profit equating to 15 per cent of the scheme's gross development value should be included in the final quarter. Advise your colleague on these two issues.

3 An investor who has £250,000 to invest and who requires a minimum rate of return of 9 per cent is considering two competing investment opportunities: Project A and Project B which have similar time horizons and risk profiles. The expected cash flows from each project are shown below, requiring you to complete the DCF appraisals in order to advise the investor on which is the preferred project.

Project A

Year	Expenditure £	Income £	Net cash flow £	PV £1 @ 9%	DCF
0	250,000	0			
1	0	60,000			
2	0	65,000			
3	0	70,000			
4	0	65,000			
5	0	60,000			
			Net Present Value £ =		

Project B

Year	Expenditure £	Income £	Net cash flow £	PV £1 @ 9%	DCF
0	250,000	0			
1	0	65,000			
2	0	65,000			
3	0	65,000			
4	0	65,000			
5	0	65,000			
			Net Present Value £ =		

4   A developer is contemplating a speculative development which will take three years to complete and which, because of the risks involved, warrants a target rate of 20 per cent. Complete the DCF below to see if it achieves the target rate.

Year	Expenditure £	Income £	Net cash flow £	PV £1 @ 20%	DCF
0	1,500,000	0			
1	700,000	0			
2	1,150,000	0			
3	150,000	5,000,000			
			Net Present Value £ =		

5   Calculate the IRR for the development considered in Question 4.

Outline answers can be found towards the back of the book.

Interest Rates and Yields

Aims

This chapter explores the different types of interest rate which may be encountered in a property context. Underlying theories of interest rates suggest that they comprise three sub-components: an allowance for time preference, an inflation element and a risk premium. Regardless of how they are constituted, interest rates influence the calibration of the different types of yield used in property appraisal. The chapter therefore rounds up by providing working definitions of the different yields which may be encountered and will be explored in more depth in subsequent chapters.

Key terms

>> **Time preference** – an investor who commits capital to a project cannot spend or invest the same money elsewhere and so the investment chosen should compensate for the deferral of consumption or the inability to earn a return elsewhere. Some prefer to use the term *opportunity cost*, but whichever term is used an allowance for time preference is normally included in an investor's target rate of return. The time preference allowance is usually benchmarked against the return which could be earned on risk-free and inflation-proof investments such as index-linked gilts.

>> **Risk premium** – an element within an interest rate which reflects the risks posed by a particular investment. Generally as the perception of risk increases then so must the risk premium to compensate investors and lenders for exposing themselves to the added risk.

>> **Weighted average cost capital (WACC)** – when some of the money to acquire an investment or carry out a development is borrowed to

supplement equity, there is an opportunity cost on the equity and a borrowing rate which will typically be much higher. The two rates are combined in proportion to the debt (borrowing) and equity being used, and the result is the weighted average cost of capital. Where borrowing is envisaged the WACC should form an element in the build-up of an investor's target rate of return

4.1 Introduction

The first part of the chapter will seek to explain how interest rates are derived. Following an era when banks colluded to fix interest rates there is obvious room for improvement in the financial system but such discussion is beyond the scope of this book. In this chapter a pragmatic stance will be taken on interest rates, accepting that they are a fact of life which will be encountered in one form or another in the world of property. At the very least, it will probably always be necessary to pool money to fund projects and it is difficult to envisage how that money will become available without a price tag called an interest rate.

The second part of the chapter links the discussion on the theory and calibration of interest rates with property yields of various types. It will define the different types of yield encountered in a property context and in that respect it could also be seen as a glossary for reference purposes.

4.2 Interest rates generally

In most countries it is the central bank which sets the minimum lending rate or base rate. In the UK the central bank is the Bank of England and its Monetary Policy Committee meets periodically to decide whether or not the base rate should be changed. Generally, central banks, which are free from political control, will consider increasing the base rate to make the cost of borrowing more expensive when they perceive inflationary pressures which need curbing. Alternatively the base rate will be reduced in the hope that banks pass on the benefits of cheaper money to borrowers, and particularly business borrowers.

Making credit available at attractive borrowing rates is one way to stimulate business activity and growth. It is not surprising, therefore, that during the difficult economic period following the global recession which began in 2008 central banks in various countries reduced the minimum lending rate to near zero, and in some cases absolute zero. The strategy aimed to ensure that businesses in growth sectors in the economy were not deterred from borrowing in order to equip, expand and take on new staff.

A series of banking scandals in the wake of the Credit Crunch suggested that the money supply chain was far from perfect in passing on to borrowers the benefits of cheap money sourced in the inter-bank market. Rather than embark on that inquiry, the focus here is on how interest rates cascade outwards, however imperfectly, from the minimum lending rates set by central banks through the banking system to customers.

At the level of property appraisal there are two fundamental effects of the cost of money, i.e. interest rates, and these relate to whether money is to be borrowed or is already possessed, i.e. equity.

Borrowing is commonly used to fund property investment and development. Generally, the cost of borrowing for investment and development is project- and borrower-specific. Investors and developers essentially shop around to source the most favourable loans from banks and other financial institutions in the context of the market at the particular time. The lenders will in turn assess the prospective borrower's credit rating, capability to complete the project and assets (if any) which have been offered as collateral.

The mark-up on the rate a bank charges a developer against the rate at which the money was originally sourced in the wholesale money markets will be influenced by the bank's risk perception. The rate in the wholesale market is sometimes referred to as LIBOR (London Inter-Bank Offer Rate), although it is not the only international money market where banks can source money at low interest rates. The LIBOR rate could normally be expected to be set at 20 or 30 basis points above the central bank's base rate. When the latter changes then so does the wholesale market and ultimately the loan rates to borrowers. Other investment media such as gilts also come into line when the minimum lending rate is changed.

If a bank can source money for 3 per cent in the money wholesale market at a particular time, a developer is unlikely to be able to borrow that money from a bank for less than a rate of 6 per cent. In fact the margin could be higher because development is an inherently risky activity and the bank may feel justified in raising the rate for exposing itself to the risk. Where a bank already has heavy exposure to development it may be indifferent about seeking additional business in that sector and might therefore set a high development loan rate. From a developer's perspective this would obviously appear as a deterrent and would incentivise the hunt to source a better rate in the market.

If the specific project is speculative and more risky than usual and there is meagre collateral and a thin equity stake from the developer, then the borrowing rate will increase steeply. The rate will also increase if it is sought on a fixed-rate basis or where pre-agreed parameters are negotiated on the extent of upward and downward rate fluctuations on a variable rate loan. The latter are sometimes referred to as 'caps and collars'.

A number of variables therefore interact to influence the interest rate for a development loan, although there is less variability regarding investment which has a lower risk profile. In this context, banks could be characterised as acting rationally, in that the lending rate is progressively increased in proportion to the perceived risks and, as in any business, a retail mark-up is added to the price of the raw material, which in this case is money.

Where a developer or an investor is able to contribute some of their own funds (equity) to a project, then the savings or accrual rate available on a safe investment becomes a relevant benchmark for the equity element. At this point the discussion can turn to the time preference, or the opportunity cost of capital. The discussion is therefore moving from what the banking system sets as interest rates for its clients to what individuals or organisations set as their desired rates of return from projects.

4.3 Time preference

Time preference, or the opportunity cost of capital, reflects the fact that, once money is invested in a project, it cannot be consumed or invested elsewhere. The concept of time preference stems from the premise that people prefer the certainty of possessing money to having to wait for it, because money available now is versatile and may be put to a number of different uses. As a result of giving up this versatility through investment, the money cannot be used until the investment matures or is sold and the money becomes liquid again. Sacrificing the time preference theoretically justifies compensation, although the concept of compensation could here be thought of as the incentive required to encourage investment and to delay consumption.

Conventionally the time preference allowance is equated to the interest rate available on gilts where the number of years to redemption matches the timeline of the investment or development. This is because the investor had the alternative of buying the gilts and benefitting from their virtually risk-free rate of return. An alternative investment should therefore provide at least the rate of return available from gilts at the time of the investment decision, and that is why a time preference allowance is included in an investor's overall target rate of return.

If an investor were using only internal funds, that is funding a project entirely with equity, then the time preference allowance is simply the rate which could have been earned by investing the money in index-linked gilts. However that simplicity seldom exists in property appraisal because of the scale of transactions, so that even a modest purchase such as a house for use as a home or as a buy-to-let investment will usually require the purchaser's equity to be supplemented with a larger borrowed element. Although most purchasers will have no choice, there are also benefits in combining equity with debt, as equity can then be spread across a number of projects rather than funding just one.

The process of borrowing against slices of equity is called gearing or leveraging and, so long as high gearing is avoided, the investor stands to gain. (These issues will be explored in more depth in Chapter 14.) At this point, the focus is on the principle that the opportunity cost of capital for a developer or investor who is borrowing will be made up by an interest rate which could have been earned by investing equity in a risk-free investment combined with an interest rate payable on borrowed money. Technically the combination is called the weighted average cost of capital (WACC), although sometimes this is simply referred to as the investor's cost of capital.

The calculation of the WACC is straightforward. For example if the risk-free rate represented by the return on index-linked gilts was 2 per cent and the cost of borrowing 8 per cent, and an investor was using 20 per cent equity and 80 per cent debt (borrowed monies), then the WACC for the project would be: $(0.2 \times 0.02) + (0.8 \times 0.08) = 6.8\%$. A rational investor who was borrowing 80 per cent of the money to fund an acquisition would therefore expect the return on that investment to be at least 6.8 per cent, but as discussed below, there should also be an allowance for the risk associated with the project and an allowance for inflation.

The time preference allowance in the discount rate for an investor using only equity would be 2 per cent, and thus the build-up of that investor's target rate will result in lower expectations than for the highly leveraged investor. Indeed, from a dispassionate market valuation perspective, the fact that there might be highly leveraged investors in the market should not affect a valuer's calibration of an allowance for time preference in a discount rate. In this example the allowance would be 2 per cent and not 6.8 per cent. However, the valuer might have been instructed to identify an asset's *investment value*, which is the worth of the asset to a specific investor who may be relying on borrowed money. The *RICS Valuation – Professional Standards* (2012: 32), known more familiarly as the Red Book, acknowledges that investment value will not necessarily accord with market value because:

> Investment value is the value of an asset to the owner or a prospective owner for individual or operational objectives.

The RICS Red Book incorporates the International Valuation Standards which confirm in paragraph 38 that investment value is entity-specific and reflects the financial performance of an asset given the entity's financial objectives.

4.4 Inflation

As well as considering an allowance for time preference, a rational investor will also be interested in investments which outperform inflation. This is for the obvious reason that there will have been no real growth from an investment earning 2 per cent per annum when the inflation rate is 3 per cent. There is some debate about the most logical inflation benchmark to use, given that the RPI (Retail Price Index) includes mortgage payments, council tax and house depreciation while the CPI (Consumer Price Index) excludes these and gives slightly different weightings to other items in the representative basket of goods. The effect is that the CPI version of inflation will tend to be lower than RPI. For example, at mid-2012 the annual CPI measure of inflation in the UK stood at 2.4 per cent while RPI was 2.8 per cent (ONS, 2012). Some feel that the RPI remains a fuller and therefore more convincing representation of inflation, and this explains its durability in terms of use in index-linked contracts. Thus if an investor feels that RPI is a more reliable benchmark, the valuer might adopt an average annual rate over, say, 10 years for inclusion in the build-up of that investor's target rate of return.

4.5 Risk premium

The concept of risk will be discussed in Chapter 13, but at this juncture it may be taken to mean the degree of uncertainty of return arising from any given investment. To compensate for this uncertainty, a risk premium is customarily added to the risk-free interest rate to reflect the additional risk posed by the particular investment. Although it is difficult to calibrate the rising scale which reflects the relationship between risk and return, there is an intuitive relationship which is conceptualised by the capital market line shown in Figure 4.1.

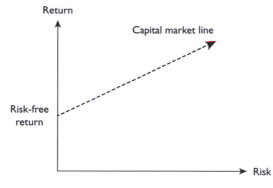

Figure 4.1 The capital market line

The assumption underpinning this relationship is that all investors are risk-averse but some of them can be persuaded to accept more risk if they are incentivised with a higher rate of return. It would be risky to invest in a start-up company with no track record in a particular sector but with an interesting product idea, a business plan and ambitious staff. However, prudent investors considering whether to back such a company would, amongst other things, look for much higher rates of return than would be available from investing in a balanced portfolio of shares in established companies. Conversely, by playing it safe and investing in FTSE 100 companies or even gilts, investors could not expect to achieve the higher rates of return which might be achieved from investing in start-up companies.

The risk differential in markets exists not just because of the inherent nature of the type of business or project but also because there may be a time or ripening dimension involved. Large property projects have this characteristic because it can be a number of years before they are completed and then fully let or sold. Over these extended timespans there can be market movements which could be conducive or which could harden against a project, and the risks are exacerbated where a project is speculative. Investment in companies whose core business is to undertake such projects is risky, and investors would need the promise of attractive rates of return in order to buy shares in such companies.

Risk and return relationships in financial markets potentially provide a benchmark for calibrating risk in a property context. However, property development and investment is qualitatively different from investing in financial products, so although the return on a representative portfolio of shares might be 4½ per cent, it does not mean that the risk premium on all property types should be 4½ per cent.

The extent to which financial market perceptions of risk could be extrapolated into a property context was examined in a Lands Tribunal case in 2006 which considered appeals against five leasehold enfranchisement decisions and became known as the *Sportelli* case. The appeals concerned, amongst other things, the assessment of the reversionary value of a number of leasehold flats and houses in parts of central London where residential property was expensive by any standards. The case subsequently went to the Court of Appeal where the decision of the Lands Tribunal was upheld, investing it with considerable weight in a legal sense.

One of the points of contention explored in *Sportelli* was the methodology which should be used to identify the risk premium, which is an important element in the deferment rate used to value reversionary properties. The Lands Tribunal considered whether the risk premium could be derived from the financial markets by using what is known as the Capital Asset Pricing Model (CAPM).

The CAPM is used in equity markets where the return on specific shares is assessed against the return on a broader representative portfolio of shares. If a particular share behaves just like the representative portfolio, it has no deviation from the norm and therefore its risk premium should be the same as for the overall portfolio. However if the particular share is more volatile than the portfolio, the CAPM will attribute to it a higher risk rate. This is consistent with the expectation that an investor would expect some compensation for accepting the risk of not receiving the average rate of return. Similarly an investment could exhibit very low volatility which would warrant a lower-than-average risk premium.

Three of the expert witnesses who gave evidence in the *Sportelli* case used the CAPM and came up with three different risk premiums for the residential properties being considered: 1.8, 2.5 and 4.5 per cent. Although the witnesses disagreed on the risk premium rate they did agree that it would be unlikely that long-term reversionary residential properties would have a higher risk premium than for a portfolio of shares.

The Lands Tribunal ultimately decided to reject the use of the CAPM as they doubted whether it was entirely pertinent to compare the risk premium on a portfolio of shares with the specific risks associated with the long-term reversionary residential properties that they were dealing with. The Tribunal felt that:

> It is merely one factor to be borne in mind, together with the valuers' evidence of the particular risks associated with investment in long term reversions and such conclusions as can be drawn from market transactions, in reaching a judgment on the risk premium (2006: para 59).

The Lands Tribunal then considered the risks associated with the particular type of property (high-value London houses and flats), noting that there was volatility in the residential market. An investor was also faced with illiquidity given the costs required to achieve a sale and the length of time that this would take. There was also a degree of deterioration and obsolescence which would be inevitable given the extended length of time to reversion in the particular cases. A rational investor would not be oblivious to these risks and would seek a rate of return which compensated for them. Having considered the evidence before it, the Lands Tribunal supported a risk premium of 4.5 per cent, a figure which had originally been suggested by one of the expert witnesses. This figure finds some support among experts such as Wyatt (2011: 324):

Therefore, given the risk premium of equities over the long run has been assessed at 4.8 per cent, it seems the risk premium of property is probably correct at 4.5 per cent, as it is slightly less volatile.

The Tribunal acknowledged that the 4.5 per cent rate was to some extent temporal and could well move around in response to wider market movements.

Although the Lands Tribunal was dealing with a particular type of property, there are some generally applicable points which arise from the decision. One of these is that the risk premium for property cannot easily be read off from a scientifically derived scale or by directly comparing data from financial markets. A number of property-specific judgements will be required to calibrate the risk premium and it will assist the valuer's task where there is comparable property market data available. When a figure emerges, it would be sensible to compare it with evidence from the financial markets at the particular time to see if the property risk premium looks credible.

4.6 Compiling an investor's interest rate

The discussion on how an investor's interest rate should theoretically comprise three components – time preference, inflation allowance and risk premium – leads to a consideration of how this may have practical effects in a property context. A bespoke interest rate might be used within a discounted cash flow (DCF) where assumptions about growth have been built into the appraisal. This calculation uses what is known as the equated yield and is applied in an appraisal of worth to a particular investor. The first step is to build up the interest rate:

The composition of an investor's equated yield

The time preference allowance – benchmarked against the return on a risk-free investment such as index-linked gilts	2.5%
An inflation allowance – derived from assessing time series data on RPI	2.5%
Risk premium – judgement and a synthesis of any property market evidence that exists	4%
Target equated yield	9%

The next step is to set out the cash flows inclusive of growth assumptions and then to discount them at 9 per cent to see if the target rate is or is not achieved. As a general rule of thumb, if the initial yield was 5 per cent, then a growth rate of approximately 4 per cent would be needed to satisfy the investor's target rate of 9 per cent. (Examples in Chapter 5 show how the precise growth rate can be calculated.) Another way to look at the overview is to start with a realistic growth rate, which might be 3 per cent, so that if a 9 per cent equated yield is sought then the investor is only going to buy if the initial yield is around 6 per cent.

If the investor is reliant upon borrowing then this changes the picture somewhat because the time preference element is replaced by the weighted average cost of capital. This will inevitably have the effect of raising the target rate of return for the investor as follows:

The composition of a leveraged investor's equated yield

Weighted average cost of capital	5.5%
An allowance for inflation	2.5%
Risk premium	4%
Target equated yield	12%

If there were two investors competing for the same asset, the investor discounting at 9 per cent would effectively be asking less of the investment and would therefore be able to pay more for it relative to its returns. The leveraged purchaser who is discounting at 12 per cent is effectively asking more of the investment or, to put it another way, is prepared to pay less for it. In that scenario the 12 per cent investor would either be bid out of the reckoning or would have to accept a lower rate of return. Leveraged purchasers might ultimately accept a rate of return which was only 1 per cent above the WACC because that represented 1 per cent of a very large sum which would have been unattainable without recourse to borrowing.

4.7 Yield definitions

Fundamentally, a yield is an interest rate which reflects the relationship between the income from a property and its capital value. However, that relationship is not fixed because either the rent or the capital value or both will change at some point in the future. In some situations it will be appropriate to estimate the amount by which they will change by factoring in an assumption about growth, while in other situations it would be inappropriate to factor in growth.

Yields in property are also not entirely independent from interest rates more generally. For example, what a property investor accepts as a yield does have some relationship with the money he could have earned in a risk-free investment such as gilts. Thus there are a number of different permutations and that is why a number of different yields have emerged to reflect different situations.

It is not surprising, therefore, that the subtle distinctions between the different yields can become blurred or that one type of yield is confused with another. The main types of yield which may be encountered in the property context are the *equivalent yield* and *equated yield*, which are often interchanged incorrectly, the *internal rate of return* and the *gross redemption yield*. Figure 4.2 shows when each yield is used and working definitions for each are given below. These topics are covered in more depth elsewhere in the book.

Internal rate of return (IRR)

As discussed in Chapter 3, the IRR is one of the outcomes from a DCF and reflects the interest rate at which the discounted income stream from a project will exactly match the expenditure. If the cash flow were to be discounted at the IRR then the Net Present Value would be zero. The DCF could be structured to reflect each and every element of the anticipated cash flow over time or cash

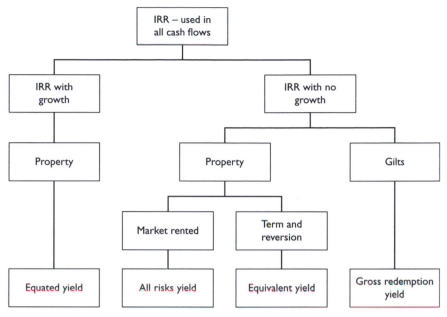

Figure 4.2 Differentiating yields

flows could be amalgamated in tranches in the short-cut format. DCF is a very flexible tool and the IRR has become the building block upon which the other yields are founded.

All risks yield (ARY)

For a market rented freehold, the ARY also equals the initial yield, although the term 'all risks yield' is preferable, because the term 'initial yield' can also apply to a situation where there is a lower-than-market rent passing on a reversionary property. The ARY is the yield that is used in conventional property investment valuations where the market rent is capitalised in perpetuity, as illustrated in worked examples in Chapter 2. The calibration of the ARY purports to reflect, in one figure, the combination of risks posed to an investment's cash flow. Although the calculation assumes that the income remains at the same level, this does not mean that there will be no change in reality.

During periods of higher than normal inflation, risk-free investments such as gilts can fail to provide returns at or above the inflation rate. As a consequence there can be a switching of money into investments such as property which are thought to have growth potential. In those circumstances the weight of money seeking exposure to particularly prime property can lead to a phenomenon known as the reverse yield gap where the ARY is driven down below the prevailing yield on gilts. This however tends to be a temporary phenomenon and the normal pattern is that the ARY on prime property will lie somewhere above the gilt yield.

Equivalent yield

The equivalent yield is a variation on the theme of the ARY. The traditional approach involves capitalising the term rent at a lower rate of interest than that used for the reversionary rent. The equivalent yield is the overall yield attached to the term and reversion and, as explained in Chapter 7, it is the internal rate of return for a term and reversionary investment. It is a weighted average yield with no allowance for future rental growth.

Although the income changes with a reversion to a market rent, the frequency of change is restricted to rent reviews in the lease. However the market rent applied to the review is the market rent at the date of the valuation (as with the ARY) and thus any expectations about future growth are not built into the cash flow. Although the cash flows do not contain an explicit allowance for growth over time, an implicit allowance is made in the discount rate chosen.

Gross redemption yield

The gross redemption yield (GRY) is an equivalent yield applied to government dated gilt-edged stock which provide a fixed percentage income and then are redeemable against their face value (par) on maturity with no growth built in. Thus for the GRY and equivalent yield, the yields are the IRR of the cash flows without growth. There is an example showing the calculation of the GRY for a gilt in Chapter 7.

Equated yield

The equated yield is the same as the IRR of a cash flow but where an allowance for growth and risk has been included in the cash flow. It is considered in Chapter 5. The discount rate is a market rate discounting the money cash flows and this is how financial analysts would look at a cash flow. Alternatively it could be a bespoke discount rate built up for a specific investor who is seeking an evaluation of worth (investment value).

The difference between general investment scenarios and property investment is that property cash flows are constrained by the lease arrangements so that changes to the cash flow will only happen on rent review or lease expiry. The cash flows from non-property investments are not so constrained and could be expected to change at least annually.

4.8 Summary

One of the objectives of the chapter has been to consider how different interest rates arise. Theoretically there are three components subsumed in an investor's interest rate: an element to compensate for the time preference of money, an inflation allowance which exists to maintain the real value of the return, and an element to compensate for risk which is called the risk premium. While it is reasonably straightforward to assess the risk-free rate from gilts and the inflation rate, judgement is required to assess the risk premium for property.

Although risk premiums were helpfully considered by the Lands Tribunal for reversionary houses in central London where 4½ per cent was adopted, it does not mean that this figure can be universally applied to all property types and locations without some assessment of the specific and contextual risks. It is helpful to have in the background the risk premium from the financial markets for a portfolio of shares, but this figure cannot be mechanically transferred to a property context where the risks encountered are different.

Assuming an acceptable risk premium can be identified, an investor could then build up a bespoke interest rate which reflects their desired rate of return. This interest rate is the equated yield and it can be used in appraisal techniques such as DCF to see if investments are able to match or exceed the desired rate.

The second part of the chapter provided working definitions of the yields likely to be encountered in a property context which will surface in subsequent chapters for more discussion. It was explained that a yield is fundamentally an interest rate arising from the relationship between the annual rental income and the capital value of a property. However, because the income and the capital value are likely to change in future and because growth might be a relevant consideration, there is a small suite of yields to try to capture each permutation. There can sometimes be a blurring of distinctions between some of these yields and perhaps this part of the chapter could be seen as a reference glossary to turn to when needed.

References

Lands Tribunal (2006) *Leasehold Enfranchisement Appeal Decision regarding* Sportelli *and others* (LRA/50/2005) (London: Lands Tribunal). Available in e-format at: www.landstribunal.gov.uk

ONS (Office for National Statistics) (2012) *Statistical Bulletin: Consumer Price Indices, June 2012* (London: Office for National Statistics). Available in e-format at: www.ons.gov.uk

RICS (2012) *RICS Valuation – Professional Standards* Coventry: Royal Institution of Chartered Surveyors).

Wyatt, J. (2011) 'Property risk premia and deferment rates', *Journal of Property Investment and Finance*, 29(3), 323–30.

Self-assessment questions

1 Theoretically an interest rate which is used in a DCF to assess the worth of an investment is built up from sub-components. What are these sub-components and how might they be calibrated?

2 Why might an investment valuation of an asset (sometimes referred to as an evaluation of *worth*) differ from a market valuation?

3 Explain why it might not always be valid to transpose the risk premium from the equities market to a property situation?

4 A buy-to-let investor is contemplating the purchase of a house as an investment property. The investor can contribute 25 per cent of the purchase price from savings but will need to raise the other 75 per cent with a specialised buy-to-let mortgage which has

an annual interest rate of 5 per cent. The investor could alternatively leave the savings in a safe high street account where it is earning 2 per cent per annum. What is the investor's cost of capital?

5   The buy-to-let investor in Question 4 wants to run the projected purchase price, cash flows and forecasted terminal sales value of the house through a DCF to see if it is able to match the target rate of return. There is reliable evidence to suggest that the risk premium for this type of property should be 4.5 per cent and that the inflation rate is 2.5 per cent. What might the target rate of return be in this case and what is another name for that rate?

Outline answers can be found towards the back of the book.

The Equated Yield

Aims

This chapter explores the concept of the equated yield which is one of a number of yields used to reflect the financial performance of investment properties. This particular yield is used when explicit assumptions can be made about future rental growth. There will be worked examples to show how the equated yield is calculated and used in financial analysis.

Key terms

>> **Equated yield** – the yield on a property investment which explicitly takes into account expectations of future rental growth.

>> **Worth** – in a property context worth is distinct from market value, because worth is specific to an individual or investor based upon certain pre-requisites or assumptions. For example, a property might be worth X to a particular investor who has a target rate of Y per cent and based upon the assumption that the property's income will grow by Z per cent per annum. X might be quite different from a market valuation which capitalises the market rent using the applicable all risks yield.

>> **Goal Seek** – a 'what-if' function in Excel® which iterates to find an unknown variable that then becomes the best fit in a calculation. It can be employed to find the equated yield or implied rental growth rate in an equation.

5.1 Introduction

Confusingly, there are a number of different yields which are used to measure different facets of the financial performance of property. It is hardly surprising, therefore, that the distinctions between these yields can sometimes become blurred and the differences misunderstood or overlooked. This chapter will define and explain the calculation and use of the *equated yield*, which takes into account assumptions about the rental growth for investment properties. This is not the same as a conventional reversionary valuation approach where the anticipated increase in income on reversion is benchmarked to the current market rent, that is, no growth above the current position is assumed.

5.2 Equated yield analysis

Before tackling the equated yield head on, it is necessary to re-visit the internal rate of return (IRR) which, as explained in Chapter 3, is one outcome from a discounted cash flow (DCF). DCF can be used to identify the IRR of an investment where rents vary or where there is a term and reversion situation. In these circumstances, the IRR could also be thought of as an overall yield. In fact, it is also called 'the equivalent yield', which is considered in Chapter 7. DCF however is very versatile and it can also be used to value freeholds where there is an explicit projection of future rental growth. The IRR produced in that context is the 'equated yield', which is the subject of this chapter.

The difference between the two similar sounding concepts is that the equated yield relates to rental values where a growth factor has been included rather than a situation where no growth is assumed. Although the distinction does not appear to be that significant, it moves property appraisals from the relatively safe position of using current and known market data to a position which relies on a forecast of future rents. There is arguably, therefore, a danger that assets could be over-valued when the equated yield is used and when growth assumptions may be too optimistic.

5.3 Assuming the rate of growth

Bearing in mind the above notes of caution, one form of equated yield analysis involves making an assumption about the expected rate of growth in the annual rental value for an investment property. The assumption could be based upon the analysis of time series data which may reveal a trend or an average annual growth rate which has occurred in the past. It could also be benchmarked against the average inflation rate experienced in recent years. For example, government policy has, on occasion, limited annual rent increases in the social housing sector to no more than the Retail Price Index (RPI) + 1 per cent. The RPI is, of course, one of the standard measures of annual inflation.

In the commercial property sector the government does not try to constrain rental levels in the same way, and rents are, therefore, a matter to be resolved by the interplay of supply and demand in the market. At the same time, property analysts must be realistic regarding the ability of business tenants to pay rents on the shops, offices, warehouses and industrial units which they use. If, for example, the income of businesses had been growing on average by 3 per cent per annum, there would have to be a very good reason why rental growth could be assumed to be 10 per cent per annum. That would be unsustainable and property would simply become too expensive, necessitating a process of market correction in which rents would have to fall back in line with the ability of businesses to pay.

When an appraiser is satisfied that a rental growth rate is realistic, it can be applied to a property's original income using the Amount of £1 formula: $A = (1 + i)^n$. Chapter 1 explained that A is the amount to which £1 compounds at the interest rate i which, in this context, is the assumed percentage growth rate over n years. The growth-adjusted rent will then be the original rent multiplied by A.

In Example 5.1, the commencement rent on a property is £70,000 per annum and an annual growth rate of 4 per cent is assumed, so that in five years' time at the first rent review, the new rent inclusive of growth would be:

$$£70,000 \times (1 + 0.04)^5 = £70,000 \times 1.2167 = £85,168 \text{ (rounded up)}.$$

The answer can also be obtained by using *Parry's Tables* (Davidson, 2013) where the Amount of £1 in 5 years at 4 per cent provides the same multiplier (1.2167) for use in the calculation. When the inflated rent has been calculated, it can be inserted into a DCF or Excel® to identify the IRR, which is also the equated yield. Both methods will be explored in the scenario in Example 5.1.

Example 5.1

The freehold of a recently developed and let retail warehouse is being marketed for sale to property investors with an asking price of £1,100,000 inclusive of purchaser's costs. The tenant is an established national retail chain which has taken a 15-year FRI lease with 5-year rent reviews at a market rent of £70,000. An analyst working for a corporate property investor wishes to see whether the company's minimum rate of return of 8 per cent could be met if the property were to be acquired at the asking price. From historic records and from assessing the state of the economy the analyst decides that it is reasonable to assume an annual growth rate for the rent of 4 per cent.

There are a number of ways that the IRR, which is the same as the equated yield, can be calculated. In all probability an analyst working for a property investment company will have a corporate software package or standardised spreadsheet into which the variables can be input to reveal the answer instantaneously. However, this being an academic book, the mathematical principles underpinning this type of software package will be considered, beginning with a short-cut DCF approach.

The first trial run of the DCF calculation adopts the 8 per cent minimum target rate to see if the property investment would clear that hurdle based upon the assumed rental growth rate of 4 per cent. The capitalisation rate of 6.36 per cent used in the DCF is simply the all risks yield which would arise from the market rent of £70,000 divided by the asking price of £1,100,000. It is a moot point whether that capitalisation rate would still apply five years later at the first rent review. However, it is assumed that the analyst is confident that this all risks yield is a relatively constant feature of the market for this type of investment property. The validity of this type of assumption and indeed the whole technique will be considered in Section 5.6.

Years	Cash flow	YP 5 years @ 8%	YP in perp. @ 6.36%	PV £1 in 5 years @ 8%	DCF
0	−£1,100,000				−£1,100,000
1–5	£70,000	3.9927			£279,489
5 into perp.	£85,169		15.7233	0.6806	£911,417
				NPV =	£90,906

The first trial run at the corporate target rate of 8 per cent, produces a positive NPV of £90,906. This tells the analyst that the investment is easily performing above the minimum expectation of an 8 per cent return. It also suggests that if there was competition to acquire this investment, there is scope to increase the offer by up to £90,900 while still preserving the corporate minimum rate of return. The analyst then tries a higher rate of return of 10 per cent to see if that hurdle can be cleared.

Years	Cash flow	YP 5 years @ 10%	YP in perp. @ 6.36%	PV £1 in 5 years @ 10%	DCF
0	−£1,100,000				−£1,100,000
1–5	£70,000	3.7908			£265,356
5 into perp.	£85,169		15.7233	0.6209	£831,471
				NPV =	−£3,173

The NPV at −£3,173 reveals that the investment does not quite achieve a 10 per cent return, but it does achieve a return somewhere above 9 per cent. The precise rate, which is the IRR, can be determined using the interpolation formula:

$$IRR = 8\% + \left[(10\% - 8\%) \times \frac{£90,906}{£90,906 - -£3,173} \right]$$

$$= 9.93\% \text{ rounded up}$$

Given that errors can easily arise in this type of modelling exercise, it is good practice to check the result using at least one alternative method. There are a number of options available and two of those have been used below to check the outcome. The first check applies the standard format DCF in which the equated yield has been inserted as the discount rate and which should produce a NPV result close to zero.

Years	Cash flow	PV £1 @ 9.93%	DCF
0	−£1,100,000	1	−£1,100,000
1	£70,000	0.9097	£63,679
2	£70,000	0.8275	£57,925
3	£70,000	0.7528	£52,696
4	£70,000	0.6848	£47,936
5	£1,409,138	0.6229	£877,752
		NPV =	−£12

The cash flow shown in the fifth year comprises the last annual rental payment plus the value of the inflated rent capitalised in perpetuity at the all risks yield:

£70,000 + ((1/0.0636) × £85,169) = £1,409,138.

The NPV of −£12 differs from zero because of rounding and is insignificant. The DCF check has confirmed that the equated yield arising from this investment is for all practical purposes 9.93 per cent.

However, if there were any lingering doubt, Excel®'s IRR function could also be called upon. This method is relatively straightforward and requires that the cash flow is entered as shown in Figure 5.1 and the IRR function is invoked in cell B8. When the IRR dialogue box appears, cells B2 to B7 would be entered together with a guess at the percentage rate of, say, 9 per cent to start the process. The corresponding string which will appear in the formula bar for cell B8 is then =IRR(B2:B7,9%), which generates the result of 9.93 per cent.

	A	B	C
1	Years	Cash flow	
2	0	−£1,100,000	
3	1	£70,000	
4	2	£70,000	
5	3	£70,000	
6	4	£70,000	
7	5	£1,409,138	
8	IRR =	9.93%	
9			

Figure 5.1 Excel® worksheet arrangement for IRR

5.4 Identifying the maximum bid using the equated yield

Thus far in the discussion the equated yield has been the unknown variable to be determined from the interplay of known variables, which were the purchase price, the initial rent and the assumed growth rate. However, any of these could become the unknown variable to be identified if the equated yield is already given and becomes one of the drivers in the calculation and not the outcome. From that standpoint, the focus may turn to identifying the maximum offer that could be made on a property while still preserving the target rate of return. Alternatively, given a fixed price asset for which the initial rent is known, the question becomes one of determining the rate of rental growth needed in order for the target rate of return to be met. The following examples in this chapter will explore these dimensions, beginning with Example 5.2 which explores what the maximum offer could be to acquire an investment property.

Example 5.2

A property investor is interested in purchasing the freehold of a shop which has been let on a long lease with 5-year rent reviews at a market rent of £100,000. The investor sets out to identify the maximum that could be offered in negotiations to acquire the shop given a target equated yield of 10 per cent. Having considered the historical performance of similar properties, the investor decides that the probable annual growth rate for the income will be 5 per cent. The investor's search to find the maximum offer which could be made to acquire the property could utilise the formula:

$$I = E - \left[\frac{E((1+G)^n - 1)}{(1+E)^n - 1} \right]$$

The variables in the formula are:

- I the initial yield or capitalisation rate which is to be determined
- E the investor's target rate of 10 per cent which is also the equated yield
- G the assumed annual rental growth rate of 5 per cent
- n the rent review period in years, which is 5

When the variables are calibrated in line with the scenario, the calculation appears as follows.

$$I = 0.1 - \left[\frac{0.1((1+0.05)^5 - 1)}{(1+0.1)^5 - 1} \right]$$

which reduces as follows:

$$I = 0.1 - \left[\frac{0.0276}{0.6105} \right]$$

$$= 0.0548 \text{ to 4 decimal places, which is 5.48 per cent.}$$

The capitalisation rate of 5.48 per cent can now be used in a straightforward investment calculation. The capital value produced is the maximum that the investor could bid for the property while still preserving the target rate of return of 10 per cent.

Market rent per annum	£100,000
YP in perp. @ 5.48%	18.2482
Capital value	£1,824,820

Again it would be prudent to check the result by using another method and so the variables could be inserted into a short-cut DCF as follows.

Years	Cash flow	YP 5 years @ 10%	YP in perp. @ 5.48%	PV £1 in 5 years @ 10%	DCF
1–5	£100,000	3.7908			£379,080
5 into perp.	£127,630		18.2482	0.6209	£1,446,087
					£1,825,167
			Less maximum bid price		£1,824,820
			NPV =		£347

The difference of £347 has arisen because of rounding at different stages in presenting the DCF calculation and is not significant. The overall result regarding the maximum offer on the property is confirmed.

5.5 Identifying the required rate of rental growth

Examples 5.1 and 5.2 have explored equated yield analysis in scenarios where the growth rate for the rent has been a given variable. Example 5.3 shows how the growth rate could be calculated when the other variables are known or could be deduced from comparable market evidence. The appraiser could then decide whether the identified rental growth rate was realistic in comparison to recent growth rates on similar properties and in the context of how the economy was performing generally.

Example 5.3

An analyst assessing possible acquisitions for a property investment company has become aware of a shop whose freehold is for sale. The shop is in an established and robust trading location. It has recently been let to a retailer on a FRI lease with 5-year rent reviews at a market rent of £70,000 per annum. Comparable market data suggest that the all risks yield for this type of property is 6 per cent. The analyst's company has a minimum target rate of return (or equated yield) of 9 per cent on this type of acquisition. The analyst decides to identify the annual rate of rental growth which would be needed for this property to meet the company requirement.

The analyst would almost certainly have access to corporate software upon which the data could be modelled. However, the discussion here will consider two alternative formulas which are capable of generating the answer, and then the focus will turn to checking the answer using Excel®. The first formula is used in a number of academic texts in this field, including Baum and Crosby (2008: 149–77) which works through various situations and examples. In this scenario the formula will be used to identify G which is the unknown variable to be determined.

$$(1 + G)^n = \frac{\text{YP in perp. @ } I - \text{YP for } n \text{ years @ } E}{\text{YP in perp. @ } I \times \text{PV £1 in } n \text{ years @ } E}$$

where, by way of reminder:

I the initial yield or capitalisation rate
E the investor's target rate of return, which is also the equated yield
G the annual growth rate for the rent which is to be determined
n the rent review period in years, which is 5

Substituting the variables in the formula to correspond to the scenario produces:

$$(1 + G)^5 = \frac{\text{YP in perp. @ } 6\% - \text{YP for 5 years @ } 9\%}{\text{YP in perp. @ } 6\% \times \text{PV £1 in 5 years @ } 9\%}$$

This progressively reduces to finally identify the annual rental growth rate, G, which would be required for the target rate of 9 per cent to be achieved.

$$(1 + G)^5 = \frac{16.6667 - 3.8897}{16.6667 \times 0.6499}$$
$$= 1.1796$$
$$(1 + G) = 1.1796^{1/5}$$
$$G = 0.0336 \text{ or } 3.36\%$$

There is an alternative formula which utilises the same set of variables – I, E and n – in order to identify the growth rate G, which should be the same as the solution above, which is 3.36 per cent.

$$G = \left[1 + \frac{(E - I)}{ASF}\right]^{1/n} - 1$$

There is, embedded in this formula, an annual sinking fund (ASF) which needs to be resolved and in which the equated yield rate is used as follows.

$$ASF = \frac{i}{(1+i)^n - 1}$$

$$= \frac{0.09}{(1+0.09)^5 - 1} = 0.1671$$

Inserting the ASF value into the formula for G produces:

$$G = \left[1 + \frac{0.03}{0.1671}\right]^{1/5} - 1 = 3.36\% \text{ rounded up}$$

Before commenting upon the significance of the outcome, its accuracy could be checked using a short-cut DCF format and Excel®'s *Goal Seek* function, which can be found under the *What-if Analysis* icon via Excel®'s Data tab. Essentially *Goal Seek* iterates rapidly until it finds the value of the chosen variable that achieves the best fit with the overall outcome in a calculation. Figure 5.2 illustrates how an Excel® worksheet could be structured to enable the *Goal Seek* function to operate effectively in this scenario. Figure 5.3 shows the values and formulas that have been used to produce the numerical results in Figure 5.2. The worksheet could have been structured differently to generate the same result, this is just one way that it can be done.

	A	B	C	D	E	F
1		3.36%	9%	6%		
2	Years	Cash flow	YP 5 years @ 9%	YP in perp. @ 6%	PV £1 in 5 years @ 9%	DCF
3	1–5	£70,000	3.8897			£272,279
4	5 into perp.	£82,577		16.6667	0.6499	£894,448
5					NPV =	£1,166,727

Figure 5.2 Excel® worksheet layout

	A	B	C	D	E	F
1		0.0336	0.09	0.06		
2	Years	Cash flow	YP 5 years @ 9%	YP in perp. @ 6%	PV £1 in 5 years @ 9%	DCF
3	1–5	70000	=(1-(1/(1+C1)^5))/C1			=B3*C3
4	5 into perp.	=B3*((1+B1)^5)		=1/D1	=1/((1+C1)^5)	=D4*B4*E4
5					NPV =	=F3+F4

Figure 5.3 Excel® cell referencing and formulas

To identify the rental growth rate of 3.36 per cent shown in decimal form (rounded up) in cell B1, Excel®'s *Goal Seek* function should be invoked in cell F5. When the *Goal Seek* dialogue box appears, the expected capital value of the property, which is £1,166,669 (a product of $1/0.06 \times £70,000$) should be entered into the dialogue box's second input window where the prompt is: 'To value'. In the third input window, which has the prompt: 'By changing cell', cell B1 should be entered or clicked upon. Given the cell linkages shown in Figure 5.3, Excel® will iterate to find the rental growth rate which generates the best fit with the predetermined answer of £1,166,669, and which in this case is 3.36 per cent. Note that it is the 'best fit' as iteration cannot always find an exact match for the outcome; hence £1,166,727 appears as the NPV in Figure 5.2. However, given the scale of the investment a difference of £58 makes no material difference.

For clarity, Excel®'s ROUND function was omitted from the formulas in Figure 5.3, so the results of these calculations will differ very slightly from those shown in Figure 5.2.

5.6 A critique of equated yield analysis

The examples considered in this chapter illustrate that the calculation of the equated yield is a delicate process involving assumptions of one kind or another. It is also a process which moves away from valuing with known market data towards assessing the worth of a property investment based upon forecasts of future rental growth. The process could be criticised as being a little one-dimensional because, if future rental growth is to be modelled, then it should perhaps include other factors such as the rate of obsolescence which is a countervailing force.

On the other hand there may be some merit in considering the potential for growth because the Investment Property Databank's (2012) representative portfolio of commercial investment properties confirms a long-term growth trend for all property sub-sectors. For example, the total returns index for a representative sample of retail properties rose from 100 at the end of 1980 to 1749 by the end of 2011, reflecting an average annual rate of growth of 9.67 per cent. Although that figure is partly composed of growth in capital values, it is also partly composed of rental growth.

Given that there has been income growth from commercial properties over the longer term, what significance can be placed on, for example, a growth rate of 3.36 per cent? At first sight, that rate of growth appears modest; however it would require the retail tenant in the scenario to cope with an increase in the rent from £70,000 over the first five years to £82,577 for the next five years. Large corporate retail chains might be able to absorb such an increase. However, for an independent retailer the initial rent is already a considerable sum for what may be a fairly modest retail unit and where additional overheads such as business rates, utility bills and staff wages have to be met.

The economic context is also important. Many town centres in the UK are facing gradual decline, a symptom of which is a steadily increasing void rate of retail properties. These characteristics are driven partly by changes in shoppers' habits and partly by increased competition from out-of-town facilities of various kinds. An increasing proportion of retailing is now being done via internet ordering and home delivery, where a shop in the traditional sense is not required. In a recessionary context, where unemployment is rising, there is simply less disposable income and the footfall in all shopping centres will decline.

These factors can combine and reinforce one another so that, rather than the sustained 3.36 per cent annual growth in retail rents envisaged in the scenario, the actual situation might be one of zero growth or a declining shopping centre where a shop rented at £70,000 per annum came to be viewed as over-rented. In the worst case scenario for the property investor/owner, the retailer might fail financially or exercise a break clause if one exists in the lease.

The point of these comments is to show that, despite the carefully structured formulas and calculations to find the equated yield, analysts will need to guard against complacency in assuming that growth will always occur for any given investment property. Even within IPD's long-term average growth trend there are some sharp peaks and troughs. A competent analyst would, therefore, consider wider social and structural changes which could have a bearing upon future property performance. The mathematics considered in this chapter should be seen as just one input into a broader decision-making process. In fact, equated yield analysis may only play a relatively small part in the final decision reached (Enever *et al.*, 2010: 107).

5.7 Summary

This chapter considered the equated yield, which is one of a number of hybrid yields used in a property context. This yield can be a given variable, perhaps reflecting a corporate target rate of return. In that scenario it is possible to use the equated yield to calculate the rate of rental growth required to meet the target rate of return. An analyst would then be in a position to assess whether or not the expectations around rental growth were realistic. The equated yield can also become the unknown variable where an assumption is made about rental growth and where the values of other variables, such as the capital value of an investment property, are known. Given that some of the calculations involving the equated yield are a little involved, it is a sensible precaution to use an alternative method for checking the accuracy of the outcome each time.

By exploring the equated yield, the chapter raises the dilemma of whether property values should be based on current market data or whether a growth factor should be included. The historic data available suggests long-term income growth for investment properties which exceeds inflation. From that standpoint, ignoring this trend might lead to under-valuing assets. There is, therefore, an argument for using the equated yield because it embodies assumptions about future growth.

The alternative and more sceptical perspective is that equated yield analysis conveniently excludes the possibility of depreciation and declining property performance. The latter scenario could arise because of structural changes in retailing, for example, or because newer properties were more sustainable and energy-efficient and thereby accelerate the rate of obsolescence in the existing stock of properties.

Perhaps one way to partly resolve the quasi-Shakespearean dilemma of '*to forecast or not to forecast, that is the question*' is to emphasise the distinction between a market valuation and an assessment of worth. Market or Red Book valuations are the province of RICS-registered valuers where the emphasis is on simplicity and transparency. The objective is to identify what the market would pay for a specific interest in a property at the valuation date. Perhaps the equated yield does not really belong in that paradigm, as it is more at home in an assessment of worth for a particular investor based upon particular growth assumptions. This is a more involved process of financial modelling which has moved away from market valuation towards investment analysis from a particular investor's perspective.

References

Baum, A. and Crosby, N. (2008) *Property Investment Appraisal*, 3rd edn (Oxford: Blackwell).

Davidson, A. (2013) *Parry's Valuation and Investment Tables*, 13th edn (London: Estates Gazette).

Enever, N., Isaac, D. and Daley, M. (2010) *The Valuation of Property Investments*, 7th edn (London: Estates Gazette).

Investment Property Databank Ltd (2012) *IPD UK Annual Property Index* (to 31.12.11) (London: IPD). Available in e-format at: www.ipd.com

Self-assessment questions

1 An investment company has a minimum target rate of return of 8.5 per cent on its commercial property acquisitions. A company analyst has identified an office building on a business park, the freehold of which is being marketed by agents with an asking price of £4 million inclusive of purchaser's costs. The building was recently let on a long lease with 5-year rent reviews to an established business at an annual rent of £260,000. Using whichever method you prefer, assist the analyst by calculating the rental growth rate needed to satisfy the company's target rate of 8.5 per cent.

2 Using an alternative method, check your answer to Question 1.

3 What criticisms could reasonably be levelled at the process undertaken in Question 1 to identify the required rental growth rate?

4 As well as identifying the required rental growth rate, what other factors might the analyst investigate before reaching a conclusion on whether the company should acquire the property at the asking price?

5 In what circumstances might it be reasonable to use equated yield analysis?

Outline answers can be found towards the back of the book.

The Hardcore Method

6.1 Introduction
6.2 A re-cap on the term and reversion approach
6.3 The hardcore method
6.4 The advantages of the hardcore method

6.5 The disadvantages of the hardcore method
6.6 Summary
References
Self-assessment questions

Aims

This chapter explores the hardcore method of valuation which separates the income arising from a reversionary investment property into horizontal layers. The chapter includes worked examples of the hardcore method to illustrate the process and to enable some evaluative discussion on the advantages and disadvantages of this method.

Key terms

>> **Reversionary property** – an investment property which is let at a rent below the market rent but where there is a reasonable prospect that a rent review or lease renewal will result in the property achieving the market rent.

>> **Hardcore method** – a technique used to value reversionary property investments by capitalising the passing rent into perpetuity and adding it to the capital value of the top slice or incremental rent which is anticipated at some future date. Given that there are differential risks associated with each layer of income, valuers would normally use a different yield when capitalising each layer of income.

6.1 Introduction

This chapter focuses upon the horizontal slicing technique known as the hardcore method which is sometimes used by valuers to appraise reversionary investment properties. The expression 'reversionary' simply means that an investment property is currently producing less than the market rent but a forthcoming rent review or re-letting will probably result in a reversion to the full market rent. This is a common occurrence where rental values have risen since the grant of a lease or perhaps because several years have passed since the last rent review or where the lessee paid a premium on entry.

In the context of traditional valuation methods, there are two main approaches to valuing reversionary investment properties: the term and reversion method, which is based on assessing vertically separated blocks of income, and the hardcore method, which separates income into horizontal layers. Although the focus in this chapter is upon the hardcore method, there is initially a re-cap on the term and reversion method as it plays a comparative role in the discussion.

6.2 A re-cap on the term and reversion approach

The term and reversion approach was explored in Chapter 2. At this point it is only necessary to summarise the principles of that method in order to provide a basis for comparison with the hardcore method.

The term and reversion technique treats the present rent as a block of income which is capitalised for the duration of the term. The market rent is then assumed to apply on reversion and it is capitalised in perpetuity to give the capital value of the reversion. The capital value of the investment property is the combined capital values of the term and reversion as illustrated in Figure 6.1.

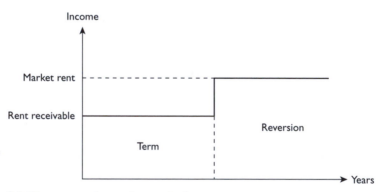

Figure 6.1 The term and reversion method

6.3 The hardcore method

In the context of traditional valuation techniques, the hardcore method, which is sometimes referred to as the layer method, is an alternative to the term and reversion method. The hardcore method capitalises in perpetuity the current rent, which is referred to as the hardcore income, and adds it to the capital value of the incremental or top slice rent expected to arise on reversion. The arrangement is illustrated in Figure 6.2. The assumptions underpinning this method are that the hardcore rent is secure and that the reviewed rent will not fall below that level.

Blackledge (2009: 215) explains that the hardcore method may have application where there is a stepped rent agreement in a lease. Stepped rents

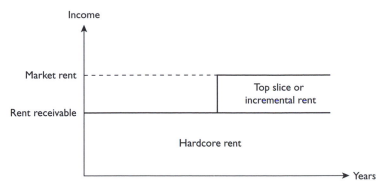

Figure 6.2 The hardcore method

have been used where, for example, a retailer is granted a lease at below the market rent with an agreement that the rent will rise to pre-agreed levels at particular staging points. This arrangement can be useful in fragile trading situations to enable a retailer to gain momentum and market share before having to meet the full market rent on a shop. The mathematics is fairly straightforward, as Example 6.1 reveals.

Example 6.1

The hardcore method and a stepped rental arrangement

A high street shop which was market rented at £70,000 per annum was sold in the investment market to reflect a yield of 7 per cent. A stepped rent agreement has been negotiated on an identical shop next door. The new lease establishes a commencement rent of £50,000 for the first two years. As Figure 6.3 illustrates, the rent will rise to £60,000 after two years and it will then increase to £70,000 after four years, and up until the first rent review (in whatever year was agreed in the lease).

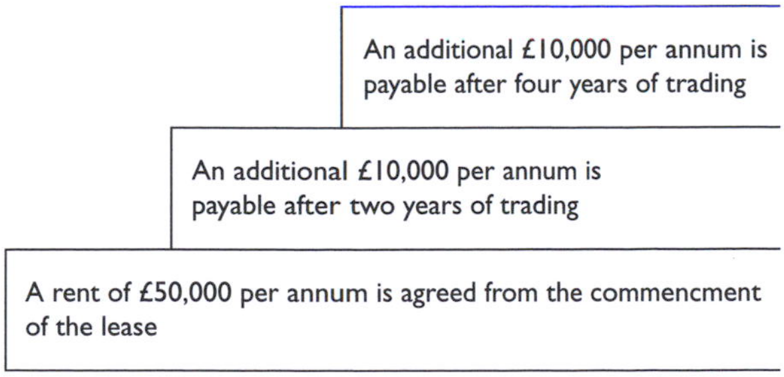

An additional £10,000 per annum is payable after four years of trading

An additional £10,000 per annum is payable after two years of trading

A rent of £50,000 per annum is agreed from the commencment of the lease

Figure 6.3

A valuer decides to use the hardcore method to determine the capital value of the property and the calculation shows how the yield has been adjusted to reflect differential risk attributed to each layer of the income.

Hardcore net annual rent	£50,000	
YP in perp. @ 6.5%	15.3846	
		£769,230
Incremental annual rent after 2 years	£10,000	
YP in perp. @ 7.0% deferred 2 years	12.4777	
		£124,777
Incremental annual rent after 4 years	£10,000	
YP in perp. @ 7.5% deferred 4 years	9.9840	
		£99,840
Capital value		£993,847

It will be explained later in the context of Figure 6.4 that further yield adjustments can be made to improve the reliability of the outcome. However at this stage of the discussion, the focus is upon establishing that the hardcore method can accommodate different income streams going forward and will normally attach different yields to each layer of income.

If the same yield is used to capitalise the layers of income and that yield is also used in a term and reversion valuation, the same overall capital value would arise, as Example 6.2 illustrates.

Example 6.2

Comparing term and reversion with hardcore results

Value the freehold interest in an industrial unit which is let at £40,000 per annum net with a rent review in four years' time. The market rent is estimated to be £55,000 and a 7 per cent yield is adopted for both blocks of income.

Term and reversion approach

Term

Net annual rent	£40,000	
YP for 4 years @ 7%	3.3872	
Value of the term		£135,488

Reversion

Reversion to market rent	£55,000	
YP in perp. @ 7% deferred 4 years	10.8985	
Value of the reversion		£599,418
Capital value		£734,906

Hardcore method

Hardcore net annual rent	£40,000	
YP in perp. @ 7%	14.2857	
		£571,428
Incremental annual rent	£15,000	
YP in perp. @ 7% deferred 4 years	10.8985	
		£163,478
Capital value		£734,906

For the purpose of comparing the two valuation methods, Example 6.2 contains a convenient simplification that the same yield is applied throughout. As Example 6.1 illustrated, some yield adjustment is usually warranted to reflect the certainty of the current known rent relative to the less certain increase expected in the future. Essentially, the known rent is viewed as being less risky and valuers have tended to ascribe a lower yield (and therefore a higher YP multiplier) to it in comparison to the more risky reversionary income, which attracts a higher yield (and therefore a lower YP multiplier). If the term yield differs from the yield used to capitalise the reversion, then the overall capital values arising from using the two valuation techniques will differ, as Example 6.3 illustrates.

Example 6.3
Adopting different yields

Value the freehold interest in an industrial unit which is let at £40,000 per annum net with a rent review in four years' time. The market rent is estimated to be £55,000. Assume that the freehold yield at the market rent is 7 per cent and the term yield is 6 per cent to reflect reduced risk to that income.

Term and reversion approach

Term

Rent received	£40,000	
YP for 4 years @ 6%	3.4651	
		£138,604
Reversion		
Reversion to market rent	£55,000	
YP in perp. @ 7% deferred 4 years	10.8985	
Value of the reversion		£599,418
Capital value		£738,022

Hardcore method

Hardcore net annual rent	£40,000	
YP in perp. @ 6%	16.667	
		£666,668
Incremental annual rent	£15,000	
YP in perp. @ 7% deferred 4 years	10.8985	
		£163,478
Capital value		£830,146

Clearly a difference of over £92,000 in the capital values in Example 6.3 could not justifiably rest upon the whim of a valuer in choosing one valuation method over another. In the background there is also the market evidence which suggests that, if this property were market rented at £55,000, it would attract an all risks yield of 7% and thus be worth around £786,000. This makes the capital value of £830,146 produced by the hardcore method look very suspect, particularly as it will be producing £15,000 per annum below the market rate for the next four years. There is an obvious need for a more rigorous approach to how the differential risks arising from the two income phases might best be represented, so that the capital value produced is more reliable.

An approach which is *potentially* capable of generating a more reliable outcome from the hardcore method begins with the premise that the incremental rent is marginal and warrants a bespoke yield which would better reflect this marginality. This requires a staged calculation which begins by ignoring the period before reversion which is shaded in Figure 6.4.

The calculation progresses on the assumption that the capital value of the market rent in perpetuity less the capital value of the hardcore rent in perpetuity produces the capital value of the incremental income. The yield used to capitalise the market rent is derived from comparison of similar market-rented properties which have been purchased in the investment market and which in Example 6.3

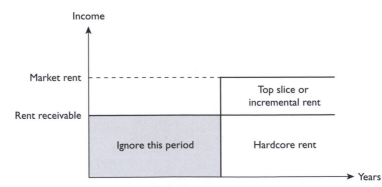

Figure 6.4 The hardcore method diagram

generate a 7 per cent yield. The yield used to capitalise the hardcore rent is adjusted downwards from that platform to reflect the greater certainty attributed to that income stream. Thus the valuer might adopt 6 per cent to produce the following calculation.

Market rent	£55,000	
YP in perp. @ 7%	14.2857	
		£785,714
Hardcore rent	£40,000	
YP in perp. @ 6%	16.6667	
		£666,668
Capital value of increment		£119,046

The calculation now requires the incremental income, which is simply the difference between the market rent and the rent passing, and which in Example 6.3 is £15,000 (£55,000 less £40,000). That figure is divided by the capital value of the incremental rent to find its yield:

$$\text{Yield on increment} = \frac{£15,000}{£119,046}$$
$$= 12.6\%$$

The next step is to complete the hardcore method valuation by inserting the bespoke yield of 12.6 per cent as follows:

Hardcore rent	£40,000	
YP in perp. @ 6%	16.667	
		£666,668
Incremental rent	£15,000	
YP in perp. @ 12.6% deferred 4 years	4.9371	
		£74,057
Capital value		£740,725

There is now a degree of similarity between this result and the valuation of £738,022 from the term and reversion method. While the exercise is not about mimicking the term and reversion approach, there is now some confidence that a more credible outcome has been produced. However this observation is not made without some misgivings, as the yield gap between 6 per cent and 12.6 per cent raises a concern as to whether a difference of 6.6 per cent really does reflect the differential risk to these two income streams. Example 6.4 illustrates how this particular approach can generate even wider yield gaps and raise doubts as to whether the process is at all reliable.

Example 6.4

Differential yields and risk reflection

A shop has recently been let for £60,000 per annum on a full repairing and insuring (FRI) lease for 15 years with five-year rent reviews. The freehold subject to the lease was subsequently sold for £750,000. You have been asked to value the freehold interest in a comparable shop nearby which was let two years ago, also on a FRI lease for 15 years with five-year reviews. The current annual rent is £50,000 with an expectation that it will increase to the market rent at the next rent review.

From the comparable property, the yield at market rent is 8 per cent, so the term yield might be adjusted by the valuer to 7 per cent to reflect the reduced risk, and that yield would be used to capitalise the hardcore income. The calculation to find the yield used to capitalise the incremental rent would appear as follows.

Market rent	£60,000	
YP in perp. @ 8%	12.5	
		£750,000
Term rent	£50,000	
YP in perp. @ 7%	14.2857	
		£714,285
Capital value of increment		£35,715

Given that the incremental rent is £10,000 (£60,000−£50,000), the yield on the increment is 28 per cent (£10,000/£35,715). A yield of 28 per cent looks incongruous when contrasted with a term yield of 7 per cent, although curiously the capital value of £731,315 which arises provides a credible comparison with that which would arise from the counterpart term and reversion calculation shown below.

Hardcore method

Hardcore rent	£50,000	
YP in perp. @ 7%	14.2857	
		£714,285
Incremental rent	£10,000	
YP in perp. @ 28% deferred 3 years	1.7030	
		£17,030
Capital value		£731,315

Term and reversion approach

Term

Rent received	£50,000	
YP 3 years @ 7%	2.6243	
		£131,215
Reversion to market rent	£60,000	
YP in perp. @ 8% deferred 3 years	9.9229	
		£595,374
Capital value		£726,589

6.4 The advantages of the hardcore method

The examples considered so far suggest that the hardcore technique appears to have a number of advantages as well as disadvantages. First, there may be some merit in isolating the less secure top slice income from the safer hardcore rent. For example, as the *Portas Review* (2011: 7–8) highlighted, conventional high street retail property has been adversely affected in the UK by a decline in expenditure in high street shops because of the increasing share of expenditure in out-of-town shops and non-store sales. These changes have taken place against the backdrop of a recession which gripped the UK and most of Europe, and this inevitably meant that consumers had less to spend. Research by GENECON in 2011 found that in UK town centres the average vacancy rate for shops was around 15 per cent as a result of reduced footfall and consumer spending. Even major retailers who had weathered the recession quite well reported that they needed fewer stores given the growth of m-commerce (sales via mobile devises) and e-retailing (internet sales). Portas (2011: 35) felt that, despite this difficult trading environment, commercial property landlords were not taking a sufficient stake in the success or failure of their business tenants.

Against this backdrop, the hardcore method would appear to have a number of benefits in that it can accommodate differential risk as rental expectations change. Indeed, in the precarious trading environment described by Portas, there would appear to be some merit, especially for high street shops, in ascribing a high yield to devalue the anticipated top-slice rent so that its contribution to overall capital value was not overstated. The hardcore method can be used in over-rented situations where the passing rent under a lease is higher than the estimated rental value which would be achieved if the property were available to let in the current market. Chapter 10 will explore the challenge presented by over-rented property and the various techniques, including the hardcore method, which may be used to value such properties.

As illustrated in Section 6.3, the hardcore technique can deal with stepped rents and it can also be adjusted to accommodate turnover rents. In the latter situation, a core income can be capitalised in perpetuity at a reduced risk rate while higher performance bands, which might be quite difficult to achieve, can be capitalised to reflect the higher risks. The hardcore method does therefore have some inherent flexibility and this might help to break a sometimes mechanistic and unhelpful use of comparables. The method is also consistent with making the commercial landlord more of a stakeholder alongside the tenant (something which Portas advocated) through the modelling of differential risks and through stepped and turnover-based arrangements.

6.5 The disadvantages of the hardcore method

In common with other valuation techniques, the hardcore method has some disadvantages and one of those is that it creates an artificial division of income. The security of the reversionary or stepped rental income is not in reality horizontally divided, because if the tenant defaults on the rent it is not just on the top slice, it is on all of the rent.

Scarrett (2008: 91) suggests that the method seems unduly complicated and, given the yield adjustments to reflect differential risk to the slices of income, the direct relationship with market evidence is lost.

The method may also lead to the over-valuation of the hardcore income, because a low yield is used to capitalise it in perpetuity. Capitalising the hardcore income as if it were a continuous unbroken stream of income is to some extent at odds with the reality of letting commercial investment properties, particularly in a recession. As the *Portas Review* confirmed, for high street shops there is a tendency towards void periods, particularly for secondary property. Although the average void rate may not be as high for other types of commercial property, there has been some company downsizing and willingness to exercise break clauses in the offices sector. The industrial, warehousing, retail warehousing and leisure property sectors are also not immune from economic downturns which make the re-letting of properties difficult when leases have expired or where break clauses have been exercised. There is, therefore, a degree of disconnection between a challenging economic climate and a valuation model based on the premise that hardcore income is reasonably secure in perpetuity.

There is a lack of transparency regarding yield calibration in the hardcore method. While it may be legitimate to reduce the yield for the hardcore income relative to yield on market-rented properties, there does not seem to be any proportionality in the margin of adjustment. Thus, if the hardcore rent were 10 per cent lower than the market rent with 3 years to reversion, the valuer might adjust the yield used to capitalise the hardcore rent down by 1 per cent. However, exactly the same yield adjustment might be made if the hardcore rent were 15 or 20 per cent lower than the market rent and, in that sense, yield calibration in this method appears arbitrary.

The method draws upon market values at the valuation date but then ascribes those values to future events. For example, the incremental rent which is expected to arise on review in several years' time is based upon the current market rental value. Thus no account is taken of inflation or growth potential in the income. Although ostensibly a weakness, this could also be seen as a strength because it curtails speculation of what the rent might be, and by doing so prevents what might otherwise be an over-valuation of assets.

Examples in the use of the hardcore method in various texts tend to revert back to a comparison with the outcome generated in the same circumstances by the term and reversion method. The implication is that the term and reversion method provides a reliable benchmark and check upon accuracy. If that is the case, it begs the question of why the hardcore method is used if it has to be re-calibrated each time to produce an answer which is more compatible with that produced by the term and reversion approach. There is, therefore, a degree of circularity associated with the hardcore method which undermines confidence in it.

6.6 Summary

The hardcore valuation technique is sometimes used to find the capital value of reversionary investment properties. The method separates rental income into horizontal layers and attributes differential risk to each layer through yield adjustment. Essentially the core income is thought to be less risk-prone and therefore justifies a lower yield (and thus a higher YP income multiplier) while the incremental or top slice income attracts a relatively higher yield (lower multiplier) to reflect additional risk. The yield adjustments have some relationship with the yields arising from transactions on comparable properties, although the magnitude of adjustment is left largely to the judgement of the valuer in the light of the circumstances.

Discussions on the hardcore method often extend into consideration of the term and reversion approach, as if that method provided a reliable second opinion on value. Given this need for affirmation and because more explicit methods of evaluation such as DCF are available, it is surprising that the hardcore method remains an option for valuers. Perhaps this is because the hardcore method exhibits some versatility and can be adapted to deal with stepped rents, turnover rents and over-rented properties, which are phenomena associated with market volatility and where greater risk-sharing between the landlord and tenant may be justified.

References

Blackledge, M. (2009) *Introducing Property Valuation* (Abingdon: Routledge).
GENECON LLP and Partners (2011) *Understanding High Street Performance* (London: Department for Business, Innovation and Skills). Available in e-format at www.bis.gov.uk
Portas, M. (2011) *The Portas Review: An Independent Review into the Future of our High Streets* (London: Department for Business, Innovation and Skills). Available in e-format at www.bis.gov.uk
Scarrett, D. (2008) *Property Valuation: The Five Methods*, 2nd edn (Abingdon: Routledge).

Self-assessment questions

1 An industrial unit is let to a reliable tenant on a long FRI lease with rent reviews every five years. The annual rent passing on the unit is £48,000 but there is market evidence to suggest that the market rent has now climbed to £62,000. Similar market-rented properties are changing hands in the property investment market to reflect a yield of 8 per cent. Use the hardcore method to produce a capital value for the property given that there are two years remaining until the next rent review.

2 What type of valuation might be invoked to provide a check on the above valuation? Why might that need to be undertaken and what might the result be?

3 An office unit on a business park is currently achieving an annual rental income of £95,000, but there is evidence to suggest that the property is over-rented. The tenant has threatened to exercise a break clause in two years' time unless the landlord agrees to reduce the rent at that point to the market rent which is estimated to be £75,000. Similar properties which are market-rented are exchanging in the investment market to reflect a yield of 7.5 per cent. Assuming the landlord wishes to keep the tenant, use the hardcore method to value this over-rented property.

4 What are some of the key criticisms associated with the hardcore method?

5 What are some of the key strengths associated with the hardcore method?

Outline answers can be found towards the back of the book.

The Equivalent Yield

Aims

This chapter discusses the concept of the equivalent yield and illustrates some of the applications of this measure of property investment performance. There are worked examples which show how this variable is calculated. The chapter explains that, while the equivalent yield is fundamentally a benchmark used in property investment analysis, it also has a degree of universality which enables comparison with the performance of alternative investments.

Key terms

>> **Equivalent yield** – is the weighted average yield of a reversionary investment where growth is not factored in. The equivalent yield is the same as the Internal Rate of Return (IRR) from an investment.

>> **Gross redemption yield** – fulfils the same role as the equivalent yield but is applied to government dated stock (gilts) which produce a fixed income and then are redeemable at face value on maturity. In common with the equivalent yield, the gross redemption yield is also the IRR from the investment.

7.1 Introduction

Earlier chapters explained that reversionary property investments can be valued using traditional valuation methods such as the term and reversion approach or the hardcore method. The discussion on those methods necessarily became embroiled in the methodology and how yields might be adjusted to take account of the differential risk posed to tranches of income. It is all too easy to become fixated on this type of process and to lose sight of the bigger picture – a client or investor may only want to know the overall rate of return being earned by a property investment. Armed with that information, the client or investor can compare rates of return on other investment media and then decide whether property investment is a sensible course of action. This chapter will explore the concept of the equivalent yield which does provide the investor with this overview.

7.2 Defining the equivalent yield

Chapter 2 explained that when appraising a reversionary property investment it would be legitimate for a valuer to use the term and reversion method. Given that choice, the valuer would normally adjust the yields used to capitalise the term and reversionary incomes to reflect the perception of differential risk. For instance, an investment's term income might be perceived as being reasonably secure and therefore valued at 6 per cent, while the reversionary income might be perceived as more risky and therefore valued at 8 per cent.

A term and reversion calculation produces a capital value for the particular property, but it does not reveal the overall yield from the investment. In the above example, the figure will lie somewhere between 6 and 8 per cent but the equivalent yield is needed to confirm the precise figure. The equivalent yield is the weighted average yield and it is the same as the internal rate of return on the cash flows from the term and reversion at current rental values. No account is taken of inflation or rental growth.

As a measure of investment return the equivalent yield differs from the equated yield, which was considered in Chapter 5. Before going further, it is worth distinguishing between these two similar sounding concepts, as it is all too easy to confuse them.

- *Equated yield* is the average annual percentage rate of return from an investment over the appraisal period, assuming a specific rental growth rate. Thus an investment property will generate an equated yield of X per cent if the rental value grows by Y per cent per annum over the appraisal period.
- *Equivalent yield* is the average annual percentage rate of return from an investment over the appraisal period based on current rental values with no growth assumed. Thus a property will generate an equivalent yield of Z per cent based on the rent passing during the term and a reversion to the current market rent.

The equivalent yield provides an overall yield for a reversionary property using known data and avoiding any forecasts of growth (or decline). The equivalent yield is the same as the IRR and this makes it a versatile benchmark, enabling comparison to be made with the rates of return on other investment properties as well as non-property investments. This book will try to reinforce these types of definitions when they arise, but for those readers who are less confident with some of the specialised property terms and expressions there are reference glossaries available such as those produced by Parsons (2005) or Jones Lang LaSalle (2002).

7.3 Calculating the equivalent yield

If the yields used to capitalise the term and reversionary incomes are the same, then the equivalent yields will be the same. However that convenience seldom applies and so Example 7.1 assumes that the term rent is more secure and has attracted a lower yield than the reversion.

Example 7.1

A shop is let at an annual net rent of £40,000. The market rent is estimated to be £60,000 per annum. Given that there are three years remaining on the lease, a valuer has used the term and reversion method to find the capital value as follows.

Term		
Rent passing	£40,000	
YP 3 years @ 5%	2.7232	
		£108,928
Reversion		
Market rent	£60,000	
YP in perp. @ 7% deferred 3 years	11.6614	
		£699,684
Capital value		£808,612

If an investor was interested in purchasing the property at around £808,612 some effort would be made to identify the annual rate of return. Although the valuer has set the parameters at between 5 and 7 per cent, the equivalent yield, which provides the precise answer, would need to be calculated using one of the following methods:

- formula;
- discounted cash flow (DCF);
- using the *Goal Seek* function in Excel®; or
- consulting valuation tables.

Most readers are computer literate and would therefore use the *Goal Seek* function in Excel® to solve the problem. As well as looking at that option, the chapter will consider the first two options listed above because they illustrate the underlying process. The fourth method – consulting valuation tables – would also produce an accurate answer, but is now probably a method of last resort for most and, given that it is essentially a reference exercise, it does not require further discussion here.

Solution by formula

$$\text{Equivalent yield} = \frac{(\text{Present income} + \text{annual equivalent of gain}) \times 100}{\text{Capital value}}$$

In Example 7.1 the present income is £40,000 and the capital value is £808,612. The remaining variable is the annual equivalent of gain which is calculated as follows:

$$\text{Annual equivalent of the gain} = \frac{\text{Gain on reversion} \times \text{PV £1 for term}}{\text{YP for the term}}$$

The gain on reversion is the difference between the capital value on reversion and the present capital value.

Thus the capital value on reversion is:

Market rent	£60,000
YP in perp. @ 7%	14.2857
	£857,142

The gain on reversion is therefore:

£857,142 − £808,612 = £48,530.

The annual equivalent of the gain is:

$$\frac{£48,530 \times \text{PV £1 @ 6.5\% in 3 years}}{\text{YP 3 years @ 6.5\%}}$$

The 6.5 per cent rate used in the calculation is a rough guess at the equivalent yield:

$$\frac{£48,530 \times 0.8278}{2.6485} = £15,168$$

Thus the first estimate of the equivalent yield is:

$$\frac{£15,168 + £40,000}{£808,612} = 6.82\%$$

The annual equivalent gain can then be recalculated using this yield in an iterative approach until the two rates equate, and that figure will be the equivalent yield. Graphically the approach is shown in Figure 7.1.

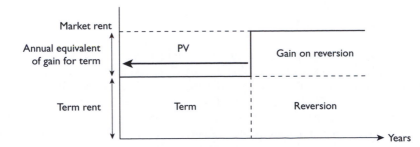

Figure 7.1 Term and reversion arrangement

The calculation converts the capital value of the gain on reversion into its present value equivalent and then annualises it for the period of the term. This gives the rental value for the period which, when added to the term rent, gives an equivalent overall rent to be used in the calculation of the yield.

Solution by DCF

Two trial rates would be used in a solution by DCF. These can be taken from the original term and reversion valuation and were 5 and 7 per cent, respectively. These figures become the two trial rates in the final part of the calculation in which the IRR (the equivalent yield) is identified.

Years	Cash flow	YP 3 years @ 5%	YP in perp. @ 5%	PV £1 in 3 years @ 5%	DCF
1–3	£40,000	2.7232			£108,928
3 into perp.	£60,000		20.00	0.8638	£1,036,560
					£1,145,488
				Less capital value	£808,612
				NPV =	£336,876

Years	Cash flow	YP 3 years @ 7%	YP in perp. @ 7%	PV £1 in 3 years @ 7%	DCF
1–3	£40,000	2.6243			£104,972
3 into perp.	£60,000		14.2857	0.8163	£699,685
					£804,657
				Less capital value	£808,612
				NPV =	−£3,955

$$IRR = 5\% + \left[(7\% - 5\%) \times \frac{£336,876}{£336,876 - -£3,955} \right]$$

$$= 6.98\% \text{ rounded up.}$$

Solution using Excel®'s Goal Seek function

The third method of identifying the equivalent yield is to use the *Goal Seek* function in Excel®'s 'What-If Analysis' suite of functions. The pre-condition is that the relevant cells in the Excel® worksheet containing the valuation are linked by formulas, as shown in Figure 7.2. In practice, the ROUND function would also be used but this has been omitted for clarity.

	A	B	C	D	E	F
1	Term					
2	Rent passing			40000		
3	YP 3 years @	0.0697		=(1-(1/(1+B3)^3))/B3		
4					=D2*D3	
5						
6	Reversion					
7	Market rent			60000		
8	YP in perp. @	=B3	deferred 3 years	=(1/B8)*(1/(1+B8)^3)		
9					=D7*D8	
10	Capital value					=E4+E9

Figure 7.2 Cell links and formula construction in Excel®

Given the cell relationships and formulas shown in Figure 7.2, the *Goal Seek* function accessed via Excel®'s Data tab could be invoked in cell F10 shown outlined in bold in Figure 7.3. When the *Goal Seek* dialogue box appears, the original capital value of £808,612 could be typed into its second input window where the prompt is: 'To value'. In the third input window, which has the prompt: 'By changing cell', cell B3 could be entered or clicked upon and as long as it is linked to cell B8 (=B3) Excel® will iterate to find the percentage value which becomes the equivalent yield in the calculation.

	A	B	C	D	E	F
1	Term					
2	Rent passing			£40,000		
3	YP 3 years @	6.97%		2.6258		
4					£105,032	
5						
6	Reversion					
7	Market rent			£60,000		
8	YP in perp. @	6.97%	deferred 3 years	11.7214		
9					£703,284	
10	Capital value					£808,316

Figure 7.3 Excel® layout enabling *Goal Seek* iteration

As the result in Figure 7.3 shows, the figure (when rounded up) is 6.97 per cent and it differs only slightly from the 6.98 per cent answer produced by DCF. Because the *Goal Seek* result has been rounded up for presentational purposes, the capital value generated of £808,316 is £296 different from the original calculation, but that is sufficiently accurate for these purposes. The un-rounded *Goal Seek* percentage result has a long string of decimal places and if that were used in the valuation it would produce a result which is only £4 different from the original capital value.

To consolidate understanding of the equivalent yield, a further scenario involving reversionary offices is considered in Example 7.2. DCF will be used to identify the equivalent yield and then Excel®'s *Goal Seek* will be employed to check the accuracy of the result.

Example 7.2

Offices have been let recently for a market rent of £120,000 per annum on a full repairing and insuring lease for 15 years with 5-year rent reviews. The freehold subject to the lease was subsequently sold for £1,500,000. A valuer has been asked to value the freehold interest in comparable offices nearby which have been let on an FRI lease for 20 years with 5-year reviews. That lease commenced one year ago when a lower-than-market rent of £90,000 was agreed to achieve a letting in a difficult market. The market rent is now estimated to be £110,000 per annum.

In these circumstances the valuer would consider the freehold yield from the comparable property which is market rented and which is 8 per cent (that is, £120,000/£1,500,000). The valuer might then choose to use the term and reversion method for the valuation in which the term yield might be adjusted downwards to 7 per cent to reflect its added security as follows:

Term rent	£90,000	
YP 4 years @ 7%	3.3872	
		£304,848
Reversion to market rent	£110,000	
YP in perp. @ 8% deferred 4 years	9.1879	
		£1,010,669
Capital value		£1,315,517

In this case, the equivalent yield, which is also the IRR, must lie somewhere between 7 and 8 per cent and thus those two figures can be used as the trial rates in the DCF calculation.

Years	Cash flow	YP 4 years @ 7%	YP in perp. @ 7%	PV £1 in 4 years @ 7%	DCF
1–4	£90,000	3.3872			304,848
4 into perp.	£110,000		14.2857	0.7629	£1,198,842
					£1,503,690
			Less capital value		£1,315,517
			NPV =		£188,173

Years	Cash flow	YP 4 years @ 8%	YP in perp. @ 8%	PV £1 in 4 years @ 8%	DCF
1–4	£90,000	3.3121			298,089
4 into perp.	£110,000		12.5	0.7350	£1,010,625
					£1,308,714
			Less capital value		£1,315,517
			NPV =		−£6,803

The final part of the calculation requires the use of the linear interpolation formula:

$$IRR = 7\% + \left[(8\% - 7\%) \times \frac{£188,173}{£188,173 - -£6,803} \right]$$

$$= 7.97\% \text{ rounded up}$$

The result using *Goal Seek* is 7.96 per cent rounded up. When that figure is inserted into the original term and reversion calculation, as shown below, it produces a capital value of £1,315,606 which is only £89 different from the original capital value (due to rounding in the calculation). This confirms that the equivalent yield in this case is 7.96 per cent.

Term rent	£90,000	
YP 4 years @ 7.96%	3.3151	
		£298,359
Reversion to market rent	£110,000	
YP in perp. @ 7.96%		
deferred 4 years	9.2477	
		£1,017,247
Capital value		£1,315,606

7.4 Comparison with other investments

The calculations which have been undertaken so far are basically the same as calculating the gross redemption yield on a fixed interest security such as dated government gilt-edged stock. Details on the performance of UK government gilts can be seen at the retail bonds section of the London Stock Exchange web site: www.londonstockexchange.com. These types of investment share some of the characteristics of a reversionary property in that there is a regular interim income. In the case of gilts with a redemption date there will be a reversion at a future date. While a property may revert to a higher rental value which is capitalised, gilts are redeemed against their face value (or par) which is usually £100.

The UK government has not so far defaulted on payment of interest on a gilt or repayment of face value on redemption. Thus gilts are about as safe as any investment can be and, given the low risk, investors cannot expect a high rate of return. Property investments on the other hand present some management responsibilities and there are risks of various kinds. Given the risk differential between these asset classes, there will ordinarily be a yield gap between the equivalent yield on a property which will normally be higher than the gross redemption yield on gilts. Example 7.3 shows how the gross redemption yield may be calculated.

Example 7.3

A UK Treasury 8 per cent fixed dated gilt matures in 9 years' time when the £100 face value can be redeemed. This type of gilt would be referred to as a 'medium' on the market because its remaining lifespan is between 5 and 15 years. The gilt is currently trading on the market above par at £155.22. Given that the base rate has remained low for some time, investors would not expect this type of low-risk investment to produce a particularly attractive rate of return in comparison with the returns which could be obtained on riskier investments.

The interest-only yield is one of the first considerations for this type of investment. It is simply the annual premium paid on the gilts, which in this case is £8 (given that this is 8 per cent stock) divided by the market price at which the gilts are currently trading (£155.22). The result is an interest-only yield of 5.15 per cent, which would be an attractive prospect in a context where high street savings accounts were only earning around 1 per cent.

The interest-only yield however, has not taken account of the receipt of £100 in 9 years' time to repay the current purchase price for the gilts of £155.22. Although an investor will receive £8 for say one year's ownership, when the gilts came to be sold one year later it is not certain that £155.22 would be received, because as gilts approach their maturity date their market value gradually converges with the face value. Thus, although £8 was received, a small loss on £155.22 might be made on re-sale one year later, so that the overall gain would be more modest than 5.15 per cent. The convergence process continues until redemption and that is why the big picture is needed. This is provided by the gross redemption yield which is the same as the equivalent yield, discussed above in a property setting. If the gross redemption yield can be identified there is then potential for comparison between the two types of investment. For the gilt example, the gross redemption yield (which is also the IRR) can be calculated by DCF using trial rates of 1 and 3 per cent as follows.

Year	Cash flow	PV £1 @ 1%	DCF @ 1%	PV £1 @ 3%	DCF @ 3%
0	−£155.22	1	−£155.22	1	−£155.22
1	£8.00	0.9901	£7.92	0.9709	£7.77
2	£8.00	0.9803	£7.84	0.9426	£7.54
3	£8.00	0.9706	£7.76	0.9151	£7.32
4	£8.00	0.9610	£7.69	0.8885	£7.11
5	£8.00	0.9515	£7.61	0.8626	£6.90
6	£8.00	0.9420	£7.54	0.8375	£6.70
7	£8.00	0.9327	£7.46	0.8131	£6.50
8	£8.00	0.9235	£7.39	0.7894	£6.32
9	£108.00	0.9143	£98.74	0.7664	£82.77
		NPV =	£4.73	NPV =	−£16.29

$$IRR = R1 + \left[(R_2 - R_1) \times \frac{NPV \ @ \ R_1}{NPV \ @ \ R_1 - NPV \ @ \ R_2} \right]$$

$$= 1\% + \left[(3\% - 1\%) \times \frac{4.73}{4.73 - -16.29} \right] = 1.45\%$$

The IRR of 1.45 per cent provides a more cautious view of what this investment is really returning, and that is before the expenses incurred in acquisition and disposal have been taken into account. Thus, if annual inflation were above 1.45 per cent (which is very likely), the investor would be making a real loss.

There are index-linked gilts available in the market where the coupon (the annual percentage rate of return) is paid to the investor plus a supplement which matches annual inflation and which protects the coupon rate from erosion by inflation. However, because index-linked gilts are traded in the same market as their non-index-linked counterparts, the market price at which index-linked gilts are traded will be higher than for non-index-linked gilts. As a result, there will be similar gross redemption yields for index-linked and non-index-linked gilts which have similar maturity dates.

Investors seeking higher rates of return than could be achieved on gilts would have to surrender some of the security which gilts provide by seeking exposure to riskier investments. Property investment might then come into view because, while the risks are higher than for gilts, there is the possibility of better rates of return, depending on the particular properties selected.

Property is not however as high-risk or as volatile as investment in equities (ordinary shares) where whole markets and the company share prices within them can fluctuate in response to global economic shocks. In some situations, companies can collapse completely, leaving investors with valueless shares. Even where companies do not collapse, company set-backs or adverse reporting of company performance will have a detrimental impact on market sentiment and share values can tumble over just a few days. Sometimes the share price recovers in the longer term and sometimes it does not – a lot hinges on the performance of companies within their particular trading environment. As well as uncertainty around share prices, there is to a lesser degree some uncertainty about the income which shares generate. A company board might decide that, during difficult trading conditions, the longer-term benefit of a company might necessitate that the dividend payable to shareholders be reduced or withheld.

There is therefore a degree of capriciousness regarding investment in shares and it is not surprising that automated 'buy' and 'sell' software has become available and can be linked by investors to market trading. The existence of this type of software reflects the fact that market players simply cannot predict the rises and falls which particular shares may experience in the market from day to day. Because of the added risks associated with shares, it would be expected that their returns to investors would on average be higher than for less risky property and gilts. The historical time-series data collected by research companies such as IPD enable this comparison to be made and it confirms that a representative portfolio of shares has tended to perform far better than gilts or property in the longer term.

Although there are long-term comparative indexes, given the risks associated with investing in shares, it is not easy to make direct comparisons between the performance of individual companies with the investment performance of gilts and property. However there are some parallels between the all risks yield in property and the Price to Earnings (P/E) ratio on shares. Basically, the value of a publicly quoted company is assessed on the market by using the latest net profits (subject to some adjustments) which are capitalised using a P/E ratio. The Years' Purchase (YP) multiplier in property plays a similar role to the P/E ratio as shown in Table 7.1.

Table 7.1 Company and property valuation compared

Valuation of a company	Valuation of a property
Net profit	Net income
× P/E ratio	× Years' Purchase
$P/E \ ratio = \dfrac{Market \ price \ of \ share}{Earnings \ per \ share}$	$YP = \dfrac{Capital \ value}{Net \ income}$

There are individual P/E ratios for all publicly listed companies on the Stock Exchange and these can be seen on share-dealing web sites or in newspapers such as the *Financial Times*. In respect of the property sector, companies are listed under *Real Estate* and are divided into those which have converted into Real Estate Investment Trusts (REITs) and those which have not. Essentially those which have converted into REITs, such as Hammerson, British Land and Land Securities, will typically have very large commercial property portfolios and will be benefitting from a favourable tax regime in return for limiting their activities to mainly managing and trading in investment properties. The REIT rules require that property development must only constitute a relatively small part of the business. Property companies which are not REITs do not benefit from the same tax advantages, but may pursue a broader business model which in some cases is dominated by riskier, but potentially more profitable, property development.

The P/E ratio for shares in these and other listed companies works in broadly the same way as the YP in property. In property YP moves in the opposite direction to the yield, so that a low yield, which implies strong growth potential, produces a high YP multiplier and therefore normally a valuable asset. Conversely a high yield implies less certain growth prospects and produces a lower YP multiplier, which in turn devalues property. The principle is similar for the P/E ratio. A high ratio suggests a low yield and the perception of a better investment in terms of the generation of future cash flows. For example, if a company's net profit from the preceding year were £15 million that figure could be capitalised using the market derived P/E ratio, which can be assumed to be 7.8:

Net profit	£15,000,000
P/E ratio	7.8
Market value of company	£117,000,000

If there were 20 million shares in the above company, then, assuming they were all issued on the same basis, the nominal share price would be £5.85. This is acknowledged to be a simple example which does not encompass capital structure, the relationship between share price and market capitalisation and how company income is assessed. The point of the example was to show that there is at least some comparability between the appraisal methods used in the different sectors.

7.5 Summary

Where the capital value of reversionary properties is evaluated, the overall rate of return is not always clear when different yields are used in different parts of the calculation to capitalise different parts of the income. The equivalent yield does provide the overall rate of return because it is the IRR of the term and reversionary income. The equivalent yield is a versatile measure because it enables comparisons with rates of return on other property investments and with returns on non-property investments. Thus for low-risk investment alternatives such as gilts, a yield gap should be identifiable between the overall returns available (reflected in the gross redemption yield) and those achievable on property which has, on average, a higher risk profile.

Although the equivalent yield usefully enables comparison within and across asset classes, it could be accused of erring on the cautious side because the calculation takes no account of the potential for future growth. Such a consideration may be unrealistic given that reversions may be several years into the future when it is unlikely that the prevailing market rent will correspond to the current market rent. By the same token, the method may have merit in avoiding forecasts of rental growth because rents may fall during recessionary cycles, resulting in over-rented property whose capital value falls on re-valuation. As a performance measure therefore, the equivalent yield could be said to be inherently conservative (and perhaps prudent) in its utilisation of known data rather than forecasts.

References

Jones Lang LaSalle (2002) *The Glossary of Property Terms*, 2nd edn (London: Estates Gazette).

London Stock Exchange web site: www.londonstockexchange.com

Parsons, G. (2005) *EG Property Handbook* (London: EG Books).

Self-assessment questions

1 A retail warehouse has been let to a national retailer on a long full repairing and insuring lease containing 5-year rent reviews and under which an annual rent of £70,000 is currently passing. There are three years remaining until the next rent review when a reversion to the market rent of £80,000 is anticipated. Using the term and reversion valuation technique, identify the capital value of this property given that similar market rented properties have recently been purchased by corporate property investors to reflect an all risks yield of 7.5 per cent.

2 Using whichever method is preferred, calculate the equivalent yield for the above property.

3 Separate the correct statements from the incorrect in the following.

   (a) The equivalent yield factors in assumptions about future rental growth and so it is a reliable measure of the overall rate of return earned by a property investment over a given appraisal period.

   (b) The equivalent yield is indistinguishable from the internal rate of return on an investment and it is therefore a convenient measure of investment performance enabling comparisons to be made within and across asset classes.

   (c) The gross redemption yield on gilts is for all practical purposes the IRR on that form of investment and so it can also be compared with the equivalent yield on reversionary properties.

   (d) Investors should find that the equivalent yield on tenanted commercial property investments should be the same as the gross redemption yield on medium dated gilts because they share the same risk characteristics.

   (e) There should be no yield gap between the overall return on investment property measured by the equivalent yield and a portfolio of company shares.

4 What is the fundamental difference between the equivalent yield and the equated yield and why might there be merit in using one of these investment measures rather than the other?

5 Why might it be slightly misleading to only consider the interest only yield on gilts?

Outline answers can be found towards the back of the book.

Equivalent Rents, Premiums and Lease Incentives

Aims

This chapter explores specialised instruments related to commercial property rents. The early part of the chapter looks at equivalent rents, which are sometimes referred to as *constant rents*. The latter part of the chapter considers the effects upon rent of premiums and incentives which may change hands between a landlord and tenant in the context of a commercial property lease. The connection between premiums and profit rents will also be explained. The chapter contains worked examples to illustrate the mathematics involved when equivalent rents, premiums and lease incentives are considered.

Key terms

>> **Equivalent rents** – also known as constant rents, reflect the adjustments made to a market rent to compensate for a non-standard rent review frequency in a commercial property lease. Where rental growth is anticipated, a landlord might expect a higher-than-market rent if the rent review cycle in the lease is longer than the norm (usually taken to be five years) to compensate for the reduced exposure to inflation. Conversely rent review intervals that are shorter than five years, say three years, would suggest that a lower-than-market rent is justified because rent reviews will more regularly be exposed to the effects of inflation.

>> **Premium** – the capital sum which is usually paid by a tenant to a commercial property landlord, often at the commencement of a lease. The premium is in effect the capitalisation of a portion of the annual rent paid up-front as a

lump sum. For the tenant, a premium normally buys a proportionate reduction in the rent for the term until the next rent review or lease expiry. During periods when the demand for properties outstrips supply, landlords will have added leverage to negotiate premiums. The payment of a premium may also create tax advantages for one or other of the parties. A premium may also arise where a *profit rent* is being purchased in the context of a lease assignment.

>> **Reverse premium** – a payment by a commercial property landlord to a tenant, usually in a situation where the market has fallen, in order to prop up the headline rent arising from a lease agreement.

>> **Profit rent** – the difference between the rent passing and the market rent when the lease rent is significantly below the market rent which would be achieved if the property were available to be re-let or subject to a rent review. This difference is enjoyed by the tenant for the remainder of the term. The capital value of a profit rent can be realised if the lease is assigned. The assignee who purchases the profit rent is effectively buying the right to enjoy a lower–than-market rent for the term remaining before the next rent review or lease expiry.

8.1 Introduction

This chapter explores specialised topics related to the analysis and interpretation of commercial property rents. The first topic for discussion is *equivalent rents*, which are sometimes known as constant rents. To reduce the potential for confusion, the term 'equivalent rents' will be used in the chapter.

The calculation of an equivalent rent applies where a commercial property has a lease containing a non-standard rent review pattern. The majority of comparable evidence in the commercial lettings market is derived from properties whose leases contain provision for rent reviews every five years. That market evidence may therefore need to be adjusted where it is to be applied to a property with a lease containing a different review pattern. The adjustments are essentially trying to create a like-for-like comparison between market data and a specific property under analysis.

The chapter will also consider the payment of premiums and incentives, both of which are capable of affecting rental values in the context of commercial property leases. The chapter will explore the process of identifying what the RICS (2012a: 282) define as the *net effective rent* which takes into account and adjusts for incentives. The RICS acknowledge that the net effective rent can sometimes be referred to as the equivalent rent so, to avoid confusion, the term 'equivalent rent' will apply throughout this chapter.

8.2 Rent review frequency and equivalent rents

The need to adjust rents would not arise in a context where there was no inflation. However there are risks for a landlord who agrees to a long lease containing no or infrequent rent reviews because the rent agreed at the outset would remain unchanged for long periods. Even in the unlikely event that there was zero inflation over a long period, other factors are likely to change so that higher rents could be obtained. For example, in the context of retail property, a strengthening economy would usually lead to increased consumer expenditure, triggering increased retail profits and increased demand for shop premises. Higher retail rents would normally ensue. Area regeneration and improved infrastructure can lead to better trading conditions for businesses, and this can lead to real growth in the rental value achievable for a property.

Conversely, in conditions of economic decline which damage the business environment in a particular area, a longer rent review period might be beneficial to a landlord. Essentially there is an element of risk to both landlord and tenant where they agree to long review periods in a lease. If inflation is accepted as the norm, as has been the experience over recent decades, then shorter rent review periods will benefit the landlord. Although that arrangement could be disadvantageous for a tenant, shorter review periods in shorter leases containing break clauses present some advantages to the tenant, particularly in periods of economic uncertainty.

The rationale for calculating equivalent rents rests on the assumption that there will be some rental growth in the future, otherwise there would be no point to the exercise because there would be no difference in value between, say, three-year and seven-year rent reviews. In common with the wider economy, the property market does experience downturns but historically there have been longer periods of growth. On average over the medium to longer term, it is therefore reasonable to assume that there will be some rental growth. However, even given reliable time-series data for the particular property sector, a forecast of the precise annual growth rate will always come with a degree of risk, simply because it is only a forecast of what might happen rather than a fact.

The general pattern of review in commercial property leases in the UK is on a five-year basis, but this will depend on the type, nature, location of the property and the covenant of the tenant. In recent years there has been a trend towards shorter leases containing more frequent rent reviews, such that the norm in some property sectors in some localities is fast becoming three-year rent reviews. The review frequency in a lease could be three, five or seven years or any other period, but it is the relationship between that frequency and the market norm that provides the comparables which suggests whether any adjustment is warranted.

The following section of the chapter will explore the mathematics which has evolved to enable adjustments to be made between comparable market evidence and a subject property. However, as the RICS (2012b: 10) reminds its valuers, the mathematical adjustments should not be applied in a mechanical fashion. The numerical solutions would still need to be considered by a valuer who had specific market knowledge and was able to evaluate whether the adjusted values were tenable in the context of other market factors. In essence the quantitative adjustments would still need to be tempered by the judgement of a valuer.

8.3 Rose's formula and equivalent rents

An early contributor to this field was Jack Rose who published *Tables of the Constant Rent* (1979). He introduced the concept of the Constant Rent Factor, the multiplier K, which can be applied to the rent payable on a normal review pattern to produce an adjusted but equivalent rent on an abnormal review pattern. In general the multiplier K will enhance the rent payable where there is a longer than normal review pattern and it will tend to reduce the rent where there is a shorter than normal review pattern. The formula which underpins the tables and provides K is:

$$K = \frac{A - B}{A - 1} \times \frac{C - 1}{C - D}$$

where:

A is the amount of £1 @ R% (the equated yield) for L years (the abnormal review period);
B is the amount of £1 @ G% (the growth rate applicable to the property) for L years;
C is the amount of £1 @ R% for Z years (the normal rent review period); and
D is the amount of £1 @ G% for Z years.

The variable L represents the abnormal rent review period which can be ascertained from the lease of the subject property, while Z represents the normal rent review period which can be gauged from standard leases which make up the majority of the market. The variable G is an assumption about the growth rate which could be expected in the rent for the subject property.

The credibility of the growth assumption can be strengthened on the back of specific research or extrapolated from time-series data. However, in the end this is still an assumption, even were it to be induced as an investor's expectation. The growth rate then becomes a minimum target rate which would need to be met in order for the investment to be viable. The required growth rate could be calculated using the growth rate formula originally considered in Chapter 5.

The purpose of Rose's formula (and tables) is to produce the constant K which, when multiplied by the market rent achievable on a standard five-year rent review pattern, will provide the adjusted rent payable on an abnormal review pattern. The rental value identified from using the multiplier K will fulfil the role of maintaining the capital value of the investment at the same level as for a normal review pattern. Thus:

$$\text{Income}^A = K \times \text{Income}^N \text{ which transposes to: } \frac{\text{Income}^A}{\text{Income}^N} = K$$

where:

Income^N is the net income obtained under a normal rent review pattern;
Income^A is the net income obtained under an abnormal rent review pattern; and
K is the constant rent factor.

An application of Rose's formula is considered in Example 8.1.

Example 8.1

Adjusting for a long review pattern

Because of the circumstances which existed at the commencement of a long lease of a major commercial property, the lease contains provision for rent reviews at 21-year intervals. Calculate the rent appropriate on review given that the lessor requires a rate of return (or equated yield) of 11 per cent and that the anticipated annual growth rate for the property's rent is 3 per cent. Market evidence suggests that the annual market rent for this property, were it to be subject to a standard five-year review pattern, would be £100,000.

Calibrating the variables in Rose's formula to reflect the scenario produces the following.

$$K = \frac{A - B}{A - 1} \times \frac{C - 1}{C - D}$$

$$= \frac{(1 + 0.11)^{21} - (1 + 0.03)^{21}}{(1 + 0.11)^{21} - 1} \times \frac{(1 + 0.11)^5 - 1}{(1 + 0.11)^5 - (1 + 0.03)^5}$$

$$= \frac{8.9492 - 1.8603}{7.9492} \times \frac{0.6851}{1.6851 - 1.1593}$$

$$= 0.8918 \times 1.3030$$

$$= 1.1620$$

Thus the annual rent appropriate on review is K multiplied by the rent achievable on a normal review pattern: $1.162 \times £100,000 = £116,200$.

There are a number of alternative ways that this answer could be found in order to provide a check on accuracy. Rose's *Tables* could obviously be consulted by cross referring the variables given in the scenario to identify K. Alternatively *Donaldson's Investment Tables* (Marshall, 1989) could be consulted. In *Donaldson's Tables* there are four variables: the equated yield, the growth rate, the review pattern and the initial yield. If, as in Example 8.1, the equated yield, growth rate and review period are known, the initial yield can be calculated. It would then be possible to calculate initial yields for the normal and abnormal rent review periods as a check to see whether they would ensure that the capital value of the investment remained the same in each scenario. The principle is that, if the capital value remained the same given standard and equivalent rents, then there must have been a proportionate change in the initial yields. This is, in fact, the basis of Rose's constant K. The constant rent factor is the ratio between the initial yield calculated on the abnormal review to the initial yield in the normal review.

Donaldson's Tables can provide initial yields for various rent review patterns if the other three variables – the rent review pattern, the equated yield and the rental growth rate – are known. This enables the establishment of a relationship involving the initial yield on a normal rent review pattern (I^N) and the initial yield on an abnormal rent review pattern (I^A). Thus:

$$I^A = \frac{\text{Income}^A}{CV^A} \text{ and } I^N = \frac{\text{Income}^N}{CV^N}$$

where CV^A and CV^N are the capital values on abnormal and normal rent reviews.

Given that the purpose of the exercise is to prove that the adjusted rents for different review patterns will still leave the investor with the same capital value (that is, $CV^A = CV^N$), the formula for K can be written as:

$$K = \frac{\text{Income}^A}{\text{Income}^N} = \frac{I^A}{I^N}$$

which, when transposed, produces: $K \times I^N = I^A$.

K can be used to adjust the ratio of the initial yields, so all that is required is the calculation of one of those yields. For convenience I^N the initial yield on a standard rent review pattern will be identified using the formula, first encountered in Chapter 5, which forms the basis for *Donaldson's Tables*. For the lease in Example 8.1, the formula utilises the known variables of rental growth, the rent review period and the investor's target rate (equated yield) to find the initial yield.

$$I = E - \left[\frac{E((1+G)^n - 1)}{(1+E)^n - 1}\right]$$

where:

I is the initial yield or capitalisation rate, which is to be determined.
E is the investor's target rate of 11 per cent, which is also the equated yield.
G is the assumed annual rental growth rate of 3 per cent.
n is the rent review period in years, which is 5 to reflect a standard lease.

Calibrating the variables to reflect the normal 5-year review period produces:

$$I = 0.11 - \left[\frac{0.11((1+0.03)^5 - 1)}{(1+0.11)^5 - 1}\right]$$

$$= 0.11 - \left[\frac{0.0175}{0.6851}\right]$$

$$= 0.0845 \text{ rounded up, which is } 8.45\%$$

The variable I is the initial yield of 8.45 per cent for the comparable property leased on standard 5-year rent review terms at an annual rent of £100,000. If that rent were capitalised at 8.45 per cent the calculation would be: YP 11.8343 × £100,000 to produce a capital value of £1,183,430. If the value of K calculated in Example 8.1 to be 1.162 is correct, it can be applied to the yield of 8.45 per cent to produce a yield for the subject property with 21-year rent reviews:

1.162 × 8.45% = 9.82% (rounded)

That adjusted yield can then be used to capitalise the equivalent rent of £116,200 as follows:

YP 10.1833 × £116,200 = £1,183,299 rounded.

The difference between the two capital values of £131 arises from rounding at various stages and, in any case, is inconsequential at this scale of investment. The point is that there is now some evidence that the adjusted rent for the non-standard rent review pattern does maintain the capital value of the property relative to properties which benefit from more frequent rent reviews.

Some readers might find the step-by-step formulaic approach a little cumbersome and might prefer to prove the relationship by using an Excel® spreadsheet. A discounted cash flow (DCF) can be structured in Excel® to enable the *Goal Seek* function to find the equivalent rent (see Figure 8.1). Given

	A	B	C	D	E	F
1	Year	Rent on 5-year reviews	Rent on 21-year reviews	PV £1 @ 11%	DCF on 5-year reviews	DCF on 21-year reviews
2	1	100,000	116,322	0.9009	90,090	104,794
3	2	100,000	116,322	0.8116	81,160	94,407
4	3	100,000	116,322	0.7312	73,120	85,055
5	4	100,000	116,322	0.6587	65,870	76,621
6	5	100,000	116,322	0.5935	59,350	69,037
7	6	115,927	116,322	0.5346	61,975	62,186
8	7	115,927	116,322	0.4817	55,842	56,032
9	8	115,927	116,322	0.4339	50,301	50,472
10	9	115,927	116,322	0.3909	45,316	45,470
11	10	115,927	116,322	0.3522	40,829	40,969
12	11	134,391	116,322	0.3173	42,642	36,909
13	12	134,391	116,322	0.2858	38,409	33,245
14	13	134,391	116,322	0.2575	34,606	29,953
15	14	134,391	116,322	0.2320	31,179	26,987
16	15	134,391	116,322	0.2090	28,088	24,311
17	16	155,796	116,322	0.1883	29,336	21,903
18	17	155,796	116,322	0.1696	26,423	19,728
19	18	155,796	116,322	0.1528	23,806	17,774
20	19	155,796	116,322	0.1377	21,453	16,018
21	20	155,796	116,322	0.1240	19,319	14,424
22	21	180,610	116,322	0.1117	20,174	12,993
23			Net present value		939,288	939,288

Figure 8.1 DCF comparing 5-year with 21-year rent review periods

the known variables in the example, the DCF would be structured to reflect 3 per cent per annum growth in the rent under the normal pattern of 5-year rent reviews. That cash flow would then be discounted at the investor's target rate of 11 per cent to arrive at a net present value (NPV) of £939,288 as shown in cell E23 of Figure 8.1.

Excel®'s *Goal Seek* function could then be used to iterate the rental value in Cell C2 (and copied down column C) so that it produces an identical NPV in cell F23 to that shown in cell E23. This confirms that an equivalent rent of £116,322 on a 21-year review pattern would maintain parity of value with the property which had the 5-year review cycle. The equivalent rent identified in the DCF is therefore very close to that found using Rose's formula. Incidentally, the NPV is not the capital value of the property but rather a like-for-like test across 21 years of income.

Example 8.2 is designed to reinforce the relationship between the DCF approach and the traditional formula approach.

Example 8.2

Adjusting for the absence of rent reviews

An office property is to be leased to a tenant of good covenant for a period of 15 years without review. Market evidence from comparable properties which have standard five-year review patterns suggest that the subject property would warrant an annual rent of £100,000 if it were to be let on a 5-year review cycle. Data shows that the average annual growth rate in the rent for this property type in this location has been 3 per cent in recent years. Given that the freeholder expects an equated yield of 10 per cent from the property, calculate the equivalent rent required using DCF and then check the accuracy of that result using Rose's formula.

The DCF in Figure 8.2 is reproduced from an Excel® worksheet in which *Goal Seek* was used to find the equivalent rent of £111,537 which would put the freeholder in exactly the same position as if the property were to be leased with standard 5-year rent reviews. That arrangement is shown graphically in Figure 8.3.

Rose's formula could then be used to check the accuracy of the DCF result as follows:

$$K = \frac{A - B}{A - 1} \times \frac{C - 1}{C - D}$$

$$= \frac{(1 + 0.1)^{15} - (1 + 0.03)^{15}}{(1 + 0.1)^{15} - 1} \times \frac{(1 + 0.1)^5 - 1}{(1 + 0.1)^5 - (1 + 0.03)^5}$$

$$= \frac{4.1772 - 1.558}{3.1772} \times \frac{0.6105}{1.6105 - 1.1593}$$

$$= 0.8244 \times 1.3531$$

$$= 1.1155$$

Year	Rent £ on 5-year reviews	Equivalent rent £ over 15 years	PV £1 @ 10%	DCF £ on 5-year reviews	DCF £ on 15-year equivalent rent
1	100,000	111,537	0.9091	90,910	101,398
2	100,000	111,537	0.8264	82,640	92,174
3	100,000	111,537	0.7513	75,130	83,798
4	100,000	111,537	0.6830	68,300	76,180
5	100,000	111,537	0.6209	62,090	69,253
6	115,927	111,537	0.5645	65,441	62,963
7	115,927	111,537	0.5132	59,494	57,241
8	115,927	111,537	0.4665	54,080	52,032
9	115,927	111,537	0.4241	49,165	47,303
10	115,927	111,537	0.3855	44,690	42,998
11	134,391	111,537	0.3505	47,104	39,094
12	134,391	111,537	0.3186	42,817	35,536
13	134,391	111,537	0.2897	38,933	32,312
14	134,391	111,537	0.2633	35,385	29,368
15	134,391	111,537	0.2394	32,173	26,702
			NPV =	848,352	848,352

Figure 8.2

Figure 8.3

The use of Rose's formula suggests that the equivalent rent on a 15-year cycle is K multiplied by the rent achievable on a normal review pattern, thus: $1.1155 \times £100,000 = £111,550$. Given that this result only differs by £13 from the result identified by DCF the check has provided some comfort that the equivalent rent has been correctly calculated.

Example 8.3 considers a situation in which the subject property is leased on shorter rent review cycles than the market norm. Again DCF will be used to calculate the equivalent rent and Rose's formula will then be used to check on accuracy.

Example 8.3

Adjusting for three-year rent reviews

A shop is to be leased for 15 years with three-year rent reviews. Comparable evidence derived from similar properties with five-year rent review clauses, suggests that the annual rent for the shop would in those circumstances be £50,000. The freeholder, who has a target rate of return of 10 per cent for this property, has asked you to calculate the equivalent rent assuming that the annual growth rate in the rent will be 3.5 per cent.

The DCF in Figure 8.4 has used *Goal Seek* in Excel® to find that an equivalent rent of £48,482 at the commencement of the lease will achieve parity with the peer group of properties.

Year	Rent £ on 5-year reviews	Equivalent rent £ on 3-year reviews	PV £1 @ 10%	DCF £ on 5-year reviews	DCF £ on 3-year reviews
1	50,000	48,482	0.9091	45,455	44,075
2	50,000	48,482	0.8264	41,320	40,066
3	50,000	48,482	0.7513	37,565	36,425
4	50,000	53,753	0.6830	34,150	36,713
5	50,000	53,753	0.6209	31,045	33,375
6	59,384	53,753	0.5645	33,522	30,343
7	59,384	59,597	0.5132	30,476	30,585
8	59,384	59,597	0.4665	27,703	27,802
9	59,384	59,597	0.4241	25,185	25,275
10	59,384	66,076	0.3855	22,893	25,472
11	70,530	66,076	0.3505	24,721	23,160
12	70,530	66,076	0.3186	22,471	21,052
13	70,530	73,260	0.2897	20,433	21,223
14	70,530	73,260	0.2633	18,571	19,289
15	70,530	73,260	0.2394	16,885	17,538
			NPV =	432,395	432,393

Figure 8.4

The comparison between the rental pattern on three- and five-year review cycles is shown graphically in Figure 8.5.

The accuracy of the result identified by DCF can be checked by using Rose's formula:

$$K = \frac{A-B}{A-1} \times \frac{C-1}{C-D}$$

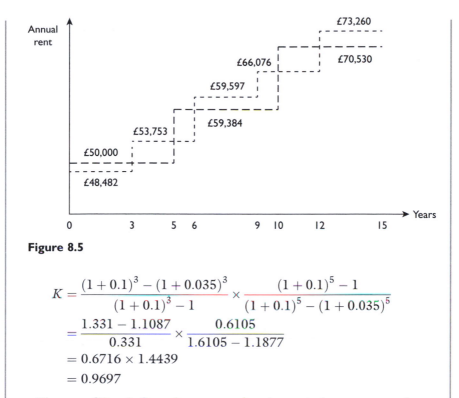

Figure 8.5

$$K = \frac{(1+0.1)^3 - (1+0.035)^3}{(1+0.1)^3 - 1} \times \frac{(1+0.1)^5 - 1}{(1+0.1)^5 - (1+0.035)^5}$$

$$= \frac{1.331 - 1.1087}{0.331} \times \frac{0.6105}{1.6105 - 1.1877}$$

$$= 0.6716 \times 1.4439$$

$$= 0.9697$$

The use of Rose's formula suggests that the equivalent rent on a three-year cycle is K multiplied by the rent achievable on a normal review pattern, thus: $0.9697 \times £50,000 = £48,485$. Given that the result only differs by £2 from the result identified by DCF, the check has provided confidence that the equivalent rent identified is correct.

8.4 Premiums and equivalent rents

In a commercial property context a premium is a capital sum which is paid, usually at the commencement of a lease, by a business tenant to a landlord with the effect that the annual rent is reduced. Although this is not the only situation where premiums are paid, the exploration of the topic will begin with that premise, before going on to consider other situations where premiums change hands.

During periods in the property market when the demand from businesses outstrips the supply of space (in quantitative or qualitative terms), commercial property landlords will find themselves in a stronger position when negotiating leases. Essentially landlords will be able to dictate terms more readily in a buoyant market than when the market is static or falling, and when incentives might be needed to attract scarce tenants.

In buoyant markets, a landlord can also be selective and might, for example, express some qualms regarding the covenant of a potential business tenant, perhaps because the potential tenant does not possess a spotless corporate credit rating or extensive trading record. In that situation, a landlord might want to reduce the risk by harvesting some of the rent up front in the form of a premium in return for taking some risk in granting the lease.

The effect of the premium will normally be to reduce the annual rent with the beneficial consequence of reducing the potential for the tenant to default, because lower ongoing costs now have to be met by the business. As Baum *et al.* (2011: 151) confirm, the payment of a premium also secures a degree of buy-in from the tenant, who will be more focused on ensuring that the venture is successful given that a portion of it has already been paid for. There may also be tax advantages for one or other of the parties in converting revenue/payment into capital receipts/payments. However it would be unwise to over-generalise on this issue, as it is contingent on the financial status of the businesses involved and the tax regime applicable at the time. Given that caveat, Examples 8.4 and 8.5 will illustrate the principles involved where a premium is required by a landlord.

Example 8.4

The effects of a premium on entry

A prime high street shop is to be let on a long lease in a prosperous town centre where some national retailers are seeking to establish a presence but where there are few vacant units. The landlord feels confident that a premium of £80,000 is realistic but accepts that this will reduce the ongoing rent for the first term below the market rent, which is estimated to be £100,000 per annum for the shop. Given that the yield for this type of property in this location is 7 per cent, what rent will the tenant be expected to meet for the first term?

Market rent		£100,000
Premium paid	£80,000	
Divide by YP 5 years @ 7%	4.1002	
		19,511
Annual rent payable up to first review		£80,489

The calculation can be restructured if necessary to find the premium required to reduce the rent to a predetermined level. Example 8.5 will use the same variables as Example 8.4 to illustrate the principles, although it is acknowledged that a potential tenant is unlikely to specify £80,489 as a precise rental target.

It is worth noting at this point that premiums do not always flow from tenants to landlords. There may be circumstances, usually in a falling market, in which a landlord pays a reverse premium to a tenant.

Example 8.5

Establishing the premium required

What premium would a retailer have to pay on the commencement of a lease on a shop in order to reduce the annual rent to £80,489 when the property's estimated market rental value is £100,000? The yield for this class of property is 7 per cent.

Market rent	£100,000	
Annual rent after premium	£80,489	
Reduction required therefore	£19,511	
Multiply by YP 5 years @ 7%	4.1002	
Premium required		£79,999

Using the same variables as Example 8.5, the calculation can be re-worked to identify the scale of reverse premium required for a tenant to meet a higher-than-market rent.

Headline rent with reverse premium	£100,000	
Multiply by YP 5 years @ 7%	4.1002	
Capital value		£410,020
Market rent	£80,489	
Multiply by YP 5 years @ 7%	4.1002	
Capital value		330,021
Reverse premium required		£79,999

8.5 Premiums and profit rents

One interpretation of Example 8.4 is that a tenant had paid a premium of £80,000 in order to enjoy a reduced annual rent for five years relative to the market rent benchmark. This principle is similar to the concept of purchasing a profit rent which had arisen because the rent passing under a lease was significantly below the market rent. This might occur, for example, in the latter years of a long lease where there are no further rent reviews but where there has been growth in prevailing market rental values. The profit rent in its capitalised form could be sold where the lease could be assigned for the remainder of the term.

An assignee who purchased a lease where there was a profit rent is effectively paying a premium to the assignor for the benefit of taking premises at a reduced rent for the remainder of the lease. As Baum *et al.* (2011: 129) confirm, the premium therefore reflects what another business is willing to pay to benefit from a reduced rent. A valuer working in this context would be aware that the 'willingness to pay' will reflect a company's cost of capital, which in turn will be influenced by prevailing borrowing rates. Example 8.6 illustrates the principles.

Example 8.6

Premium payable on lease assignment

A bank which is restructuring and consolidating its property holdings wishes to assign the lease on one of its high street properties. A building society is expanding but does not yet have a branch in that high street and is therefore interested in taking the lease on assignment. The lease has eight years remaining under which an annual rent of £55,000 is passing without further review. Because of infrequent rent reviews in this particular lease, a significant gap has opened up between the rent passing and the estimated annual market rent for this property, which is now £75,000. What premium might be paid by the building society to purchase the remaining eight years of the lease from the bank given that internal funds priced at 7 per cent will be used?

Estimated market rental value	£75,000	
Rent passing for remainder of term	£55,000	
Profit rent	£20,000	
YP 8 years @ 7%	5.9713	
Estimated premium		£119,426

Should a check on the answer be required, a DCF could be constructed as follows:

Year	Annual profit rent £	PV £1 @ 7%	DCF £
1	20,000	0.9346	18,692
2	20,000	0.8734	17,468
3	20,000	0.8163	16,326
4	20,000	0.7629	15,258
5	20,000	0.7130	14,260
6	20,000	0.6663	13,326
7	20,000	0.6227	12,454
8	20,000	0.5820	11,640
		NPV =	119,424

This confirms that the premium might well be of the order of £119,424 (the difference of £2 is due to rounding).

In recessionary markets where properties are over-rented, the assignment might have to be accompanied by a reverse premium from the bank (the assignor) in order to induce the building society (the assignee) to take the lease. In that context the premium acts like a bursary, enabling the building society to continue to meet the higher-than-market rent which is contractually due to the landlord. Transposing the variables from Example 8.6 so that the passing rent under the lease was £75,000 but the market rent had fallen to £55,000, the bank might have to pay the building society a reverse premium of around £119,426 to offload the now-unwanted lease.

8.6 Adjusting for lease incentives

As Jayne (2008: 337–42) notes, the equivalent rent may be required for rating purposes where incentives have been given by the landlord when granting a commercial lease. The headline rent, which the RICS (2012a: 282) confirms is the contracted rent which the tenant will meet after the incentives have ended, is not sufficient in these circumstances. The headline rent will, however, feature as one element in the reconciliation process between the actual lease agreement and a hypothetical tenancy where no inducements apply. Example 8.7 illustrates the principles involved.

Example 8.7

Adjusting for rent-free periods

A business was given a two-year rent-free period as an inducement to take a long lease on a suite of offices at a headline rent of £90,000 per annum on a five-year rent review pattern. Determine the equivalent rent for the first term given a capitalisation rate of 7 per cent for this type of property.

Headline rent for years 3 to 5 inclusive		£90,000
YP 3 years @ 7%	2.6243	
Deferred 2 years @ 7%	0.8734	
	2.2921	
Capital value of term		£206,289
Decapitalise for 5 years @ 7%	4.1002	
Equivalent rent		£50,312

The calculation suggests that an equivalent rent of £50,312 applies. That answer could be checked using a DCF constructed in Excel® in which the cells could be linked and formulas structured to enable *Goal Seek* to find the equivalent rent. In the DCF below there is a very minor difference of £2 in the outcome due to rounding, but essentially there is confirmation that the annual equivalent rent in this case is £50,312.

Year	Headline rent £ and rent-free period	Equivalent rent £	PV £1 @ 7%	DCF £ on headline rent	DCF £ on equivalent rent
1	0	50,314	0.9346	0	47,024
2	0	50,314	0.8734	0	43,944
3	90,000	50,314	0.8163	73,467	41,071
4	90,000	50,314	0.7629	68,661	38,385
5	90,000	50,314	0.7130	64,170	35,874
			NPV =	206,298	206,298

Incentives do not always take the form of rent-free periods and may be offered as stepped rents. The steps would normally begin with a first year's rent which was significantly below the market rent for the property. In subsequent years the rent would increase to specified levels set out in the lease. This method of offering incentives has particular applicability for secondary retail property, where a retailer may need the opportunity to establish a presence and some trading momentum before meeting the full market rent.

The following DCF illustrates the principle and shows that the stepped-rent arrangement can be engineered to leave a landlord in the same position as if a two-year rent-free period had been granted. It can be seen that the equivalent rent of £50,300 is materially the same as in Example 8.7 where a two-year rent-free period was granted.

Year	Stepped rents £	Equivalent rent £	PV £1 @ 7%	DCF £ on stepped rents	DCF £ on equivalent rent
1	30,000	50,300	0.9346	28,038	47,010
2	40,000	50,300	0.8734	34,936	43,932
3	62,500	50,300	0.8163	51,019	41,060
4	62,500	50,300	0.7629	47,681	38,374
5	62,500	50,300	0.7130	44,563	35,864
			NPV =	206,237	206,240

8.7 Summary

Rose's formula provides one way of identifying an equivalent rent where a commercial property has an abnormal rent review pattern relative to the market norm. In most situations the market norm is a five-year rent review pattern. Where a subject property has a shorter review pattern, its rent would normally be adjusted below the prevailing market rent, and where the review pattern is longer than five years then the equivalent rent will normally be above the market rent. The adjustments pre-suppose inflation, which will normally see market rents gradually increase year on year.

The payment of premiums by one or other of the parties in a landlord–tenant relationship will normally affect the ongoing rental value. When undertaking comparative exercises or assessing the rental value for rating purposes, valuers will normally need to look beyond the headline rent to identify the underlying equivalent rent. This chapter illustrated both calculation and DCF methods for determining the equivalent rent in these situations.

Profit rents arise when the contractual rent under a lease is below the estimated market rent for a property. Profit rents have a latent capital value which may be realised in the form of a premium if a property is successfully assigned. The premium paid for a profit rent will reflect what one business is willing to pay another to occupy premises below the market rent.

Particularly in recessionary situations commercial landlords may offer incentives to businesses to commit to long leases. The incentives can take a number of forms, although the most common are rent-free periods and sometimes stepped rents. In each case the underlying equivalent rent can be identified using one or other of the methods illustrated in the chapter.

For all the adjustment techniques explored there is an Excel®-based DCF alternative, in which the *Goal Seek* function can be used to find the unknown variable. However the mathematical result is found, the RICS (2012b: 10) advises that there is still a role for an experienced valuer who is conversant with the specific market to judge whether the outcome is credible in the light of other qualitative and market factors.

References

Baum, A., Mackmin, D. and Nunnington, N. (2011) *The Income Approach to Property Valuation*, 6th edn (Oxford: EG Books).

Jayne, M.R. (2008) 'Rating' in R. Hayward (ed.), *Valuation: Principles into Practice*, 6th edn (London: EG Books).

Marshall, P. (1989) *Donaldson's Investment Tables* (London: Donaldson's).

RICS (2012a) *RICS Valuation – Professional Standards* (Coventry: Royal Institution of Chartered Surveyors).

RICS (2012b) *Comparable Evidence in Property Valuation – Information Paper* (Coventry: Royal Institution of Chartered Surveyors).

Rose, J. (1979) *Tables of the Constant Rent* (Oxford: The Technical Press).

Self-assessment questions

1 A landlord, who has a minimum target rate of return of 10 per cent, has agreed to let a high street shop to a tenant on a 15-year lease with rent reviews at three-year intervals. The market evidence from properties which have five-year rent reviews suggests that the rental value for this property would be £65,000 per annum if it were let on that basis. A recent recession has curbed expectations about growth, although the property is in a prime location in a robust high street setting and so a conservative growth rate of 2.5 per cent per annum is felt to be justified. Given that assumption, use Rose's formula to calculate the equivalent rent which should apply for this property and then use DCF to check the answer.

2   You have been asked to represent a manufacturing firm which occupies an industrial unit under a 30-year lease which was granted 15 years ago. The lease provides for only one mid-term rent review which will soon take place. Your research suggests that comparable industrial units which have been let on leases with rent reviews every five years are achieving annual rents of £50,000 and initial yields of 8 per cent. Investors in these properties expect an overall rate of return of 10 per cent. Given that the landlord is professionally advised, provide your client with an indication on the scale of rent that is likely to arise from the rent review and which will apply for the remaining 15 years of the lease.

3   A national retailer is paying an annual rent of £45,000 for a shop whose lease contains no further rent reviews until expiry in four years' time. The retailer is downsizing and no longer needs this property. Given that the estimated market rent for the shop is £60,000 what premium might be achieved if the lease was assigned? Retailers who might be interested in taking the lease are assumed to have a cost of capital of 9 per cent to fund this type of acquisition.

4   The estimated market rent for a suite of recently refurbished, prime, city-centre offices is £85,000 per annum. The lessor feels that the covenant of the lessee, who would like to take a 15-year lease, is not as robust as it might be. Given that there is a lack of supply of this type of high quality space and that there is buoyant occupier demand, the lessor feels justified in seeking a premium on entry of £65,000. The parties accept that the premium will reduce the rent for the term up until the first rent review in five years' time. Assuming that the premium is paid, and that the market capitalisation rate is 8 per cent for this type of property, what annual rent might the tenant be expected to meet?

5   An industrial unit has been let at a headline rent of £65,000 at the commencement of a 20-year lease containing provision for five-year rent reviews. The tenant was granted a two-year rent-free period as an incentive to commit to the lease. What is the equivalent rent given that the freehold yield is 8% for this type of property?

Outline answers can be found towards the back of the book.

The Frequency and Timing of Rental Payments

Aims

This chapter investigates the frequency of rent payments by business tenants on the commercial properties which they lease. Given that rent is normally paid quarterly in advance rather than annually in arrears in a commercial lease, the chapter outlines the mathematic principles involved in converting a valuation calculation from annual in arrears to quarterly in advance. The chapter also tries to establish whether a move to quarterly in advance assumptions would make a material difference to the capital values of investment properties.

Key terms

>> **Quarterly in advance** – the principle which is usually written into a commercial lease that an annual rent for an investment property be paid by the tenant in four instalments, each becoming due at the start of a quarter.

9.1 Introduction

In Chapter 2, where the traditional method of valuation was discussed, the rental income arising from investment properties was capitalised on the assumption that rent was received annually in arrears. This key assumption, which still underpins much valuation practice, has arisen because, conventionally, valuation tables were based on interest compounded annually. However this principle does not sit easily with reality, where the majority of commercial property leases require the rent to be paid by business tenants on a quarterly in advance basis.

Although this discrepancy has some implications for the capital value of investment properties, it has not been assimilated into valuation practice in a systematic way, perhaps illustrating the power of established convention and inertia in this field.

9.2 Adjusting the compound interest formula

The cornerstone of most property valuations, and indeed wider financial analysis, is the compound interest formula for the *Amount of £1*:

Amount of £1 $= (1 + i)^n$

where, as explained in Chapter 1:

i is the interest rate; and
n is the number of time periods, normally years.

A simple example in which £10,000 is to be invested for four years in an account which earns 8 per cent interest per annum will provide a reminder of how the formula works. Ignoring the effects of tax, at the end of four years the original sum will have compounded into:

$$£10,000 \times (1 + i)^n = £10,000 \times (1 + 0.08)^4$$
$$= £10,000 \times 1.3605$$
$$= £13,605$$

The same result can be obtained by consulting the Amount of £1 tables in *Parry's Tables* (Davidson, 2013) as follows.

Sum invested: £10,000
Amount of £1 in 4 years @ 8% $= 1.3605$
£10,000 $\times 1.3605 = £13,605$

However, when interest is paid more frequently than once a year, the formula requires modification as follows.

$$\left(1 + \frac{i}{m}\right)^{nm}$$

where

n is the number of years; and
m is the number of payments per year.

For example, given the same investment of £10,000 over four years but where interest is paid every six months, the resulting calculation would be:

$$£10,000 \times \left(1 + \frac{0.08}{2}\right)^{4\times2}$$
$$= £10,000 \times (1.04)^8$$
$$= £13,686 \text{ (rounded up to the nearest pound)}$$

If interest is paid quarterly over the same period for the same initial investment of £10,000 then the calculation becomes:

$$£10,000 \times \left(1 + \frac{0.08}{4}\right)^{4 \times 4} = £10,000 \times (1.02)^{16}$$

$$= £13,728 \text{ (rounded up to the nearest pound)}$$

Although the Amount of £1 in *Parry's Tables* (Davidson, 2013) is compounded annually, it is possible to use the tables if the 'years' are regarded as the number of period payments. For example, using the same amount invested – £10,000 over four years at 8 per cent annual rate – but with interest paid on a quarterly basis, the steps taken using *Parry's Tables* would be as follows:

Amount of £1 in 16 'years' @ 2% from *Parry's Tables* = 1.3728

£10,000 × 1.3728 = £13,728

Regardless of whether *Parry's Tables* or the formula is used, these calculations show that the more frequently interest is paid, the greater will be the amount earned.

Should the interest payment only be required, then the formula is modified again as follows:

$$(1 + i)^n - 1$$

When it is applied to the example, the calculation appears as:

$$(1 + 0.08)^4 - 1 = 0.3605$$

The amount of interest is then:

£10,000 × 0.3605 = £3,605.

In a quarterly scenario the calculation becomes:

$$(1 + 0.2)^{16} - 1 = 0.3728$$

The amount of interest is then:

£10,000 × 0.3728 = £3,728.

9.3 Adjusting the discounting formula for in advance payments

As pointed out in Chapter 1, for discounting purposes the formula is inverted and therefore becomes:

$$\text{Present Value of £1} = \frac{1}{(1 + i)^n}$$

This formula also needs to be adapted when rental payments are made more frequently than annually:

$$\text{Present Value of £1 (interest paid } m \text{ times per annum)} = 1 \left/ \left(1 + \frac{i}{m}\right)^{nm} \right.$$

The importance of this formula for valuation purposes is that modern commercial property leases usually require the rent to be paid quarterly in advance whereas conventionally the underlying assumption has been that the rent is received annually in arrears. The RICS (2010: 7), in its guidance to registered valuers, advises that when undertaking discounted cash flows such appraisals should reflect the actual cash flow frequency.

Income being capitalised in a quarterly in advance situation is affected not only by the increased frequency of payment, but also because tranches of income are being received earlier and this makes the overall cash flow worth more in present value terms. This is an application of the concept of discounting, which was explained in Chapter 3, and is based upon the principle that an income received now is worth more than an equivalent sum to be received in the future. So, once again, the formula must be modified.

The modification to give the Years' Purchase for n years is simply that one period of income will be received now, leaving $(n - 1)$ periods remaining. This can be expressed as:

YP in advance for n periods $= 1 + $ YP in arrears for $(n - 1)$ periods

For example, for annually in advance:

$$\text{YP in advance 10 years @ 8\%} = 1 + \text{YP in arrears } (10 - 1) \text{ years @ 8\%}$$
$$= 1 + \text{YP in arrears 9 years @ 8\%}$$
$$= 1 + 6.2469$$
$$= 7.2469$$

The effect on capitalisation becomes obvious when an income of £10,000 per annum is assumed for 10 years and YP in arrears is compared with YP in advance.

Net annual income	£10,000
YP 10 years **in arrears** @ 8%	6.7101
	£67,101

Net annual income	£10,000
YP 10 years **in advance** @ 8%	7.2469
	£72,469

The difference will not be as great when rent is paid quarterly:

Net quarterly income	£2,500
YP 10 years quarterly **in arrears** @ 2% per quarter (YP 40 'years' @ 2%)	27.3555
	£68,389

Net quarterly income:	£2,500
YP 10 years quarterly **in advance** @ 2% per quarter (1 + YP 39 'years' @ 2%)	27.9026
	£69,757

A difficulty arises when deciding on the quarterly interest rate to be used. It was shown above that the return is higher if interest is paid more frequently than annually. If interest is paid quarterly at 2 per cent, then the annual equivalent rate becomes:

$$(1 + 0.02)^4 - 1 = 0.0824 = 8.24\%$$

This means that the income will have been undervalued using a quarterly discount rate of 2 per cent if the nominal annual rate is supposed to be 8 per cent. In that scenario the quarterly rate would need to be adjusted using the following formula, which is endorsed by the RICS (2010: 7) for practice purposes and by academics such as Fraser (2004: 21).

$$\left((1 + i)^{1/4}\right) - 1 = \left((1 + 0.08)^{0.25}\right) - 1$$

$$= 0.0194$$

$$= \text{Quarterly rate of } 1.94\%$$

As discussed in Chapter 1, the Years' Purchase for n years formula is:

$$\frac{1 - [1/(1 + i)^n]}{i} \quad \text{which can be re-writtten as} \quad \frac{1 - (1 + i)^{-n}}{i}$$

Therefore at 1.94 per cent for 39 'years' the formula produces:

$$\frac{1 - (1 + 0.0194)^{-39}}{0.0194} = 27.1819$$

YP quarterly in advance 10 years @ 8% is therefore:

$$1 + 27.1819 = 28.1819$$

Valuing the quarterly income becomes:

$$\text{YP quarterly in advance 10 years @ 8\%} = 28.1819 \times £2,500$$

$$= £70,455$$

Recent editions of *Parry's Tables* include Quarterly in Advance tables. Using the *Tables*, the calculation becomes (with a slight difference in the result due to rounding):

Annual income	£10,000
YP Quarterly in Advance 10 years @ 8%	7.0424
	£70,424

Banfield (2009) has produced further scenarios and worked examples for readers who wish to practise the technique of valuing on a quarterly in advance basis. *Parry's Tables* also provides Dual Rate Quarterly in Advance Adjusted for Tax tables for valuing leasehold profit rents where income is received quarterly in advance.

Whether a valuation is calculated on in advance or in arrears assumptions, it is important that the valuer knows the date of completion of sale, which is unlikely to be when rent payment is due. 'In advance' means that a period payment is to be made immediately; should this not be the case, then the income pattern is effectively received in arrears. Recognition of the rent income is essential for analysis so that the correct discount rate is used for the income pattern being valued. The investor may have a different view of an acceptable rate for in advance and in arrears incomes received quarterly or annually.

9.4 Summary

Conventional valuation formulas originally developed on the basis that the compounding of sums against given interest rates would take place annually in arrears. Similarly, incomes arising from investments were assumed to be paid annually in arrears and were capitalised on that basis. This convention has shown remarkable durability in valuation practice, given that it is at odds with reality where rents are normally paid quarterly in advance under commercial leases. In recent years however, there has been growing recognition that the valuation toolkit should try to reflect reality and recent editions of *Parry's Tables* (Davidson, 2013) now give prominence to 'in advance' tables and corresponding formulas. This chapter illustrated the principles involved where a valuer or client felt that it was more appropriate to conduct an appraisal on a quarterly in advance basis.

References

Banfield, A. (2009) *Valuation on Quarterly in Advance Basis and True Equivalent Yield* (Reading: College of Estate Management).

Davidson, A.W. (2013) *Parry's Valuation and Investment Tables*, 13th edn (London: Estates Gazette).

Fraser, W.D. (2004) *Cash-Flow Appraisal for Property Investment* (Basingstoke: Palgrave Macmillan).

RICS (2010) *Discounted Cash Flow for Commercial Property Investments* (London: Royal Institution of Chartered Surveyors).

Self-assessment questions

1 A builder is going to borrow £500,000 from a bank at an annual interest rate of 8 per cent in order to undertake some projects over a three-year period. Using the appropriate formula, calculate the interest which will be added to the original capital when it is to be repaid in three years' time.

2 Convert an annual interest rate of 9 per cent into its quarterly equivalent rate.

3 Calculate the present value of five years of annual income of £25,000 at a 6 per cent discount rate, assuming that the income will be paid annually in advance.

4 Repeat the above calculation but with the condition that the income will now be received quarterly in advance.

5 An investor wishes to know the difference between the present value of an annual income of £80,000 over 5 years valued on an annual in arrears basis when compared to valuing the income on a quarterly in advance basis which would reflect reality. Advise the investor on the basis that the annual interest rate is 7 per cent.

Outline answers can be found towards the back of the book.

10

Over-rented Property

Aims

This chapter will focus on over-rented commercial property, which is a common occurrence during recessionary periods. The task of identifying the capital value of over-rented properties exposes a number of weaknesses in conventional valuation techniques. The chapter will explain that the challenge of accurately valuing over-rented property has strengthened the case for adopting growth explicit discounted cash flow-based appraisal methods.

Key terms

>> **Estimated rental value (ERV)** – the value of a property calculated by reference to recent market transactions. The rent passing under a commercial lease may have been agreed several years previously and will remain liable until the next rent review or break clause or on lease expiry. Meanwhile the market will probably have changed and the ERV will better represent current market conditions. In strengthening markets the ERV will typically be higher than the lease rent and the tenant will be enjoying a profit rent. When the market has fallen the tenant will typically be paying a higher rent than the ERV and the property is then said to be over-rented.

>> **Overage** – sometimes referred to as *froth*, is a characteristic of over-rented properties and is the difference between a property's ERV and the higher rent passing under the lease. The overage can be significant for some over-rented properties and for that reason valuers will tend to apply a higher capitalisation rate to the overage to reflect increased risk.

10.1 Introduction

Over-rented commercial property is a characteristic associated with recessions when prevailing market rents fall back to leave the rents passing under existing leases higher than would be achieved in the market. Where the degree of over-renting is marginal and the market is gradually recovering, the situation will in all probability resolve itself. Market rents would climb under the effects of inflation to eradicate the difference between the lease rent and the market rent and the situation could be rectified at the next rent review. However, that might not occur for several years and in the meantime the property will be considered over-rented and valued as such.

In circumstances where the gap which has opened up between the lease rent and market rent is too large to be 'caught up', the situation is unlikely to be resolved at the next rent review. The point of convergence might well be beyond the next rent review and indeed there can be situations where the gap does not close until after the following rent review or beyond the termination of the lease. The historical legacy of upwards-only rent review clauses in long institutional leases with no break clauses can commit some tenants to meeting continued rental obligations which significantly exceed the ERV for a property.

Assumptions regarding the rate of catch-up by market rents can also be problematic, because in some situations there is underlying structural decline which will prevent rents from recovering over the short or medium term. For example, retail property in some high street locations can be adversely affected by retail impact from out-of-town malls which have a superior quality and quantity of retail offer. The *Portas Review* (2011: 8–9) confirmed that high streets in some suburban centres and small towns are particularly prone to retail impact which leads to key retailers vacating units in the prime frontages, leading to a loss of confidence in the centre.

Portas identified a spiral of decline which increases the likelihood of further store closures and which had already left close to one-in-six shops in the UK vacant by 2011. Shopping centres were also losing footfall due to changes in shopping habits, because there is an increasing propensity for consumers to make on-line purchases with home deliveries.

Over-renting is, of course, not unique to retail property and Baum and Crosby (2008: 279) describe widespread and significant over-renting of office property in established business centres such as the City of London in the wake of development booms.

10.2 Assessing the capital value of over-rented properties

The rent passing on over-rented properties under an occupational lease is higher than would be achieved if the property were available for re-letting in prevailing market conditions. The margin between the lease rent and the lower ERV in the market is sometimes referred to as overage, which can occur for any type of commercial property, especially during recessionary periods. As noted in the introduction to this chapter, retail property and parts of the office stock seem particularly prone to overage.

Overage sometimes occurs when a property is let on a lease containing abnormally long rent reviews (i.e. longer than five years), but in that context the term is a little misleading because the property has a market value but on unique terms.

Determining the capital value of over-rented properties presents a challenge which exposes some of the weaknesses in the traditional methods of valuation considered earlier in the book. The discussion here will begin by considering traditional methods in an over-rented context before moving on to consider some of the alternative methods available to a valuer. In each case, the strengths and weaknesses of each technique will be discussed.

The situation in Example 10.1 will be used to illustrate all three methods of determining the capital value of an over-rented property.

Example 10.1

A high street shop was let two years ago on a 20-year lease containing provision for rent reviews at five-year intervals. The annual net rent passing under the lease is £100,000. However the market has fallen since the lease was agreed and the ERV is now £90,000. The capitalisation rate for market-rented properties is currently 6.8 per cent.

10.3 The hardcore method and over-rented property

The hardcore or layer approach, which was first explored in Chapter 6, can be used to assess the capital value of over-rented commercial properties. Where this method is used, the overage is treated differently from the core rent, which is the ERV that could be achieved in the market. The justification is that the overage is seen as temporary additional income until the next rent review when it is assumed that it will evaporate. The assumption is that the ERV will remain below the lease rent which will fall to the level of the ERV without the hindrance of any upwards-only rent restrictions. Given that there are three years remaining before the next rent review, the hardcore method could be used to calculate the capital value of the freehold by combining the value of the core income and the overage (see Figure 10.1).

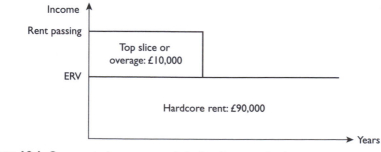

Figure 10.1 Over-rented property and the hardcore method

The calculation which accompanies the hardcore approach adopts differential yields to reflect the relative security of the income of each layer. The market-derived capitalisation rate of 6.8 per cent, which is applied to the core income, implies growth in that layer but is not explicit about the expected rate of rental growth. The capitalisation rate of 10 per cent applied to the overage reflects risk and the unlikelihood of growth in that element.

Valuation experts such as Saunders (2011: 90–7) illustrate how judgement is exercised when calibrating the capitalisation rate for the top slice to reflect factors such as the covenant strength of the tenant, the remaining duration of the lease and the presence or absence of break clauses. Essentially, where there is a tenant of good covenant in place on a long institutional lease and where the degree of over-renting is relatively modest, the differential between the core and top slice yields will be relatively narrow. Conversely, where the situation is less certain because the tenant represents a relatively weak covenant and the margin of over-renting is significant, then the differential between the core and top slice yields will widen to reflect the increased risk.

Scarrett (2008: 92) confirms that the degree of security embodied in a rent which is greater than the ERV is difficult to judge because it rests on the interplay of a number of factors. The margin chosen between the core and top slice yields is reliant upon a judgement call on the part of the valuer in the light of the circumstances and against the backdrop of similar exercises. There is no prescriptive formula or sliding scale that can be conveniently applied in these situations, hence the expression that this type of traditional valuation is more of an art than a science.

Using the situation in Example 10.1, the calculation of capital value by the hardcore method is as follows.

Hardcore method			
Core rent = ERV	£90,000		
YP in perp. @ 6.8%	14.7059		
		£1,323,531	
Top slice			
Lease rent	£100,000		
Less core rent	£90,000		
Overage	£10,000		
YP 3 years @ 10%	2.4869		
		£24,869	
Capital value			£1,348,400

Although there is some merit in the way that this approach differentiates risk by using two capitalisation rates, it rest upon an unrealistic fiction that the rental income is receivable in two layers, when in fact there is one income which is prone to a uniform risk. The method does not deal explicitly with the possibility of convergence between the market rent and the lease rent which could occur at some point due to the effects of inflation. However, the use of the market-rented yield of 6.8 per cent implies that there will be growth in this layer, leading to the suggestion that there could be double counting of part of the overage.

10.4 The term and reversion method and over-rented property

Given the conceptual uncertainties raised by the use of the hardcore method for valuing over-rented properties, a valuer might turn to the term and reversion method to see if it could provide a more convincing capital value.

The situation in Example 10.1 is illustrated in Figure 10.2 and the accompanying calculation follows.

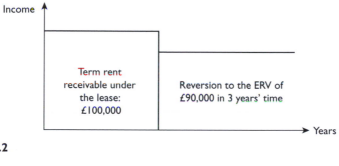

Figure 10.2

Term and reversion

Term rent	£100,000	
YP 3 years @ 10%	2.4869	
		£248,690
Reversion to ERV in 3 years	£90,000	
YP in perp. @ 6.8%	14.7059	
PV £1 in 3 years @ 10%	0.7513	
		£994,368
Capital value		£1,243,058

The term and reversion method does have the merit of treating the term rent as a cohesive income which has a uniform risk rate. In common with the hardcore method there is implied growth in the capitalisation rate for the reversion but there is a questionable assumption that the market rent has not changed over three years. This could be viewed as a strength in a market which has recently fallen because it would lead to a more conservative valuation than one which contained an assumption about rental growth.

10.5 Short-cut DCF and over-rented property

Given that neither the hardcore or term and reversion methods are explicit about the possibility of rental growth, a valuer might turn to a method which does model rental growth. Such a choice might arise where it was assumed that inflation would progressively narrow the gap between the lease rent and market rent to the point where they converged. In the scenario in Example 10.1, convergence at the next rent review in three years' time would require an annual growth rate in the rent of 3.6 per cent:

$$((1 + 0.036)^3) \times £90,000 = £100,074$$

(assuming that the £74 would be rounded down).

At reversion the risk to the reviewed rent reduces, as it has now harmonised with prevailing market values, as illustrated in Figure 10.3.

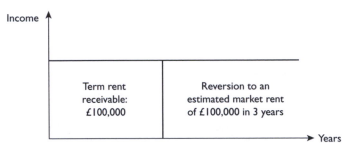

Figure 10.3

Because an assumption is being made about rental growth, the capital value produced by the calculation could be expected to be higher than in previous calculations where no explicit allowance for rental growth was made. The assumed increase in the market rent to a specific figure also changes the nature of the technique, which would be referred to as a short-cut DCF rather than a term and reversion valuation.

Short-cut DCF			
Term rent	£100,000		
YP 3 years @ 10%	2.4869		
		£248,690	
Reversion in 3 years	£100,000		
YP in perp. @ 6.8%	14.7059		
PV £1 in 3 years @ 10%	0.7513		
		£1,104,853	
Capital value			£1,353,543

The 10 per cent capitalisation rate used for the term rent reflects its relatively high risk given that it is divorced from market conditions and has low growth potential. The reversionary rent is inflated at the implied growth rate and then capitalised at the all risks yield. The short-cut DCF does not inflate the rent throughout the reversionary period, thus the discount rate for the all risks yield is used to capitalise the reversionary rent as it stands at Year 3.

In this example, the reversionary market rent has been made to conveniently harmonize with the lease rent at £100,000 under the effects of an assumed annual rental growth rate over three years of 3.6 per cent. This assumption might be suspect in a market which has recently fallen, leaving the subject property over-rented in the first instance. It is possible that the market has even further to fall or may plateau for a few years at close to zero growth, so that an assumption that rental growth can be sustained at 3.6 per cent might not be credible in the particular circumstances.

An assumed growth rate of 3.6 per cent is also arbitrary and might or might not match the specific expectations of the property investment community. Chapter 5 considered the relationship between the annual growth in rental values that was needed in order to satisfy investors' target rates of return, which are more formally referred to as 'equated yields'. If that logic were applied to the scenario in Example 10.1, the rental growth rate required could be calculated using the formula used in Chapter 5:

$$(1 + G)^n = \frac{\text{YP in perp. @ } k - \text{YP for } n \text{ years @ } E}{\text{YP in perp. @ } k \times \text{PV £1 for } n \text{ years @ } E}$$

where:

$G=$ implied annual rental growth (%) which is the variable to be determined
$E=$ equated yield (%)
$n=$ rent review pattern (years)
$k=$ all risks yield (%)

Inserting the values for Example 10.1 and assuming an equated yield of 10 per cent, the rental growth rate required by investors would be:

$$(1 + G)^5 = \frac{14.7059 - 3.7908}{14.7059 \times 0.6209} = 1.1954$$
$$G = (1.1954^{1/5}) - 1$$
$$= 3.6\%$$

The coincidence of 3.6 per cent has, of course, been engineered in this case. The point is that, while the investment community may require this rate of return, there is no guarantee that it is deliverable. The growth in rents in any commercial property market is contingent upon the interplay of a number of variables which include the balance reached between the supply and demand for floorspace in the particular occupational rental market. The supply side is determined largely by the rate at which existing stock becomes vacant and the rate at which new stock emerges from the development pipeline. The demand side is influenced by the economic outlook and how firms who make up the occupational market are responding to that environment by either expanding or downsizing or re-locating to more affordable locations.

10.6 Full DCF and over-rented property

The short-cut DCF approach does seem to have the advantage of explicitly incorporating an assumption about rental growth. A full DCF is capable of extending transparency further by explicitly modelling the income from each year at the growth rate which is felt to be justifiable in the circumstances. A DCF can also incorporate a sale value based upon an exit yield selected by the valuer which would normally reflect some loss of competitiveness due to depreciation as the building aged. The Gross Present Value (GPV) which emerges from such a DCF represents the capital value of the property, inclusive of purchase costs, stemming from the application of an investor's target rate of return. This is represented by the discount rate, which is 10 per cent in this case.

The DCF which follows models the scenario in Example 10.1 with the assumed annual rental growth rate of 3.6 per cent. The property is assumed to be sold in Year 8 on the basis of the reviewed rental value at that stage:

$$1.036^8 \times 90,000 = £119,432$$

which is capitalised at an exit yield of 8 per cent, so that the capital value arising is:

$$12.5 \times £119,432 = £1,492,900.$$

The eighth year's income of £1,592,900 shown below is the sum of the capital value and the last year of rental income of £100,000.

Year	Income £	PV £1 @ 10%	DCF
1	100,000	0.9091	90,910
2	100,000	0.8264	82,640
3	100,000	0.7513	75,130
4	100,000	0.6830	68,300
5	100,000	0.6209	62,090
6	100,000	0.5645	56,450
7	100,000	0.5132	51,320
8	1,592,900	0.4665	743,088
		GPV =	£1,229,928

This DCF was produced on a conventional annual in arrears basis, although it is reasonably easy to model the income on a quarterly in advance basis in Excel® with quarterly equivalent growth and discount rates. For those who wish to explore this degree of detail, Baum and Crosby (2008: 285–94) have produced a worked example of an over-rented office block valued on a particular set of assumptions on a quarterly basis.

The calculation of the present value of the asset in our example, which is the GPV of £1,229,928, rests upon two key assumptions: the rental growth will average 3.6 per cent per annum and the exit yield will be 8 per cent. Given that the problem of over-rented properties has arisen because the market has fallen, appraisers would obviously search for evidence to substantiate such assumptions.

Rental growth at 3.6 per cent per annum appears to be a fairly modest expectation but, given the 'fallen market' context, an appraiser might usefully explore variations in this assumption to gauge the effect on the outcome. Similarly, an exit yield of 8 per cent assumes that the property has become less competitive due to the effects of depreciation by the time of disposal in Year 8. While that might be a justifiable stance to take, it would again be prudent to try to support that assumption with historic trends for similar property types as depreciation will affect properties in different ways.

Recognising the potential for change in the key variables going forward Havard (2004: 114) has produced a summary sensitivity table for an over-rented property where marginal percentage changes to the investor's target rate interact with stepped changes to the exit yield and rental growth assumptions. A *high combination* and a *low combination* emerge, showing potential swings in the present value of the property either side of the core value. It is not necessary here to go into that degree of modelling. However, the DCF which follows adopts a more pessimistic 2.6 per cent annual rental growth rate. The effect of that single change is that the ERV will remain below the lease rent at the time of the first rent review. This assumes that the lease does not contain an upwards-only rent review clause and that the rent has therefore fallen back marginally to harmonise with the market. By the time of next rent review in Year 8, just prior to disposal, the reviewed rent has inflated to £110,515. That figure is capitalised and added to the remaining income of £97,200 to produce a Year 8 total of £1,478,638.

Year	Estimated rental value £	Income £	PV £1 @ 10%	DCF £
0	90,000		1	–
1	92,340	100,000	0.9091	90,910
2	94,741	100,000	0.8264	82,640
3	97,204	100,000	0.7513	75,130
4	99,731	97,200	0.6830	66,388
5	102,324	97,200	0.6209	60,351
6	104,984	97,200	0.5645	54,869
7	107,714	97,200	0.5132	49,883
8	110,515	1,478,638	0.4665	689,785
			GPV =	1,169,956

10.7 Summary

Given the reality of market movement juxtaposed with lease structures which fix rents (normally) for five-year intervals, it is perhaps not surprising that over-rented commercial properties will be encountered from time to time. During recessionary periods, which follow a few years after a property-market boom, there may be many thousands of such properties in the market. The margin of over-renting, or overage, is reflected in the difference between the lease rent passing and the ERV that a property could achieve if it were to be let in prevailing market conditions. In some cases the overage can be quite significant and it may take several rent reviews before the ERV closes the gap on the original lease rent.

There are a number of techniques which valuers could use when trying to put a capital value on over-rented properties. The chapter suggested that the traditional hardcore and term and reversion methods have some shortcomings in this context, which cast doubt on the reliability of the valuations. Short-cut DCF and full DCF methods seem to have the advantage because they are able to explicitly model specific assumptions about rental growth and exit yields. However, given that there are often extended timeframes involved, it would seem prudent to try to substantiate the assumptions being made with data and to model changes in the variables to gauge the scale of variance in the outcome.

References

Baum, A. and Crosby, N. (2008) *Property Investment Appraisal*, 3rd edn (Oxford: Blackwell).

Havard, T. (2004) *Investment Property Valuation Today* (London: Estates Gazette).

Portas, M. (2011) *The Portas Review: An Independent Review into the Future of our High Streets* (London: Department for Business, Innovation and Skills). Available in e-format at: www.bis.gov.uk

Saunders, O. (2011) *Valuation Calculations: 101 Worked Examples*, 2nd edn (Coventry: Royal Institution of Chartered Surveyors).

Scarrett, D. (2008) *Property Valuation: The Five Methods*, 2nd edn (Abingdon: Routledge).

Self-assessment questions

1 A retail firm is the tenant of a retail warehouse under a 15-year lease which contains provision for rent reviews every five years, coinciding with break clause options. The retailer has been in occupation for three years and is currently paying an annual rent of £70,000 to the freeholder. During the three years since the lease was signed, trading conditions on the retail park have become increasingly difficult. Recently-agreed leases on comparable terms for similar properties suggest that the ERV for the warehouse is now close to £55,000. Recent investment transactions also suggest that the initial yield for market-rented retail warehouses on the retail park is 7.5 per cent.

   Assuming that the tenant will remain in occupation beyond the next rent review (and making any other necessary assumptions), use the hardcore method to calculate the capital value of this over-rented property.

2 Using the term and reversion format, re-calculate the capital value for the over-rented retail warehouse in Question 1. Explain why the capital value identified using this method might differ from that produced by the hardcore method.

3 Calculate the annual growth rate which would be required for the ERV to inflate and converge with the current lease rent in two years' time when the next rent review takes place. Comment on whether this growth rate appears to be a realistic prospect in the scenario.

4 Regarding the retail warehouse scenario in Question 1, assume that, after difficult trading conditions when rents fell, there is a gradual recovery. Over the remaining two years leading up to the next rent review there is therefore an assumption that rents will grow by 3.5 per cent per annum. Use the short-cut DCF method to re-calculate the capital value of the retail warehouse taking into account the assumed annual growth rate.

5 A corporate property investor who has a target rate of return (or equated yield) of 10 per cent on property assets is interested in acquiring the retail warehouse in Question 1. The purchase would secure the remaining two years of rental income at £70,000 per annum and then five years of the reviewed rent before the asset was disposed of at the following rent review. The capital value on disposal is expected to reflect an exit yield of 8.5 per cent as the building will have experienced some depreciation over the intervening seven years.

The investor is aware that the property is currently over-rented but feels confident, on the basis of research, that market rents for retail warehouses on the retail park will grow by 3.5 per cent per annum going forward. Produce a DCF to ascertain the maximum the investor could pay (which will be the GPV) to acquire the retail warehouse as an investment on these assumptions.

Outline answers can be found towards the back of the book.

11

Residential Leaseholds and Enfranchisement

Aims

This chapter focuses on residential property which is held on long leases and where leaseholders wish to either extend their lease or to enfranchise the freehold. The evaluative process used in these cases to determine the compensation payable to the freeholder in the form of a premium will be explained. The discussion and examples in the chapter focus upon leasehold flats because they are now a very common housing type in towns and cities. However, virtually the same process and legal principles apply for leasehold houses.

Key terms

>> **Deferment rate** – is the interest rate offered as an incentive for investors to purchase residential freehold properties. Residential leasehold property reverts to the landlord when the lease expires and thus the value of the reversion to the freeholder is said to be deferred until that time. There is some risk involved in waiting for an investment like this to mature, because the ultimate value might not be as expected. Because there is some risk, investors require an incentive to purchase residential freeholds in the form of an interest rate known as the deferment rate. Examples in this chapter illustrate how the deferment rate is derived and then used in the valuation of a premium to extend a lease or enfranchise a freehold.

>> **Enfranchisement** – is a right which can be exercised by qualifying leaseholders of houses or flats to enable them to acquire the freehold out of which their leases have been created. The leaseholders of flats have to *collectively* enfranchise their freehold which is then held by them in common and out of which they would customarily grant themselves 999-year leases. Enfranchisement is a form of compulsory purchase for which compensation must be paid to the freeholder. An example in the chapter illustrates the process used to calculate the premium payable.

>> **Relativity** – is the proportionate relationship between the value of the lease and the value of the freehold of a residential leasehold property, measured at a particular point in the timeline of a lease. When a long lease has just been granted the relativity might be 99 per cent, reflecting the fact that nearly all of the value is held in the lease and only 1 per cent resides in the freehold. On lease expiry, however, all value will have transferred into the freehold with no value remaining in the lease and so relativity at that point is zero. Between these two ends of the spectrum, relativity records the gradual decline in the value of a lease and the gradual increase in the value of the freehold.

11.1 Introduction

Flats and houses can be held on long leases created out of the freehold of the particular property. The freeholder (landlord) and leaseholder (tenant) enjoy certain rights and responsibilities under the terms of the lease. In essence the landlord owns a long-term investment which produces a modest annual ground rent before reverting to the landlord on expiration of the lease. The leaseholder enjoys the use of the property for the term of the lease, but it is a wasting asset which will have no value when it expires.

Since the 1960s leasehold reform legislation has made it progressively easier for the leaseholders of flats and houses to either extend their leases (by 90 years) or to buy out the freeholder entirely through the process of enfranchisement. The exercise of these rights by qualifying leaseholders is a form of compulsory purchase which requires the freeholder to be compensated for the loss of property rights acquired by the leaseholder(s).

Where leaseholders successfully extend their leases or enfranchise the freehold, the scale of compensation (called a 'premium') payable to the freeholder can be considerable, and disputes can arise over the precise figure. Where compromise cannot be reached, the matter goes before a Leasehold Valuation Tribunal (LVT) which assesses the evidence before determining the premium to be paid. If either party remains aggrieved by the findings of a LVT and sufficient grounds can be shown, there is a right of appeal to the Lands Tribunal in the first instance and the courts following that.

Using worked examples, this chapter will explore the calculation of the premium required when the right to extend a residential lease or to enfranchise the freehold is exercised. The discussion will focus upon leasehold flats which have become synonymous with urban living in recent decades and which for many represent the first step on the housing ladder. However the same principles and rights exist for leasehold houses, albeit under a different Act.

11.2 Leasehold flats

Flats are a common housing format in the UK, particularly in urban areas where land is in short supply. The development of flats on brownfield sites close to employment and services is consistent with government policy which supports sustainable development. In some towns and cities flatted developments have dominated the output of new housing stock in recent years. Flats are an inherently flexible building type which can be developed in medium- and high-rise blocks on relatively small sites where it would be difficult to accommodate houses. As well as modern purpose-built flats, most towns and cities also possess a sizeable stock of flats which have been created by the conversion of large houses.

Flats have always been a popular housing format in the social housing sector but there are now approximately 1.3 million privately-owned flats in the UK. The vast majority of these have been purchased on a long lease, which is usually 99 years, although in recent years there has been a trend towards 125-year leases.

Leaseholders (sometimes referred to as 'tenants') of privately-owned flats will, under the terms of their leases, have to pay an annual ground rent to a freeholder (sometimes referred to as the 'landlord'). The ground rent in most cases is a nominal sum which in many residential leases will rise in set increments after long intervals such as 25 or 33 years. Thus the ground rent for a flat held on a 99-year lease might be £100 per annum for the first 33 years, rising to £125 for the next 33 years and then £150 for the final 33 years.

The annual ground rent from an individual flat is not of any great significance to a landlord. Ground rents from a block of flats only have significance when they are pooled. For example, a block of 20 flats whose annual ground rents were £150 each would provide an annual income of £3,000.

The freeholds of blocks of flats are occasionally sold at property auctions where the low risk of default on the ground rents warrants a relatively low yield. For example, if the annual ground rents from a block of flats were £3,000 that income might be capitalised with a 6 per cent yield to produce a capital value of £50,010 (the product of YP 16.67 × £3,000). The purchasers of residential freeholds are likely to be individuals or companies who already own similar investments and have experience of meeting the management responsibilities required of residential landlords.

Where freeholds are subject to long residential leases, the collection of ground rents by the landlord is only likely to be part of the business model because tenants also pay an annual service charge for the estate management of blocks of flats.

The service charge is divided up to pay for a number of things. Part is spent on regular cleaning and maintenance of the common areas within and outside blocks of flats. Another portion of the service charge is pooled in a sinking fund to pay for periodic decoration and strategic repairs to parts of the building and another part is used to pay for annual buildings insurance premiums. Residential estate management comes with legal responsibilities, and this is why landlords sometimes contract out the work to managing agents who specialise in this type of work.

The leaseholders of modern purpose-built flats might face an annual service charge of around £1,200. If there are lifts in a block of flats and landscaped grounds which require regular maintenance, the service charge could be around £2,000 per annum. Service charges, which tend to rise in line with inflation, represent a significant bill for those who live in flats. Given the scale of expenditure, leaseholders could reasonably expect their landlords to operate an effective estate management programme. In most situations that expectation is met and there are some exemplary landlords and effective managing agents with good reputations.

Leaseholders have legal rights to be consulted and to have inputs into the estate management service operated by their landlords. However, there are reports of landlords who are difficult to contact and are unresponsive when maintenance or repairs to common areas are needed. In these situations leaseholders may feel that they have lost any meaningful control over the quality and timing of the work undertaken. There have also been cases where landlords have exploited the system by instigating expensive repairs which are charged to the leaseholders and where the contract has been awarded to a company connected to the landlord.

As well as these potential problems, leaseholders have to contend with the wasting nature of the lease. Leaseholders who have 'bought their flat' have in reality paid a premium for a long lease which enables the quiet enjoyment of the property during the term and which may be sold in the property market. The premium has the effect of keeping the ground rent at a nominal level but it does not prevent the reversion of the property to the landlord at the end of the lease. Ultimately the lease becomes valueless, albeit in most cases at the end of a very long term. There are rights to a new periodic tenancy should the situation go that far, but the issue is more about the gradual deterioration in the value of the lease during the interim years.

In the early years of a long lease, the diminution in the value of the lease is barely detectable as most purchasers of flats are unlikely to distinguish in value terms between a lease of say 95 years and one of 85 years. Prospective purchasers will tend to be more interested in the location, general condition, space standards, parking availability and amenity enjoyed by a flat in comparison to other potential purchases in the market at similar asking prices.

As time passes, however, a loss of value in a lease can begin to be detected at or around 80 years because beyond that point leaseholders will have to compensate landlords in the event of a lease extension or enfranchisement. When a lease has 70 years or less remaining, most building societies will be reluctant to provide potential purchasers with a mortgage and this will effectively dry up most of the market for such properties.

Where leases have run down, the sales prospects and hence the values of flats in this predicament are deleteriously affected. A gap has effectively opened up in comparison to un-eroded long leases on new flats. Freehold houses in the same price bracket also become comparatively more attractive. For these reasons, long-term statistics show that average annual price growth for houses has outperformed that for flats.

11.3 Residential leasehold reform

It is not surprising, given the combination of factors discussed above, that many leaseholders of flats feel that the landlord and tenant arrangement is unfair. Legislation began to address these concerns for the leaseholders of houses as early as the Leasehold Reform Act in 1967 which, following a series of amending acts, now empowers most leaseholders to either extend their lease by 90 years or to enfranchise the freehold. The leaseholders of flats have similar powers arising from the Leasehold Reform, Housing and Urban Development Act 1993 with subsequent amendments and secondary legislation.

A key difference between the leasehold reform legislation for flats and for houses is that the leaseholders of flats have to act collectively to enfranchise their freehold while the leaseholders of houses can act individually. Thus the term 'collective enfranchisement' applies for flats where the leaseholders act collectively to acquire and hold the freehold, out of which they grant themselves very long leases such as 999 years.

In some situations, enfranchising leaseholders will form themselves into a Right to Enfranchise (RTE) company, although this is not a mandatory requirement. Regardless of whether a formal company is established, if the enfranchisement process if successful, the leaseholders have effectively become masters of their own destiny. There are also a few more qualifying hurdles faced by the leaseholders of flats in comparison to the leaseholders of houses and some of those are touched upon below.

The leasehold reform legislation contains basic qualifying hurdles which must be met by leaseholders who are considering action to extend their leases or to enfranchise. For example, where leaseholders in a block of flats wish to enfranchise the freehold, at least half of them must participate in the action and they must be qualifying tenants. The latter would include those whose lease was originally at least 21 years in length and those who were originally shared-ownership tenants but who have now purchased 100 per cent of the lease. A qualifying tenant is also somebody who has exercised their right to buy a long lease from a local authority.

If there are shops or other commercial premises in a block of flats (usually on the ground floor) then the residential element must account for at least 75 per cent of the internal floor space. Enfranchisement action cannot be taken against landlords such as the National Trust or charitable housing trusts where the flats or houses are leased as part of the charitable activity.

In some situations the qualifying criteria might mean that collective enfranchisement is not possible, perhaps because there is insufficient interest or financial ability to participate from a sufficient number of qualifying tenants. The alternative for a leaseholder is to extend the lease by 90 years because fewer eligibility criteria apply in that scenario and action can be taken independently.

Despite resistance from some high-profile residential landlords, leasehold reform legislation has gradually re-engineered the power relationship between the freeholder and leaseholder in favour of the leaseholder. The empowerment of leaseholders has created a specialised form of compulsory purchase which enables property rights to be acquired from a freeholder subject to payment of compensation in the form of a premium. The premium which the leaseholder pays to the freeholder is commensurate with the rights acquired.

The overriding principle of compensation applies in enfranchisement cases, in that those who have their rights in land compulsorily acquired should be left no better or no worse off following the payment of compensation. The leaseholders must therefore pay both the premium and the landlord's costs arising from the action, which are primarily fees for legal and valuation advice.

The final bill to enfranchising leaseholders is therefore the sum of their own costs of legal and valuation advice plus the premium payable to the landlord plus the landlord's legal and valuation costs. Because the process is now established and there are a number of decided cases concerning the award of landlord's costs, that particular issue should not be seen as an impediment to leaseholders contemplating action. The tribunal and court decisions on costs have created a tone of reasonableness around what a landlord can legitimately claim and this is benchmarked against the cost of a few hours' work by appropriately qualified solicitors and valuers. Although leaseholders should not overlook the costs of taking action, the costs are unlikely to be exorbitant in most cases.

The most significant issue for both landlord and leaseholder is the valuation of the rights to be acquired and the premium payable, and this is where a specialised branch of valuation practice has evolved. Valuers in this context could be working for either the landlord or the leaseholder(s) or for a Leasehold Valuation Tribunal (LVT). Under s.48 of the 1993 Act LVTs are called upon to resolve a dispute where the parties cannot voluntarily agree on the premium to be paid. Whoever the client may be, the *RICS Valuation – Professional Standards* (2012: 17), otherwise known as the Red Book, reminds registered valuers that they have a professional duty to ensure that they are suitably experienced and qualified to undertake the work competently. Such valuers would also be aware of the RICS (2011) practice guidance produced for this specialised field of practice.

A valuer in this context will almost certainly be working closely with the client's legal advisors to ensure that the calculation of the premium is based on firm legal foundations. The solicitor is likely to be a specialist who will have checked that the parties met all of the necessarily qualifying criteria and who will ensure that the exchanges between the parties are handled correctly.

11.4 The deferment rate

Sometimes a case may go before a LVT, not because there is a fundamental objection to a lease extension or enfranchisement, but because the parties cannot agree on an aspect of the valuation methodology. An issue of contention which sometimes arises is the deferment rate used in the term and reversion valuation. This is used in these situations to combine the value of the term income (the ground rent) with the value of the reversionary interest in the property which arises for the landlord at the end of the lease. Readers who might want to refresh their understanding of the term and reversion technique could refer back to Chapter 2 where the method is explained.

Advisors acting for leaseholders will sometimes claim that, because of particular circumstances or the characteristics of the subject property, a higher-than-normal deferment rate should be applied. An increase in the deferment rate has the effect of lowering the premium payment by the leaseholder(s) to the landlord. Conversely, advisors acting for landlords will sometimes argue that a lower deferment rate should be applied, which produces a higher premium payment to the landlord. The deferment rate is effectively a discount rate which as it increases will reduce the present value of a future sum. Conventionally, where the risks are felt to increase, then the discount rate will increase and the present value will reduce.

There are influential cases which have considered the compilation and setting of deferment rates. One of these was *Sportelli*, which was appealed to the Lands Tribunal (2006) and subsequently the Court of Appeal. The decision in that case, which concerned a prime high-value central London residential property, was that a deferment rate of 4.75 per cent for houses and 5 per cent for flats was applicable. However, it was acknowledged in that case that, given the heterogeneity of property, there might be subsequent cases where a variation in the indicative deferment rates might be warranted, perhaps because of a higher rate of obsolescence and the potential for deterioration in lower-value property.

The issue of whether the *Sportelli* deferment rates could be varied was explored in a decision by the Leasehold Valuation Tribunal of the Midland Rent Assessment Panel in 2008. It was established in that case – known as the *Zuckerman* case – that there was an evidential test which would need to be passed by either of the parties to warrant a departure from the deferment rates established in *Sportelli*. Thus it would be insufficient to rely solely on professional opinion that a development was at a higher risk of obsolescence and deterioration because it had lower value than central London property and therefore warranted a different deferment rate. The parties would have to prove this assertion to the satisfaction of the LVT by reference to convincing evidence.

When conducting a determination, LVTs therefore start from the premise that *Sportelli* deferment rates should apply unless either of the parties can demonstrate with convincing evidence that those rates should be varied. This is a stiff test which is only occasionally passed in special circumstances where the weight of evidence supports a variation.

11.5 Relativity

Another contested issue where lease extensions or enfranchisements are sought can be the *relativity* between the market value of a lease at the valuation date in comparison with the value of the freehold. The RICS (2009: 5) defines relativity as:

> the value of a dwelling held on an existing lease at any given unexpired term divided by the value of the same dwelling in possession to the freeholder, expressed as a percentage.

Thus, where a 99-year lease is created for a newly-developed flat which is then purchased at a market value of £250,000, the value of the lease at that moment is worth virtually all of the value of the freehold out of which the lease has been created. To put it another way, the relativity is 99 per cent because virtually all of the value is represented by the market value of the lease and adding the freehold at that point would make very little difference. A nominal 1 per cent is attributed to the value of the freehold to reflect the fact that there are two interests in the property: a leasehold and a freehold. As time passes the value gradually transfers from the leasehold to the freehold, so that if the full term of 99 years were to expire, the lease would no longer have any value, as all value would then be vested in the freehold.

In the context of lease extensions and enfranchisement cases, the two ends of the spectrum are seldom at issue and it is more likely that a determination of the value split is required at some intermediate point. For a 99-year lease with, say, 50 years remaining, it might be supposed that there was a linear relationship, so that about half of the value resided in the market value of the lease and about half of the value latent in the freehold. However, the situation is not that straightforward, as the data points in the relativity table reveal (Table 11.1).

Disagreement on relativity can arise because there is sometimes a paucity of comparable market evidence in the particular locality, which is not surprising given the specialised nature of the process. Valuers have shown great ingenuity in trying to adapt tangential market evidence and by making assumptions about the no-Act world in which lease values are not affected by the possibility of enfranchisement or lease extension. However, this can amount to fragile assumptions layered upon fragile assumptions and ultimately distortion, which the LVTs correctly reject.

Where comparable market evidence is scarce or of flimsy relevance, LVTs have been willing to consider graphs of relativity which have been produced by firms of chartered surveyors and reputable property research organisations. The graphs are based upon empirical data collected from the property market and from decisions handed down by LVTs. They have effectively correlated evidence arising over a number of years across broad geographical areas. Thus several of the graphs in circulation focus upon the prime central London market while others model the wider market across Greater London and the South East, and others represent data arising from across the whole country. The RICS (2009) has collated the recognised graphs of relativity into one document for ease of reference.

Given that the graphs of relativity are based upon information from the market, albeit over slightly different time frames and geographies, it is not surprising that there is some similarity in the data points. These are used to plot the declining value profile of a residential lease. Table 11.1 shows the data points used by the Leasehold Advisory Service to produce its graph, which are based on LVT decisions in England and Wales between 1994 and 2007. The corresponding graph can be viewed in the RICS (2009) document or at the Leasehold Advisory Service web site: www.lease-advice.org. This web site also contains broader independent advice on both lease extension and enfranchisement.

Table 11.1 Relativity of unexpired leases

Leases – years unexpired	Relativity (% of freehold)	Leases – years unexpired	Relativity (% of freehold)
0	0	55	83
5	18	60	87
10	34	65	91
15	45	70	93.5
20	53	75	95
25	59	80	96
30	63	85	97
35	67	90	98
40	71	95	99
45	75	100	99
50	79		

Source: Leasehold Advisory Service data in RICS (2009: 42).

In the context of a lease extension or enfranchisement for a flat with 60 years remaining on the lease, one of the issues to resolve would be the proportionate value held by the landlord and tenant at that point in time. If there were market evidence to suggest that the flat could be sold for £85,000 then that sum would reflect the leaseholder's interest and (using the data in Table 11.1) would represent 87 per cent of the value of the freehold in vacant possession. The landlord's interest at that point would have reached: (£85,000/0.87) – £85,000 = £12,701 or 13 per cent of the reversionary value of £97,701.

Even when the parties agree on most issues in a case, differing judgements made by them when calibrating the relativity and the deferment rate can have significant effects on the calculation of the premium. This is illustrated in Table 11.2, which gives the summaries of six randomly selected LVT decisions from 2012 where leaseholders had sought 90-year extensions to their existing leases. The parties had been unable to agree the premium and hence under s.48 of the 1993 Act the cases were referred to the LVT. Despite the fact that the flats are in different locations with different characteristics and intrinsic values, the small sample still reveals the effect of the lease running down upon the premium a leaseholder will have to pay to extend a lease. The same principle applies to enfranchisement.

11.6 The premium calculation for lease extensions

The process of calculating the premium for a lease extension to a flat will be illustrated using the scenario in Example 11.1. This is a commonly occurring situation where leaseholders occupy flats which were developed in the 1970s and 1980s.

Table 11.2 Randomly selected premium determinations by LVTs in 2012 where 90-year lease extensions were sought for flats, in order of lease length

Existing lease length and market value	Assessment of premium by		
	Freeholder's representative	Leaseholder's representative	LVT ruling
With 83 years remaining the lease was valued at £120,000.	£4,200	£3,000	£4,200
With 75½ years remaining the lease was valued at £156,400. Following lease extension the value was £170,000.	£24,900	£6,700	£9,300
With 68 years remaining the lease was valued at £173,000. Following lease extension £190,000.	£17,500	£9,700	£12,750
With 64 years remaining the lease was valued at £146,000. Following lease extension £165,000.	£39,100	£11,000	£13,300
With 51½ years remaining the lease was valued at £136,600. Following lease extension £175,000.	£28,250	£21,500	£26,750
With 23 years remaining the lease was valued at £54,600. Following lease extension £167,500.	£113,400	£58,000	£70,100

Example 11.1

The leaseholder of a 2-bedroom flat, which has an unexpired term of 64 years and 6 months on what was originally a 99-year lease, wishes to seek a 90-year lease extension. The ground rent on the flat for the first 33 years of the lease was set at £75 per annum, rising to £100 for the following 33 years and then £125 for the final 33 years.

The leaseholder has explored the possibility of enfranchisement with others in the block but an insufficient number were willing to take action to satisfy the 50 per cent participation criterion in the 1993 Act. The leaseholder has, therefore, decided to seek a 90-year lease extension under the 1993 Act. Valuers acting for both parties have agreed the calibration of variables in the valuation of the premium to be paid to the landlord and so have avoided going to a LVT for a determination.

There has recently been a lease extension of a virtually identical flat and the market value of that property with its new 153-year lease was agreed to be £170,000.

The leaseholder and landlord must first agree on the value in possession. Although ground rent is no longer payable on the new lease, there is still a distant reversion to the landlord and continuing involvement in estate management and service charging. Thus, although a very long lease extension is possible, it still does not exclude the landlord, and the lease extension is not quite the same as a fully-fledged enfranchisement. Thus, the parties agree that the value in possession for a landlord would be £170,000 plus 1 per cent to reflect the fact that there is still some landlord involvement. The value in possession for calculation purposes is therefore taken to be £171,700.

Graphs of relativity suggest that, for a lease with 64.5 years remaining, the relativity should be 90 per cent. The existing lease value is therefore agreed to be £171,700 × 90% = £154,530. Recent purchases of the freeholds of blocks of flats in the area suggest a capitalisation rate of 7 per cent. There are no special circumstances to warrant a departure from the 5 per cent deferment rate arising from the *Sportelli* case.

The agreement between the landlord and the tenant must include the 'marriage value' of the property. This is the difference between the total value of both parties' interests after the extension and the total value of their interests before. The marriage value has to be shared equally between the parties where a lease has fewer than 80 years remaining.

A term and reversion valuation to identify the premium payable to the landlord for a 90-year lease extension might look as follows.

Diminution of landlord's interest
Term ground rents

31.5 years @	£100		
YP 31.5 years @ 7%	12.5902		
		£1,259	
33 years @	£125		
YP 33 years @ 7%	12.7538		
PV £1 in 31.5 years @ 7%	0.1187		
		£189	
Reversion to freehold vacant possession	£171,700		
PV £1 in 64.5 years @ 5%	0.0430		
		£7,383	
Landlord's present interest			£8,831

Less
Landlord's interest after grant of new 154.5 year lease

Reversion to freehold vacant possession	£171,700		
PV £1 in 154.5 years @ 5%	0.0005		
		£86	
Diminution of landlord's interest by grant of a new lease			£8,745

Marriage value

Landlord's interest after new lease	£86		
Tenant's interest after new lease	£170,000		
		£170,086	
Less value of existing interests			
Landlord's interest	£8,831		
Tenant's interest	£154,530		
		£163,361	
Marriage value			£6,725
Premium payable for new lease			
50% share of marriage value to landlord			£3,363
Plus diminution of landlord's interest			£12,108

The leaseholder would therefore have to pay the landlord a premium of £12,108 plus the costs of both parties, which might add another £2,000. The overall bill to the leaseholder might be around £14,000. Against that outlay, the leaseholder has a potential increase in the value of the flat of £15,500 from £154,500 to £170,000. Assuming that the flat was in reasonable condition, the extended lease would make the flat more saleable. Mortgage-reliant purchasers would now be factored back into the pool of potential purchasers whereas a new mortgage could not be secured on it before extension of the lease. The sum of £14,000 is, however, a significant outlay for most individuals, and illustrates how the value slips away from the leasehold to the freehold as time elapses.

The premium will now be calculated for the same scenario and set of variables but where the original lease has 81 years and 6 months unexpired. Because action is being taken earlier in the timeline of the lease, there is a marked reduction in the premium which the leaseholder has to pay to the landlord. The prime reason for this is that the 1993 Act excludes the payment of any share of the marriage value to the freeholder if the unexpired term of a lease is 80 years or more. Thus the calculation of the marriage value is no longer needed in the valuation. For this reason, professionals involved in lease extension and enfranchisement work normally advise leaseholders who are contemplating action to do so before the lease runs down below 80 years.

Diminution of landlord's interest

Term ground rents			
15.5 years @	£75		
YP 15.5 years @ 7%	9.2801		
		£696	
33 years @	£100		
YP 33 years @ 7%	12.7538		
PV £1 in 15.5 years @ 7%	0.3504		
		£447	*cont. overleaf*

Totals from previous page		£1143
33 years @	£125	
YP 33 years @ 7%	12.7538	
PV £1 in 48.5 years @ 7%	0.0376	
		£60
Reversion to freehold vacant possession	£171,700	
PV £1 in 81.5 years @ 5%	0.0188	
		£3,228

Landlord's present interest		£4,431
Less		
Landlord's interest after grant of new 171.5 year lease		
Reversion to freehold vacant possession	£171,700	
PV £1 in 171.5 years @ 5%	0.0002	
		£34

Diminution of landlord's interest by grant of a new lease	£4,397
Premium payable for new lease	£4,397

Because the lease has not run down significantly, the relativity between the current lease value and the vacant possession value has changed. By reference to one of the recognised graphs of relativity (see Table 11.1), the current lease would be worth approximately 96 per cent of the vacant possession value of £171,700, which is £164,832. Although the current lease value plays no part in the valuation, it is important information for the leaseholder, because it signifies that there is a potential increase of £5,168 in the value of the lease from £164,832 to £170,000.

When the costs of both parties are added to the lease premium payable of £4,397, there will be very little difference between the value uplift and the outlay. However, by taking action, the leaseholder has created a more valuable and saleable asset. The leaseholder has also avoided the heavier expenditure necessary for lease renewal if the situation had been allowed to drift beyond the 80-year boundary when 50 per cent of the marriage value becomes payable.

11.7 The premium calculation for collective enfranchisement

The scenario in Example 11.1, in which the leaseholder held a 99-year lease with 64.5 years unexpired, will now be reactivated with the assumption that all ten leaseholders in the block qualify for and wish to participate in the enfranchisement of the freehold. It is assumed that this is purely a residential block containing no commercial uses such as shops or offices. The calculation of the premium also takes the form of a term and reversion valuation, although the figures are scaled up by a factor of ten to represent the number of flats involved.

Diminution of landlord's interest
Term ground rents from 10 flats

31.5 years @	£1,000		
YP 31.5 years @ 7%	12.5902		
		£12,590	
33 years @	£1,250		
YP 33 years @ 7%	12.7538		
PV £1 31.5 years @ 7%	0.1187		
		£1,892	
Reversion to freehold			
possession (10 flats)	£1,717,000		
PV £1 in 64.5 years @ 5%	0.0430		
		£73,831	
Value of landlord's interest			£88,313

Marriage value

Aggregate value of			
10 enfranchised flats		£1,717,000	
Less value of existing interests			
Landlord's interest	£88,313		
Aggregate of 10 tenants'			
interests	£1,545,300		
		£1,633,613	
Marriage value			£83,387

Aggregate premium payment for enfranchisement

50% share of marriage value to landlord	£41,694
Plus diminution of landlord's interest	£130,007
Premium payable per flat therefore	£13,001

Because the landlord is entirely removed by enfranchisement, the premium payable per flat (£13,001) is higher than if the leaseholders had sought 90-year lease extensions (£12,108). However, the costs involved in enfranchisement would now be shared by the ten leaseholders and those costs would not have factored up by a scale of ten, so there would be some saving on that element. Overall, the participants are achieving a better outcome from the same order of magnitude of expenditure in comparison with the 90-year lease extension. Of course they will now collectively have to take responsibility for the estate management of the block and be responsible for setting and spending the service charge. However, crucially they have gained control and if they wish to contract out those roles to a managing agent whom they will control then it is within their power to do so.

These examples of premium calculation for lease extensions and collective enfranchisement have been based upon deliberately straightforward scenarios so that the principles involved are not obscured. Those wishing to explore the topic in more depth could consult Hubbard (2008: 45–83) who navigates through examples which contain additional layers of complexity.

11.8 Summary

This chapter has examined the principles which enable residential leaseholders to either extend their lease by 90 years or to enfranchise the freehold on payment of a premium to the landlord. The legislative reforms which have taken place in this field over several decades now empower the leaseholders of flats and houses with what is really a specialised form of compulsory purchase.

Where leaseholders choose to take action, the professional teams acting for the landlord and tenant can usually come to an agreement on the premium payable to the landlord. However, disagreements can arise because there are a number of variables in the term and reversion valuations used in these circumstances, and because there is often a paucity of comparable market evidence against which to calibrate those variables. There is a tendency for the professional team acting for the landlord to place a higher value on the premium than the team acting for the tenant(s). Where the gap cannot be bridged by negotiation, the issue is resolved by a LVT. The LVT considers the evidence from each party before determining the value of the premium to be paid, which usually comes somewhere between the values proposed by each party. There is a right of appeal to the Lands Tribunal if either party feels that the LVT ruling has been unjust, although most cases are satisfactorily resolved by the LVT ruling.

As well as paying a premium for either a lease extension or enfranchisement, leaseholders will have the expense of instructing specialist solicitors and valuers and they will have to meet similar costs arising for the landlord. However the LVTs have shown themselves capable of scrutinising claims for costs and the resulting tone of decisions has largely prevented unwilling landlords from succeeding with unreasonable claims against leaseholders.

A lease extension or enfranchisement can be a sensible action for a leaseholder to take because it removes the requirement for ongoing ground-rent payments and it may buoy up a flagging leasehold market value for the flat or house. In the case of enfranchisement, the tenant(s) also has added control over the cost, timing and quality of maintenance and repairs because the landlord is entirely removed.

From a leaseholder's perspective, timing is of the essence because, as the lease reduces in length, the premium payable to the landlord will increase. If a lease has fewer than 80 years remaining, the premium payable to the landlord must include a 50 per cent share of the marriage value. However, even in that eventuality, it can still be cost-effective for a leaseholder to take action. For example, a premium plus the costs of both parties might amount to £10,000 for the owner of a flat whose lease has 75 years remaining, but the extension of a lease by 90 years or enfranchisement will probably produce an uplift in the market value of the property which exceeds £10,000. There is little difference in terms of the costs and value uplift between a 90-year lease extension and enfranchisement, and perhaps the main difference is that enfranchisement extinguishes any further involvement by the landlord in the property.

Leaseholders of flats or houses contemplating a lease extension or enfranchisement should first check whether they are qualifying tenants under the Acts and they should also consider whether they realistically have the funds to progress a case. In the event of a defective claim in which leaseholders were subsequently found not to be qualifying tenants, they will not only have to meet their own abortive costs but those of the landlord.

References

Hubbard, C.C. (2008) 'Leasehold enfranchisement', in R. Hayward (ed.) *Valuation: Principles into Practice*, 6th edn (London: EG Books).

Lands Tribunal (2006) *Leasehold Enfranchisement Appeal Decision regarding* Sportelli *and others* (LRA/50/2005) (London: Lands Tribunal). Available in e-format at: www.landstribunal.gov.uk.

Leasehold Valuation Tribunal of the Midland Rent Assessment Panel (2008) Zuckerman and others *v.* Trustees of the Calthorpe Estate, *Lease Extension Decision Regarding Properties at Carpenter Road, Edgbaston (BIR/00CN/OLR/2008/0013-0032)* (Birmingham: Midland Rent Assessment Panel). Available in e-format at: www.lease-advice.org/lvtdecisions/.

RICS (2009) *Leasehold Reform: Graphs of Relativity, RICS Research Report* (London: Royal Institution of Chartered Surveyors).

RICS (2011) *Leasehold Reform in England and Wales: Guidance Note*, 2nd edn (London: Royal Institution of Chartered Surveyors).

RICS (2012) *RICS Valuation – Professional Standards* (Coventry: Royal Institution of Chartered Surveyors).

Self-assessment questions

1 Why might the leaseholder of a flat with an unexpired term of 82 years be in a better position than a leaseholder of an identical property with an unexpired lease of 79 years?

2 A leaseholder of a 2-bedroom flat in a large purpose-built block is considering whether to embark on enfranchisement. What elementary things might the leaseholder do before contacting professional advisors to assist in the process?

3 Although the principle of a lease extension or enfranchisement might not be at issue, why might there still be disagreement on the deferment rate which is needed to calculate the premium?

4 What are graphs of relativity and what role do they play in lease extension and enfranchisement cases?

5 Assuming that a group of leaseholders in a block of flats successfully enfranchise their freehold, what are some of the principal rights and responsibilities which then arise?

Outline answers can be found towards the back of the book.

12

Development Valuation and Cash Flows

Aims

This chapter considers the valuation of property which has latent development potential and which is conventionally appraised using the residual valuation technique. The residual method aims to establish a site value which is independent of the development costs. The technique is not capable of delivering a high degree of accuracy, so it is often linked to a period by period cash flow to strengthen the appraisal.

Key terms

>> **Residual method** – a development valuation that deducts the costs of development from the estimated development value to obtain a site value.

>> **CIL** – the Community Infrastructure Levy Regulations 2010 – empower local authorities to operate a charging schedule against which money is collected at a rate per square metre of development to pay for infrastructure. The CIL is gradually replacing negotiated planning agreements under which the value capture to pay for infrastructure was variable and the contribution expected of developers uncertain.

>> **BREEAM certification** – non-statutory criteria contained in the Building Research Establishment Environmental Assessment Method against which the degree of sustainability achieved by a development can be certified on a

rising scale from Pass, Good, Very Good, Excellent to Outstanding. Although not the only green building accreditation, BREEAM is currently the most recognised method in the UK and it is cited by corporate property investors as a value-adding criterion with regards to their property portfolios.

>> **Affordable housing** – has a lower rent or capital value than the market and it is required in housing developments whose size exceeds locally established thresholds. Affordable housing can take various formats including social rented, market rented and shared ownership. In a residual valuation, each type of affordable housing will make a different value contribution to the gross development value of a mixed tenure scheme.

12.1 Introduction

The valuation of properties which have development potential, such as vacant sites with planning consent or obsolete buildings that can be redeveloped or improved, is customarily undertaken using the residual valuation method. Although the comparison method should still be considered in a development context, the residual method is often favoured because it is more capable of identifying the specific value arising from a particular development. This is because, although two development sites might appear to be similar, they will still differ in certain ways and their planning status may be entirely different in terms of the permitted use and density of development. Thus the value arising from the exchange of a similar site is useful information for the valuer, but it may not be a good enough guide to the value of another site where a different set of circumstances exist.

In essence, the residual method begins with an estimate of the future value of an envisaged project and then all of the project costs are deducted to leave a residual sum which can be used to pay for the land. Although the residual method does have its merits, this chapter will explain that it also has weaknesses, so it should only be seen as a guide to what a site is worth. The reasons for this include the reliance on historic data to calibrate the numerous variables which interact. For high-value projects, analysts and valuers will normally link the residual model to a period by period cash flow, and some form of sensitivity testing would also be undertaken to improve the quality of the output.

12.2 The principles of the residual valuation technique

The basis of the residual method is that it works backwards from an estimate of the value of the completed project. The development costs are then deducted to leave a site value as follows:

	Estimate of developed value:	$£X$
Less	Estimate of development costs	$£Y$
	(Residual) Value of site =	$£X - Y$

Development costs include all of the expenditure required to complete the development, such as the construction costs, professional fees and interest charges arising from funding the project. The developer's profit is also treated as a cost because it is a sum of money which the project has to bear, albeit that the profit will ultimately be taken by the developer. Example 12.1 contains a simple development scenario to illustrate the principles underpinning the method.

Example 12.1

Four houses are to be built on a site fronting a road with all services. From comparable sales, the houses are expected to sell for £280,000 each. It is anticipated that the houses will take a year to build and the construction costs for each one will be £110,000. The annual cost of borrowing for the project is 10 per cent. A simplified residual valuation for the project would look as follows. The calculation of the development costs is quite straightforward. The conversion of the site value in 1 year to its current value is explained under the valuation.

Estimated development value of 4 houses @ £280,000 each		£1,120,000
Development costs		
Construction costs, 4 houses @ £110,000 each	£440,000	
Professional fees @ 12% of building costs	£52,800	
Total borrowing	£492,800	
Interest on borrowing @ 10% over 6 months	£24,640	
Agent's sales fees @ 2% of value	£22,400	
Developer's profit @ 15% of value	£168,000	
Total costs therefore		£707,840
Amount available for site in 1 year (estimated value less total costs)		£412,160
PV £1 in 1 year @ 10%		0.9091
Present amount for site		£374,695
Less land acquisition costs @ 4%		£14,411
Site value today		£360,284

The sum of £412,160, which is available for site acquisition in 1 year's time, includes interest which has accumulated throughout the development period. The amount needs to be discounted back to the present day to find the acquisition price now; hence it is multiplied by the present value of £1 in 1 year.

The developer will incur legal and valuation fees relating to the acquisition of the site, which are estimated to be 1 per cent of the site's value. In addition, the developer will have to pay Stamp Duty Land Tax (SDLT) to the government. At the time of writing (2013), the SDLT rate for housing sites with values between £250,000 and £500,000 was 3 per cent. Thus the total site acquisition costs are the fees plus SDLT, which add up to 4 per cent benchmarked against the discounted site value. This is not, however, 4 per cent of £374,695 but the value that becomes £374,695 when 4 per cent is added to it (£374,695/1.04). The acquisition costs are therefore:

£374,695 − (£374,695/1.04) = £14,411.

Given that a developer will want to protect the profit margin, the significance of the calculation is that the site should not be purchased for more than the *site value today* which is £360,284. Fees of £14,411 will be added to that figure to produce a total of £374,695 which attracts interest at 10% so that by the end of the development period, the figure becomes £412,160.

The method would be the same for a commercial development except that the estimated developed value would be calculated using a simple investment valuation in which the net income would be capitalised by an appropriate Years' Purchase in perpetuity. There is an example of this approach in Section 12.6.

As well as appraising the development of new buildings, the residual method can be adapted to appraise the viability of renovation projects. For example, the method could be used to identify the maximum which could be offered for a derelict house or dilapidated commercial building. In those contexts the residual would begin with the estimated market value of the renovated property from which the costs of repairs and improvement would be deducted to give the unimproved value of the property. This would represent the maximum bid which could prudently be made to acquire the property in its derelict state. As Wyatt (2007: 322) confirms, the residual method can also be re-structured to identify the developer's profit where the land value is already known and cannot be varied.

12.3 A critique of the residual method

The fundamental principle underpinning the residual method is defensible because it correctly contrasts the costs of realising a project against the end value. It is a relatively quick and straightforward way to identify whether a development opportunity is fundamentally financially viable. However there are weaknesses in the approach which stem from some of the simplifications in the model and the need to make estimates in order to calibrate the variables in the calculation.

The residual method envisages that the funding of a project relies on borrowing at a uniform rate throughout the development period as if a loan facility were gradually being drawn upon. In practice, 'straight line' borrowing does not take place because, for projects of any scale, most of the building costs are incurred in the second half of the building period when more expensive materials and labour are used in fitting out and installing services. The expenditure profile therefore follows an 'S curve', but this subtlety cannot be accommodated in a residual valuation which assumes that interest accrues on costs over half the timescale. For most projects this will result in an over-estimation of interest charges, thus reducing the amount available for site purchase.

Another simplification in the residual method is the assumption that borrowing will be at a simple annual rate, but in fact it is more likely to be compounded on a period by period basis, which could be monthly or quarterly. As explained in Chapter 9, 3 per cent paid quarterly produces an annual equivalent rate of 12.55 per cent $(100 \times (1.03^4 - 1)\%)$ not 12 per cent. Alternatively, if the loan agreement is pegged to an annual rate of say 10 per cent (as in Example 12.1) the quarterly equivalent rate is not 2.5 per cent but 2.411 per cent (i.e. $100 \times (1.1^{1/4} - 1)\%$). As shown in the cash flow in Table 12.1, the monthly equivalent rate is 0.797 per cent which is derived from $100 \times (1.1^{1/12} - 1)\%$. For high-cost projects the correct interest rate needs to be applied or an inaccurate sum for the site will emerge.

It is common under the terms of a construction contract for a developer to retain around 5 per cent of the contract sum. Part of the retained money is released to the contractor on completion and the remainder after a period following completion, usually six months, during which minor defects might appear. The retention provides the developer with sufficient leverage to ensure that the contractor remedies any defects. It is difficult for the residual format to reflect this staggered pattern of payments to the contractor and so it is ignored in that model, although in reality it will have some effect on the interest charges generated within a high-value project.

Although a residual valuation can to some extent be structured to suit the particular circumstances, it cannot represent the fine grain of the timing of costs and values within the overall development timeline. Thus a reading of a residual appraisal might suggest a linear process in which development begins immediately after site acquisition and completed schemes are sold as soon as construction has finished. Of course this convenient representation seldom exists in reality, apart from in exceptional boom periods or occasionally when developments have been pre-let or pre-sold.

In most situations there will be lead-in times before construction can start, and this particularly applies for brownfield sites where there will be demolition and other site-preparation activity. Although outline planning consent may exist, detailed planning permission may not have been achieved prior to the purchase of some sites and nor will detailed construction plans always be available. Finance details will need to be settled and contractors appointed between site acquisition and commencement of building work, during which time the cost of purchase must be funded. In more challenging market conditions, completed speculative developments can remain unlet or unsold for long periods during which an appraisal will need to account for the funding.

Even when a diligent approach is taken in order to model some of the above complications, the timeline of most developments is lengthy and not all of the costs and values will remain fixed over the duration of the project. During periods of growth in the property market, rising property values will tend to compensate for any under-estimation of costs. Thus by the end of a project, which may have taken three years to complete, the costs may have been 5 per cent above what was predicted at the outset. However, the value of the finished building(s) may also be at least 5 per cent above what was originally estimated. In that situation there is no need for a post-mortem on the valuation process, as all parties should be happy with the outcome. Inflation has increased the costs but also the end value and, as value is the bigger part of the equation, all stakeholders in a scheme would have been satisfied.

The situation changes during cyclical market downturns when a 5 per cent under-estimation of the costs may not ultimately be balanced by rising values at the end of the project. When market values fall, developers engaged in speculative projects who are highly geared become very exposed. In these situations developers are sometimes forced into administration and the banks have to take partially-completed schemes into possession in order to try to recover loans made on them. Between 2009 and 2012 this was a common situation in a number of European countries.

When things go wrong in the property market and considerable sums of money disappear from the value of a project, it is perhaps not surprising that a developer or bank in possession might sue a valuer on the grounds of professional negligence. However, this might be clutching at straws because the valuer's role in most projects is to provide an estimate of how much a property would exchange for at the valuation date, and not to provide a forecast of what the value might be perhaps three years later when the market will almost certainly have changed. It is unlikely that a financial advisor or broker who advised a client to buy shares in a leading company would be held accountable for a drop in the share price (by whatever margin) three years later. Risks exist in share transactions, and property development is also acknowledged to be a risky activity.

If there is a culprit for large discrepancies in value over time then it might be the residual valuation methodology itself because it is essentially backward-looking in the way it benchmarks variables against comparable data. The method is, therefore, based upon where the property market has been rather than where it is going.

Another culprit could be the culture of over-optimism which seems to pervade the world of property most of the time. This may stem from the fact that banks make money from lending to developers, so they are inherently predisposed to do business with them. Developers need projects to stay employed and, after all, development is their *raison d'être*. Landowners will naturally make their land available in buoyant markets when the best prices can be achieved. Thus none of the key stakeholders are predisposed to turn down a proposition which looks viable and which could potentially make all of them lots of money.

Long periods of steady growth are a characteristic of property markets but these periods seem to nurture complacency and result in little weight or acknowledgement being given to warning signs. An executive in a bank who suggests that no further loans should be made to property developers is unlikely to be looking forward to a large Christmas bonus or promotion. Business is fundamentally an optimistic activity and in property development those who are most optimistic about the potential of a site will secure it. Thereafter the most optimistic scenario has to materialise to make good the financial commitment made.

Given that development valuation takes place in an entrepreneurial and risk-taking culture and there are acknowledged weaknesses in the residual method, the RICS (2008: 17) advises that sensitivity testing would be a wise precaution in some circumstances. The RICS also suggest that it would be prudent to conduct a broad reality check by comparing the site value identified using a residual approach with any comparable market data on site values which may exist. The RICS advises valuers to consider (in conjunction with the client) whether in some situations it might be more realistic to report a range of possible site values. A single figure suggests absolute precision and certainty, when in fact neither of these conditions is consistent with the development process.

12.4 Strengthening the residual approach with cash flows

Despite the criticisms of the residual model, it can still be a useful appraisal tool, particularly as some of its shortcomings can be overcome by linking it to a period by period cash flow. This enables a more detailed modelling of cash flows into and out of a project than is possible by relying solely on the residual method. For example, where projects such as business and retail parks and industrial estates are phased, a cash flow can more accurately reflect the expenditure profile and the timing of income. Phasing is an acknowledged technique for reducing borrowing requirements and, therefore, risks to the developer.

For simple residential schemes such as that in Example 12.1 the conversion of the residual valuation into a cash flow is reasonably straightforward, as illustrated in Table 12.1. The cash flow shows that the first house is assumed to be completed and sold after 9 months, with the remainder being completed and sold over the ensuing 3 months.

The ability to introduce more project detail into a cash flow brings with it an added responsibility because more judgements are needed about how the project will roll out over time. Given the culture of over-optimism in property (discussed above), it is important for analysts and valuers to realise that they are effectively modelling a version of the future and it is beholden upon them to be as realistic as possible. Even in this simple example, there is an assumption that the houses will sell in sequence and at the pre-determined prices. Such optimism can founder in times of economic difficulties, when changes in bank base rates increased mortgage borrowing costs and adverse changes in tax relief and credit restrictions can make housing sales very difficult. History shows that the construction industry is usually among the first to suffer in such times.

Table 12.1 Monthly cash flow for residential development – site value as outcome

Annual borrowing rate: 10%   Monthly equivalent rate: 0.797%

Month	1	2	3	4	5	6	7	8	9	10	11	12
Expenditure												
Construction costs	22,000	22,000	22,000	33,000	33,000	33,000	44,000	44,000	55,000	55,000	44,000	33,000
Professional fees	26,400			10,560				10,560				5,280
Developer's profit												168,000
Balance b.f.		48,786	71,350	94,094	138,751	173,120	207,763	253,770	310,787	92,115	−128,299	−361,558
Total monthly expend.	48,400	70,786	93,350	137,654	171,751	206,120	251,763	308,330	365,787	147,115	−84,299	−155,278
Income												
Sales									280,000	280,000	280,000	280,000
less Agent's fees									5,600	5,600	5,600	5,600
Total net income	0	0	0	0	0	0	0	0	274,400	274,400	274,400	274,400
Outstanding balance	−48,400	−70,786	−93,350	−137,654	−171,751	−206,120	−251,763	−308,330	−92,387	127,285	358,699	429,678
Interest on balance	−386	−564	−744	−1,097	−1,369	−1,643	−2,007	−2,457	−728	−1,014	2,859	3,425
Cumulative balance c.f.	−48,786	−71,350	−94,094	−138,751	−173,120	−207,763	−253,770	−310,787	−92,115	128,299	361,558	433,103

Balance available for site in 1 year   433,103
PV £1 in 1 year @ 10%   0.9091
Present amount for site   393,734
Less acquisition costs @ 4%   15,144
                                   _____
Site value today   378,590

Summary
Construction costs   440,000
Professional fees   52,800
Interest payments   3,697
Developer's profit   168,000
Agent's fees   22,400
                        _____
Total costs   686,897

Balance available for site in 1 year
Total income from house sales   1,120,000
Less total costs   686,897
                                   _____
     433,103

The monthly cash flow in Table 12.1 shows that a higher proportion of the professional fees are paid towards the front end of the project, reflecting the fact that most of the design and contract work takes place then. The profile of payments to the construction contractor follows a different pattern, which accelerates as work progresses and when more tradesmen are active on the site.

The effect of the income from house sales in the latter months is that the developer's overall balance becomes positive from Month 10 onwards and the accrued amount is assumed to be deposited in a bank to attract interest. On that issue, the cash flow contains a simplification that the borrowing and deposit interest rates are the same. In reality that is most unlikely, because if the annual borrowing rate were around 10 per cent for a scheme like this, then the deposit rate would be much lower, at perhaps 3 per cent. Example 12.2 is based upon an office development where differential interest rates are applied and illustrates the principle.

The final balance, shaded in the cash flow in Table 12.1, is £433,103, and it is the sum available to acquire the site inclusive of purchase costs and finance. The summary below the cash flow confirms that its ability to absorb more detail on the timing of costs and receipts has reduced the interest charges in comparison with those arising in the residual method. The result is that more money is retained in the cash flow model for the site, so that its estimated value today is £378,590 compared with the residual method which produced £360,284.

The cash flow in Table 12.2 uses the same scenario but assumes that the cost of the site is a known and fixed variable, enabling it to be inserted in the cash flow as a cost from the outset. The role of the cash flow then becomes the identification of the developer's profit as the unknown residual outcome. Because the site value is the same in both illustrations, the profit arising at the end of the cash flow in this case could be predicted to be £168,000 (the £17 difference is an inconsequential effect of rounding at the various stages in the model). If the profit were to be re-inserted in the cash flow as a cost in month 12, the result would be a nil balance at the end of the cash flow, signifying that all the costs plus the developer's profit would be covered by the sale of the houses. This is confirmed in the summary below the cash flow, where the total cost, including site acquisition and developer's profit, is balanced by the income from housing sales.

Table 12.3 develops the scenario a little further by envisaging a slightly more realistic situation in which building work does not commence until one month after the purchase of the site. The first house is now expected to be sold in the eleventh month and the last house is not sold until one month after completion. Thus the development timeline is extended by two months. The summary below that cash flow confirms that, because the project has been extended, interest charges have increased. As a consequence, there is now less available to purchase the site: £428,981 in comparison to the original sum which was £433,103 (Table 12.1). Considering the alternative situation, a developer who had paid the original price would have to absorb a loss of around £4,000. In this case the extended project duration does not threaten viability because the overall profit margin is estimated at £168,000. However, for speculative commercial projects where void periods can extend beyond a year, the accumulation of compound interest on borrowing can lead to serious problems for a developer.

Table 12.2 Monthly cash flow for residential development – inclusive of site value to identify profit

Annual borrowing rate: 10%   Monthly equivalent rate: 0.797%

Month	1	2	3	4	5	6	7	8	9	10	11	12
Expenditure												
Site cost	378,590											
Site acquisition costs	15,144											
Construction costs	22,000	22,000	22,000	33,000	33,000	33,000	44,000	44,000	55,000	55,000	44,000	33,000
Professional fees	26,400			10,560				10,560				5,280
Balance b.f.	442,134	445,658	471,385	497,317	545,188	582,796	620,704	670,002	730,337	515,009	297,965	68,103
Total monthly expend.	442,134	467,658	493,385	540,877	578,188	615,796	664,704	724,562	785,337	570,009	341,965	106,383
Income												
Sales									280,000	280,000	280,000	280,000
less Agent's fees									5,600	5,600	5,600	5,600
Total net income	0	0	0	0	0	0	0	0	274,400	274,400	274,400	274,400
Outstanding balance	−442,134	−467,658	−493,385	−540,877	−578,188	−615,796	−664,704	−724,562	−510,937	−295,609	−67,565	168,017
Interest on balance	−3,524	−3,727	−3,932	−4,311	−4,608	−4,908	−5,298	−5,775	−4,072	−2,356	−538	
Cumulative balance c.f.	−445,658	−471,385	−497,317	−545,188	−582,796	−620,704	−670,002	−730,337	−515,009	−297,965	−68,103	

Summary

Site and acquisition costs	393,734
Construction costs	440,000
Professional fees	52,800
Agent's fees	22,400
Total interest	43,049
Profit arising in Mth 12	168,017
Total costs	1,120,000

House sales	1,120,000
Less	
Total costs	1,120,000
Balance therefore	0

Table 12.3 Monthly cash flow for residential development – extended development timeline

Annual borrowing rate: 10%   Monthly equivalent rate: 0.797%

Month	1	2	3	4	5	6	7	8	9	10	11	12	13	14
Expend.														
Constr. costs		22,000	22,000	22,000	33,000	33,000	33,000	44,000	44,000	55,000	55,000	44,000	33,000	
Prof. fees		26,400			10,560				10,560				5,280	
Dev. profit														168,000
Bal. b.f.	0		48,786	71,350	94,094	138,751	173,120	207,763	253,770	310,787	368,702	150,492	−80,545	−319,189
Tot. mth exp.	0	48,400	70,786	93,350	137,654	171,751	206,120	251,763	308,330	365,787	423,702	194,492	−42,265	−151,189
Income														
Sales											280,000	280,000	280,000	280,000
less agent											5,600	5,600	5,600	5,600
Net inc.	0				0	0	0	0	0	0	274,400	274,400	274,400	274,400
Out. bal.	0	−48,400	−70,786	−93,350	−137,654	−171,751	−206,120	−251,763	−308,330	−365,787	−149,302	79,908	316,665	425,589
Int. on bal	0	−386	−564	−744	−1,097	−1,369	−1,643	−2,007	−2,457	−2,915	−1,190	637	2,524	3,392
Cum. bal. c.f.	0	−48,786	−71,350	−94,094	−138,751	−173,120	−207,763	−253,770	−310,787	−368,702	−150,492	80,545	319,189	428,981

Balance available for site in 1 year	428,981
PV £1 in 14 months @ 10%	0.8949
Present amount for site	383,852
Less acquisition costs @ 4%	15,144
	―――――
Site value today	378,590

Summary

Construction costs	440,000
Professional fees	52,800
Interest payments	7,819
Developer's profit	168,000
Agent's fees	22,400
	―――――
Total costs	691,019

Balance available for site in 1 year	
Total income from house sales	1,120,000
Less total costs	691,019
	―――――
	428,981

12.5 Schemes containing affordable housing

For the purposes of establishing basic principles, Example 12.1 considered a straightforward scenario in which four houses were developed on a small plot of land. When the scale of residential development increases to a threshold set out in the local authority's Local Development Framework (LDF), a requirement to include affordable housing will be triggered. The inclusion of affordable housing changes the dynamics of a residual valuation. It would not, therefore, be appropriate to assume that, because the development of four houses generated a site value of £378,000 (or a value per plot of £94,500), a development of 40 similar houses at the same density would create a site value of ten times that value, i.e. £3.78 million.

In a rural area the affordable housing threshold can be quite low, so that for example a development of 6 or more dwellings might be required to provide 25 per cent affordable units. In urban and suburban settings the thresholds will tend to be higher. The levels of the threshold and the target percentage for affordable housing will depend on the degree of housing need encountered in a particular district. The council's housing needs survey will influence the levels set in the LDF.

In localities where affordable housing is in short supply and there are long council house waiting lists and where property prices are relatively high, the planning system may be hard-pushed to deliver additional affordable housing. For example, because of the degree of housing need relative to the high value of market housing in the London Borough of Camden, its LDF (2010) contained a sliding scale policy. On sites capable of delivering 10 or more residential units, there is an expectation that 10 per cent of the units will be affordable and this expectation rises to 50 per cent when a site has capacity for 50 or more dwellings.

Before affordable housing policies like Camden's are adopted by councils, the policy thresholds and percentage targets are required to undergo viability testing, which is then independently scrutinised by an inspector. If the policy is adopted it could be thought of as robust. While there remains some variation in the ability of local authorities to implement these policies, there is now acceptance that housing developments above the specified threshold will be required to include a proportion of affordable housing.

For a residual valuation of a housing development of any scale, valuers therefore have to ensure that they understand the relevant affordable housing policy. As well as factoring in the affordable housing quota, the valuer will have to assess the value of the sub-components within the affordable housing element. The Department for Communities (2012: 50) confirms that in England, affordable housing can take a number of formats which include social rented, affordable rented (in which rents can be up to 80 per cent of market rents) or intermediate housing (such as shared ownership). Most local authorities have LDF policies which express weighted preferences for particular affordable housing formats. For example, some councils seek 60 per cent social rented and 40 per cent intermediate housing on sites where affordable housing is to be provided.

In practice, the tenure split is not as starkly defined as there is normally some negotiation on a site by site basis. The registered provider which is usually (but not exclusively) a housing association will be involved in these discussions alongside the local authority and developer. In the background there may be a capital grant available to support the funding of the affordable units, although during an era of public spending austerity the government's expectation is that the majority of schemes will be self-financing.

In this setting the registered provider, who will become the recipient of the affordable housing units, will be expected to borrow and pool surplus money from the rents on existing properties in order to fund the acquisitions from the developer. However creatively that funding package is put together, it is unlikely to reach the open-market value of the properties, hence the need for a specialised valuation to ascertain the worth of the units in a situation where the market is effectively excluded.

In most situations, the valuer will have access to the relevant planning consent and Section 106 agreement which together confirm the housing tenure split for a particular site. For example, a valuer might be instructed to assess the value of a consented scheme for 30 dwellings in which there are 21 open market and 9 affordable dwellings. The affordable dwellings might be sub-divided into 5 social rented, 2 affordable rent and 2 shared ownership units. The gross development value of the scheme will therefore be the sum of the receipts arising from the open market sales plus the value of the affordable units.

Using market comparison, the valuer will be able to assess the value of the 21 open market dwellings relatively easily. However, the challenge lies in assessing the value of the affordable dwellings. The RICS (2010: 5) advises that the value of the rented units can be found using a discounted cash flow (DCF) of the net rental income to the registered provider (more commonly referred to as a social landlord or housing association). The value of the shared ownership units can be built up by adding the value for the first tranche sold (often 25 per cent benchmarked against the open market value) plus the discounted value of the future net rents on the unsold equity plus receipts arising when remaining tranches are sold.

The rate at which shared ownership tenants are likely to purchase further shares in their properties on the way to full ownership is a delicate modelling exercise in which assumptions will be needed. There is anecdotal evidence that this does not happen as often or as rapidly as might be supposed, perhaps because some inertia may develop around settling for ownership of a share of a property while paying a discounted rent on the un-purchased share. There will therefore need to be a dialogue between the valuer and the registered provider around the adoption of realistic assumptions to shape the valuation process.

The rents on social rented properties in England are ultimately controlled by the Homes and Communities Agency rent guidelines with the intention that these properties remain among the most affordable tenure types. The valuer of the scheme with 21 open market, 5 social rented, 2 affordable rent and 2 shared ownership dwellings might find that, when the annual net rent from the social rented units is assessed using a DCF, they tend to have the lowest capital value in the scheme. The affordable rent properties will be more valuable as their rents are benchmarked at 80 per cent of market rents, although they are unlikely to be as valuable as the shared ownership properties whose value is more closely linked to the market. The highest value units in the scheme will be the open market properties. There is thus a staggered profile in the build-up of the value of the scheme.

It is sometimes supposed by those coming to the topic of affordable housing valuation for the first time that, because the value contribution of the affordable units in a scheme is less than for comparable open market sales units, compensatory savings might be made in the build costs for the affordable units. This is not the case because the affordable units have to meet more exacting standards set out by the Homes and Communities Agency and achieve higher levels of the Code for Sustainable Homes. Thus the build costs of the affordable housing units could actually be higher than for the open market sales units where quality-related regulation is less demanding.

It follows from the above discussion that the valuation of a scheme containing affordable housing is specialised work and the *RICS Valuation – Professional Standards* (2012a: 17) confirms that registered valuers should not accept instructions unless they can competently undertake the work by virtue of their qualifications and experience.

12.6 Residual valuation and commercial developments

Residential development scenarios have been used up to this point in the chapter to establish the principles of the residual method. Example 12.2 will illustrate that the method is also applicable to commercial property development which in this scenario takes the form of an office development.

Example 12.2

The development of a low-rise office building is proposed on an edge of a city business park. The building will have a gross floor area of 1,920 square metres and the net lettable floor area will be 82 per cent of that area. Comparable market evidence suggests that a yield of 7.5 per cent is appropriate for this type of property and that a net rental value of £260 per square metre is realistic. Construction is scheduled to commence 6 months after the site has been acquired and the work will take 15 months to complete. The offices will be let and sold as an investment 6 months after completion. Because the base rate is very low, the developer expects to source funds for the development at an annual rate of 9 per cent.

The development is taking place in a borough which has a Community Infrastructure Levy (CIL). The CIL charging schedule requires developers to pay the local authority £70 per square metre of net commercial floor space in a scheme. The planning application fee is an additional £8,000 so the total payment to the local authority will be £118,180. (Further observations are made regarding CIL and development viability in Section 12.7.)

The developer is conscious that to increase the prospects of a sale to a corporate property investor when the building is completed and let, it will need to achieve at least a BREEAM *Very Good* certification. That quality will necessitate the expenditure of at least £1,280 per square metre on construction.
A conventional residual valuation would be as follows.

Gross floor area m²		1,920	
Net floor area m² @ 82% of gross		1,574	
Rent per m²		£260	
Annual rental value			£409,240
YP in perp. @ 7.5%		13.3333	
Gross development value (GDV)			£5,456,520
Less purchaser's costs @ 5.75%			£296,690
Net development value (NDV)			£5,159,830
Development costs			
Construction costs 1,920m²			
@ £1,280	£2,457,600		
Professional fees @ 12.5% of construction costs	£307,200		
Contingencies @ 5% of both of the above	£138,240		
Local authority CIL and planning fees	£118,180		
Costs sub-total		£3,021,220	
Finance on costs sub-total over 7.5 months @ 9%	£3,021,220 0.0553		
		£167,073	
Finance on accrued amount for letting period over 6 months @ 9%	£3,188,293 0.0440		
		£140,285	
Letting and legal fees 12% of annual rental value		£49,109	
Developer's profit 15% of GDV		£818,478	
Total development costs			£4,196,165
Amount for site on completion			£963,665
PV £1 in 2.25 years @ 9%		0.8237	
Present amount for site			£793,771
Less site acquisition costs @ 4%		£30,530	
Site value today			£763,241

Table 12.4 Quarterly cash flow for office development – site value as outcome

Annual borrowing rate:	9%	Quarterly equivalent rate:	2.178%
Annual deposit rate:	3%	Quarterly equivalent rate:	0.742%

Quarter	1	2	3	4	5	6	7	8	9
Expenditure									
Construction costs			245,760	430,080	516,096	614,400	651,264		
Professional fees	61,440	61,440	30,720	30,720	30,720	30,720	30,720	15,360	15,360
Contingencies	3,072	3,072	13,824	23,040	27,341	32,256	34,099	768	768
Local authority fees	118,180								
Less retention			−12,288	−21,504	−25,805	−30,720	−32,563		
Release retention								61,440	61,440
Letting and legal fees									49,109
Developer's profit									818,478
Balance brought forward		186,671	256,654	546,315	1,030,619	1,613,361	2,309,240	3,057,942	3,203,801
Total quarterly expenditure	182,692	251,183	534,670	1,008,651	1,578,971	2,260,017	2,992,760	3,135,510	4,148,956
Income									
Sale realises NDV	0	0	0	0	0	0	0	0	5,159,830
Outstanding balance	−182,692	−251,183	−534,670	−1,008,651	−1,578,971	−2,260,017	−2,992,760	−3,135,510	1,010,874
Interest on balance	−3,979	−5,471	−11,645	−21,968	−34,390	−49,223	−65,182	−68,291	7,501
Cumulative balance	−186,671	−256,654	−546,315	−1,030,619	−1,613,361	−2,309,240	−3,057,942	−3,203,801	1,018,375

Balance for site in 2.25 years	1,018,375
PV £1 in 2.25 years @ 9%	0.8237
Present amount for site	838,835
Less acquisition costs @ 4%	32,263
Site value today	806,572

The net development value is based on the capitalised net rent (based on the net floor area) less the investment purchaser's costs. It is something of a curiosity that the developer has to absorb the investment purchaser's costs which include stamp duty and legal fees. This has been an enduring practice in this setting and relates to the investor, which may be a pension fund or insurance company, being able to report a rate of return from acquired assets unencumbered by entry costs. To some extent developers have little alternative if they wish to secure a sale in a restricted market.

The building costs are estimated against the gross floor area and the professional fees are assessed at 12.5 per cent of construction costs. A contingency allowance of 5 per cent is allowed for both the construction costs and professional fees. Finance is taken for half the construction period, followed by six months during which finance will be paid on the total costs which have accrued by that stage and which include rolled-up interest charges. The amount for the site will have to be financed from the date of purchase and therefore the final sum is discounted for the total period of 27 months (2.25 years) of the project. The result is that up to £763,241 could be bid to purchase the site.

The residual valuation on p. 164 provides the basis for the cash flow in Table 12.4.

Summary of costs

Construction costs	2,457,600	Sale income	5,159,830
Professional fees	307,200	Less costs	4,141,455
Contingencies	138,240	Balance for site	1,018,375
Local authority CIL and fees	118,180		
Letting and legal fees	49,109		
Developer's profit	818,478		
Interest	252,648		
Total costs	4,141,455		

In this case, the local authority fees and a proportion of the professional fees are paid in the first quarter with construction commencing in the third quarter. The developer is assumed to retain 5 per cent of the construction money from the contractor with staggered release to the contractor at the end of the project to ensure that defects are remedied.

In a situation where the offices had been let before being sold as an investment, any interim rent received by the developer would appear in the cash flow as income, thus reducing costs and interest charges. However, in this scenario the first rental income is assumed to go to the investment purchaser and not the developer. In the final quarter when the developer's budget moves from debit to credit, money may be deposited to earn some interest. However in the guise of a depositor, the developer will not be able to earn the quarterly equivalent of 9 per cent annual interest, as that is the borrowing rate. Deposit rates will be much lower and so an annual rate of 3 per cent is envisaged, the quarterly equivalent of which is shown at the top of the cash flow (Table 12.4).

As for the housing example (Example 12.1), the cash flow here has 'found' more money for the site than in the corresponding residual appraisal. In this case the cash flow suggests an uplift in the site value from £763,241 in the residual valuation to £806,572 in the cash flow. Essentially a developer could have some confidence in bidding an additional £43,331 to secure the site if that were needed. As well as strengthening appraisals, cash flows produced in Excel or other software packages can play a role in project monitoring as they can easily be updated when any of the variables change during the project.

12.7 Development viability and planning

The exercise in Section 12.6 recognised CIL as a development cost and in that guise it is passed on in the land bid. CIL rates will vary between authorities because they arise from the interplay of a number of factors, such as the estimated cost of infrastructure required to support development, the extent of existing infrastructure budgets and the ability of the local property market to absorb CIL charging. In the example, the application of the CIL rate of £70 per square metre does not appear to have jeopardised what is a substantial site value. However more would need to be known about the sales of similar plots on the business park and the local land market generally before a definitive conclusion could be drawn on whether it was a competitive site bid.

CIL charging brings into focus the potential tension between a local authority's legitimate desire to achieve sustainable planning objectives (by using CIL and its predecessor, Section 106 agreements) and a developer's natural ambition to achieve profitable development. Historically the achievement of planning objectives was separated from the assessment of development profitability. However that situation has evolved and development viability is now a material planning consideration which is formally acknowledged in the National Planning Policy Framework (NPPF). This policy shift recognises the fact that most development is carried out by private developers and, therefore, the implementation of sustainable planning policies will require developments that are otherwise acceptable to be financially viable. The NPPF (Department for Communities and Local Government, 2012: 41) expresses it in these terms:

> To ensure viability, the costs of any requirements likely to be applied to any development, such as requirements for affordable housing, standards, infrastructure contributions, or other requirements should, when taking account of the normal cost of development and mitigation, provide competitive returns to a willing land owner and willing developer to enable the development to be deliverable.

Viability appraisals have now become a part of the planning process and they may be undertaken to test the viability of policy in a LDF, where for example a district-wide affordable housing policy is under review. Viability appraisals may also be undertaken for specific developments in the context of local authority development management and viability appraisals will be conducted to test the reasonableness of proposed CIL charging schedule rates. In whatever context they may be used, viability appraisals will be subject to public scrutiny by independently appointed inspectors before the policy or CIL charge can be adopted by a local authority.

The RICS (2012b: 2) confirms that developers, planners, landowners and other stakeholders in the development process need to have a shared awareness of the relationship between sustainable planning and development viability. The RICS (2012b: 4) has produced a definition of financial viability in planning:

> An objective financial viability test of the ability of a development project to meet its costs including the cost of planning obligations, while ensuring an appropriate site value for the landowner and a market risk adjusted return to the developer in delivering that project.

Fulfilling the landowner's expectations is explicitly recognised in the definition because there could be fragile market situations where the value side of the equation is not sufficiently robust to leave a satisfactory land value. In those situations it is doubtful that the land would be put forward for development. There is thus a temporal dimension in that, as markets fluctuate, there might be occasions when the full complement of planning policy expectations cannot be carried by a development. During recessions, some planning policy expectations may have to be relaxed in order for development to remain viable. These circumstances occurred from 2009 when the full affordable housing quota could not always be carried by some housing developments. In order for those schemes to progress the affordable housing element has had to be reduced with the agreement of the local authority. However objective evidence for this type of adjustment will be needed in the form of an agreed viability study. This is an evolving area of practice at the interface between local authorities and developers which is creating interesting consultancy opportunities for chartered surveyors.

12.8 Summary

This chapter has explored the circumstances in which the residual valuation method might be used. The discussion highlighted a number of shortcomings associated with the method, which has led to the use of linked period by period cash flows in an attempt to improve the accuracy of the output. As well as being more efficient in modelling money flows in and out of a development project, a cash flow can also play the role of a development monitoring tool. For example, changes in interest rates, delays in the construction programme and variations in costs and sales forecasts can be incorporated into a cash flow spreadsheet to ascertain the effects at each stage of a project.

Despite some of the criticisms, the residual valuation model still has its uses, especially where a quick appraisal is required to see if a project has any potential. The more forensic approach possible in a cash flow can follow up in circumstances where some potential is identified. The related topic of sensitivity testing and the role that it can play in development appraisal will be discussed in Chapter 13.

References

Department for Communities and Local Government (2012) *National Planning Policy Framework* (London: Department for Communities and Local Government).

London Borough of Camden (2010) *Local Development Framework – Camden Development Policies 2010—2025* (London: Camden Council).

RICS (2008) *Valuation of Development Land – Valuation Information Paper 12* (Coventry: Royal Institution of Chartered Surveyors).

RICS (2010) *Valuation of Land for Affordable Housing – RICS Guidance Note* (Coventry: Royal Institution of Chartered Surveyors).

RICS (2012a) *RICS Valuation – Professional Standards* (Coventry: Royal Institution of Chartered Surveyors).

RICS (2012b) *Financial Viability in Planning – RICS Guidance Note* (Coventry: Royal Institution of Chartered Surveyors).

Wyatt, P. (2007) *Property Valuation in an Economic Context* (Oxford: Blackwell).

Self-assessment questions for Chapter 12

1 What are some of the key weaknesses associated with the residual valuation technique?

2 What steps could be taken to strengthen the reliability of the outcome from a residual appraisal?

3 Complete the final stages of the residual valuation below by inserting appropriate figures in the relevant boxes so that the site value today can be identified.

Amount available for site in 1 year's time (estimated value less total costs)	£475,000
PV £1 in 1.75 years @ 10%	
Present amount for site	
Less site acquisition costs @ 4%	
Site value today	

4 Complete the monthly cash flow below by inserting appropriate figures into the empty boxes to identify the deficit which is the cumulative balance at the end of Month 6.

Annual borrowing rate:	9%		Monthly equivalent rate:			
Month	1	2	3	4	5	6
Costs incurred in month	20,000	22,000	24,000	26,000	28,000	30,000
Balance brought forward	0					
Total monthly expenditure	20,000					
Income from sales	0	0	0	0	0	0
Outstanding balance	−20,000					
Interest on balance						
Cumulative balance						

5 Complete the quarterly cash flow below by putting appropriate figures into the empty boxes. Given that the expenditure of £250,000 in the first quarter is payment for the land, the cumulative balance in the sixth quarter will be the developer's profit. When the cash flow has been completed, confirm whether the present value of the developer's profit is superior or inferior to the return to the landowner.

| Annual borrowing rate: | 10% | | Quarterly equivalent rate: | |
| Annual deposit rate: | 2% | | Quarterly equivalent rate: | |

Quarter	1	2	3	4	5	6
Costs incurred in quarter	250,000	60,000	80,000	120,000	140,000	160,000
Balance brought forward	0					
Total quarterly expenditure	250,000					
Income from sales	0	0	0	0	750,000	450,000
Outstanding balance	−250,000					
Interest on balance						
Cumulative balance						

Profit arising in 1.5 years	
PV £1 in 1.5 years @ 10%	
Present value of profit	

Outline answers can be found towards the back of the book.

Risk

Aims

This chapter discusses some of the risks which apply to property development and investment. It will consider methods which are commonly used to assess risk and the extent to which some of those risks may be controlled, mitigated or transferred.

Key terms

>> (**Sensitivity testing** – normally focuses upon variables in a property appraisal which are more likely to affect the outcome because they have a large monetary value.) These would normally include the gross development value and the construction costs. Marginal adjustments are made to these variables to gauge the effect on the outcome. Thus, if the construction costs were increased by 10 per cent and this reduced the residual sum available to purchase the site by 20 per cent, then this variable is sensitive because change in it has a disproportionate effect on the outcome. Measures to reduce the risk of variation in a sensitive variable need to be considered. However, while some controls can be exerted on the cost side of the equation, such as through diligent project management or fixed price contracts, it is less easy to control market-driven variables, such as commercial rents or house prices.

>> **Scenario testing** – develops the concept of sensitivity testing further by making a series of changes to sensitive variables to reflect pessimistic and optimistic scenarios. Risk-conscious developers will tend to focus upon the most pessimistic scenario in which the gross development value would be marginally reduced and the costs increased so that the residual outcome is squeezed from both sides. If a development (or investment) were able to withstand a worst case scenario by remaining financially viable, it could be thought of as a robust prospect worthy of further investigation.

13.1 Introduction

Risk is an ever-present fact of life and it is doubtful that any business or property-related venture could be undertaken without encountering some risks in one form or another. The expression 'Nothing ventured, nothing gained' applies in a property-development or property-investment context.

In most situations the risks are remote, enabling them to be tolerated without the necessity of introducing special risk-reduction measures. In other situations the risks might need to be insured against or the project re-designed to reduce risk. Thus, while the risk to the average home of flooding, fire or damage from strong winds is statistically quite low, it is still a sensible precaution to have adequate home insurance to cover these eventualities because of the scale of loss which could arise. However, even in insurable situations or where a project can be re-designed, there will still be some residual risk. While it may be possible to reduce or transfer most of the risks, it is seldom possible to remove risk entirely from any situation. Residual risk is therefore a condition which has to be accepted.

In business and property contexts, attempts are often made to quantify risk in the form of a percentage risk rate. The basic principle is that as the perceived risk increases the expected financial reward will also increase to compensate. Before exploring risk rates and their application, the distinction between 'risk' and 'uncertainty' must be considered. While both imply that a given outcome is not guaranteed, a probability can be attached to risk whereas it cannot to uncertainty. Thus an actuary could assess insurance risk but could not attach a probability to uncertainty. For the purposes of this chapter no such rigid distinction is drawn and a simpler umbrella definition of risk is adopted, characterising it as the level of probability that a required return will be achieved.

In a property context, risk manifests itself in a number of ways. For the property investor there are risks to the income flow because future outgoings could increase and the anticipated growth in capital value might not ultimately be realised. For the property developer there are risks that projected sales or rental values might not be realised at the culmination of a project and/or that the project might be delayed, preventing the value from being realised while the costs escalate. The chapter will explore some of these risks and some of the techniques which have evolved to try to evaluate risk. The chapter will also consider some of the practical steps which may be taken to control, mitigate or transfer the identified risks.

13.2 Sources of risk in a property context

Property developers and property investors are dealing with tangible assets which are prone to a wide variety of risks. Baum and Crosby (2008: 39–44) have categorised a number of sources of risk in a property context: tenant risk, sector risk, taxation risk, planning risk and legal risk. These categories are not exhaustive but they do help to stimulate thought about the range and type of risks that could be encountered. It will become evident that some risks have more significance for property investors while other risks are more applicable to property development; some types of risk cross over to affect both developers and investors. For example, tenant risk might at first sight appear to be more relevant to a property investor, but business tenants' decisions on whether and on what terms to take a lease in a new development holds considerable risk for a property developer.

In a harsh economic climate business tenants, such as healthcare companies, electrical retailers and hotel operators, may find it difficult to meet rental obligations on properties which were leased during more optimistic periods. In some cases the inevitable outcome is that investors are left holding empty properties after a business tenant has become insolvent. Of course it is possible to investigate the covenant strength of a potential business tenant before a lease is granted, but this does not guarantee that several years into a lease the market for that tenant's products or services will remain strong.

One of the roles of a property portfolio manager is to ensure that the portfolio does not become over-exposed to a particular sector of industry which may be facing turbulent trading conditions. This could apply equally to the public sector where large properties are leased to government agencies but where leases are due to expire or are subject to break clauses which are more likely to be exercised in the context of public spending cuts. This type of risk prompts major property investors, such as Real Estate Investment Trusts (REITs) to confront and report to shareholders on the degree to which a property portfolio is exposed to particular sectors of industry or agencies or departments of government. A property portfolio that had a diversity of exposure across business and government sectors would be at reduced risk compared to a portfolio which had, for example, a high concentration of tenants who were involved in a particular type of retailing.

In recent years the policy drive towards fostering more sustainable buildings is likely to have the effect of hastening the depreciation rate of the stock of existing buildings which were designed and built before sustainability became an explicit criterion in the development process. Ideally, where a property is at risk from obsolescence, the owner or potential purchaser will build estimates of future refurbishment into the initial investment appraisal. As well as policy changes presenting a risk, there can also be changes to legislation, which, for example, shift the power relationship between landlord and tenant in the residential property sector. As discussed in Chapter 11, gradual change to the legislation in that sector has made the option of extending a lease or enfranchising a freehold more practical for residential leaseholders and those changes therefore represent risks for the landlords involved.

Periodic government budgets can result in unforeseen changes to tax rates, thresholds and qualifying criteria for VAT, stamp duty, inheritance tax, capital gains tax and business rates. These changes will affect everyone involved in property investment or development in one way or another. For example, a 'mansion tax' on high-value residential property has been proposed as one way to reduce the scale of government debt. Although technically not a tax, some developers would see the locally operated Community Infrastructure Levy as a tax which increases development costs, although the impact is mainly felt by the landowner through reduced site values.

Developers are often faced with the risk that planning consent may not be granted for a scheme or that it comes with limiting conditions which were not originally anticipated. There can also be strategic decisions on the part of government agencies about when and where to locate major infrastructure projects. For example, in 2013 a new London airport was being promoted in North Kent and plans for a high speed train link (HS2) between London and the Midlands were presented. The decision on whether or not to proceed with these types of projects, and then on the timing and specific location and routing, embodies risk which ultimately generates winners and losers in the property market.

Even at the routine scale of buying a house, the exchange of legal title embodies some risks for a purchaser and requires careful verification of the specific bundle of rights being purchased. Some high-profile property acquisitions have stalled because of deficient title or because restrictive covenants were discovered which presented insurmountable problems for a purchaser. Property is an illiquid asset and it is seldom easy to convert property rights into their money equivalent at short notice, particularly where the lot size is significant. Property markets are also volatile and vendors always face the potential risk of trying to achieve a sale in a falling market.

Climate change has added to the potential risks faced by property owners. Even within the sub-category of flooding, far more properties are being included in the Environment Agency's flood risk maps as an allowance for climate change is factored in to periodic re-modelling and re-mapping exercises with improvements in data and knowledge around climate change.

Overall, it is evident that, whether the activity is property development or property investment, there is always likely to be an overlay of risk factors which need to be considered in the decision-making process.

13.3 Determining the risk rate for property investment

Regarding property investment, there are different risk implications depending on whether a single property or a portfolio of properties is under consideration. For a single asset, one way that risk can be incorporated is to embed a margin for it in the investor's discount rate. This *risk-adjusted discount rate* can then be used to price the asset.

The risk-adjusted interest rate (I) applicable in a market for particular assets is theoretically made up of two main elements which are the *risk-free rate* (RFR) plus the *risk premium* (RP):

$$I = \text{RFR} + \text{RP}$$

For practical purposes the RFR is the same as the interest rate on index-linked gilts where the effect of inflation has been removed. Alternatively, ordinary gilts could be used and a deduction made for inflation but the resulting risk-free rate of interest will be the same. Given that the risk posed by the corrosive effect of inflation has been removed, it is not surprising that the RFR will be very low, moving in harmony with the minimum lending rate set by the central bank. So if 1 per cent could be obtained on index-linked gilts and a particular property asset class is known to have a 5 per cent risk premium then the investor's minimum discount rate for that particular asset would be 6 per cent.

The composition of the discount rate looks beguilingly simple, especially since the RFR can be identified from the markets. However it is not such an easy task to pin down the risk premium for a particular property asset class. This was one of the issues explored in the *Sportelli* Lands Tribunal (2006) case discussed in Chapter 11. In that case the Tribunal sought an acceptable methodology for composing the risk premium applicable (in that case) to prime central London residential property.

Having considered an array of evidence from financial experts and valuers the Lands Tribunal ultimately rejected the use of the Capital Asset Pricing Model (CAPM) to determine the risk premium. The CAPM essentially transposes the equities market risk premium for a property company trading in similar assets to the risk attributable to actual properties. The Tribunal felt that, although it was interesting background information, in the end the data from the financial markets such as share price performance was not directly translatable to the risks suggested by a particular type of property asset.

Rather than use the CAPM as a benchmark, the Tribunal felt that it was more defensible to build up the risk premium for a particular type of property by looking at the constituent parts of the risk posed to that type of asset. In the case of prime central London residential property the Lands Tribunal in *Sportelli* thought the risk factors primarily related to illiquidity and volatility in the market for high-value residential properties. Thus, while an investor in such properties had a reasonable expectation of capital growth over the long term, this did not remove the risk that it might be difficult to realise a sale for these high-value lots at an acceptable price at certain points in the property cycle. There were also the lesser risks of deterioration and obsolescence to consider.

After deliberating upon the evidence in *Sportelli*, the Tribunal decided to support a risk premium of 4.5 per cent for this type of asset. That risk premium was added to the risk-free rate prevailing at the time (0.25 per cent) to arrive at an overall deferment (or discount) rate of 4.75 per cent for high-value houses. The Tribunal felt that a marginal uplift to 5 per cent for flats was warranted to reflect a slightly higher risk for those types of property in that area.

It is not possible here to do full justice to the delicacy and reasoning of the 40-page Lands Tribunal decision in *Sportelli*, but there are a number of points of principle which are pertinent to this chapter and its discussion on the composition of a risk premium for any particular property investment.

Market volatility, illiquidity, deterioration and obsolescence are of course not unique risks for prime central London residential investment properties, as these factors are present for other types of investment property. The risk factors, however, will combine differently depending upon the particular property asset class under consideration. There will also be specific risk factors which will need to be considered such as location, tenant covenant strength, legislation, planning and potentially some of the other risks discussed earlier in the chapter.

Depending on the circumstances, some risk factors will be seen as relatively insignificant and consequently given no weight in the composition of a risk premium. However, other risks might raise real concerns to the point where they warrant some adjustment to the risk premium. It would therefore be convenient but over-simplistic to assume that the risk premium of 4.75 per cent for prime central London houses adopted by the Lands Tribunal in *Sportelli* could be mechanically applied to all property investment classes in all locations.

Judgement will be required when framing the risk premium to suit a specific set of circumstances, although this is not to say that the wheel would need to be re-invented each time. Investment transactions will provide a means for deducing the tone of risk perception prevalent in the market for particular types of property assets. Against that backdrop, it will be possible for valuers with the requisite experience to fine-tune the risk premium against market norms to reflect the perception of greater or lesser risk in a particular asset. Identifying the appropriate risk premium is therefore a process based on judgement and interpretation. It is not something that can be generated from a standard formula or read from a sliding scale of values.

Assuming that a risk-free rate at a particular point in the market cycle is 1 per cent and that an appropriate risk premium is felt to be 6 per cent for a particular property asset, the risk-adjusted market rate would then be 7 per cent. That rate could be used in discounting the anticipated income stream to identify the capital value, as illustrated in Example 13.1.

Example 13.1

An annual income of £70,000 has been secured under a lease for 5 years and following a rent review the asset is to be sold in Year 6 for £1,014,365. Table 13.1 shows the NPV for different situations based on a risk-adjusted rate of 7 per cent. The discounted cash flow (DCF) of 7.5 per cent reflects the viewpoint of a slightly more risk-averse investor who requires a higher rate of return to persuade them to accept the particular investment risk. The DCF at 6.5 per cent reflects an investor who is more risk-tolerant and will accept a marginally lower rate of return for bearing the same risk. The NPV in each case indicates what each investor is prepared to bid for the asset. The investor who is willing to accept 6.5 per cent could bid up to £986,043 and will therefore probably secure the asset.

Table 13.1

Year	Net income £	PV £1 @ 7%	DCF @ 7%	PV £1 @ 7.5%	DCF @ 7.5%	PV £1 @ 6.5%	DCF @ 6.5%
1	70,000	0.9346	65,422	0.9302	65,114	0.9390	65,730
2	70,000	0.8734	61,138	0.8653	60,571	0.8817	61,719
3	70,000	0.8163	57,141	0.8050	56,350	0.8278	57,946
4	70,000	0.7629	53,403	0.7488	52,416	0.7773	54,411
5	70,000	0.7130	49,910	0.6966	48,762	0.7299	51,093
6	1,014,365	0.6663	675,871	0.6480	657,309	0.6853	695,144
			NPV = 962,885		NPV = 940,522		NPV = 986,043

Example 13.1 illustrates that an investor who is overly risk-averse and expects above-normal returns relative to market's perception of risk is unlikely to be successful in acquiring assets where there is market competition for them. The investor who has discounted at the lower rate has implicitly accepted more risk by showing a willingness to pay more for the asset relative to market competitors. However, if there was subsequently no growth in the investment, one interpretation would be that the investor had failed to give proper weight to the risks.

The *all risks yield* (also referred to as the initial yield) is an implicit version of the DCF principle explored above, in that it reflects the property investment market's perception of risk through its purchasing behaviour. Thus an initial yield of 6 per cent suggests that the investment community is willing to pay up to 16.7 times the net annual income of a property because there is confidence that there will be rental and/or capital growth. Investors are not accepting a 6 per cent return for the duration of the investment, but they are showing a willingness to accept that rate of return as a minimum at the outset. The implicit assumption is that, with growth, the investment will ultimately perform above 6 per cent.

The same investment community might only be willing to pay up to 10 times the net income for another property, reflected by an all risks yield of 10 per cent, because in that case there was less confidence that the asset had much growth potential. That property might, for example, be several decades old and perhaps viewed as secondary rather than prime. The property might have a tenant who was not considered to be a strong covenant and who might not be able to 'stay the course' for the remainder of the lease. There might be a break clause in the lease and some concern that, if it were exercised, there would be difficulties in re-letting the property. The asset is simply viewed as being more risky and worth fewer multiples of its annual income and, consequently, the all risks yield reflects that interpretation.

For each property, the combination of risk factors will be unique and, in the context of the implicit traditional method of valuation, judgement is required of a valuer to fine-tune the yield. Saunders (2011: 16–47) illustrates this type of implicit process by showing how a combination of risk factors affects the calibration of the yield used to value commercial properties.

13.4 Risk and the cost of capital

The comparative DCF exercise in Example 13.1 assumed that the investors had sufficient flexibility to adapt their rates of return, enabling them to vary their bids for an asset dependent upon the perceived risk. However, some investors will be more constrained than others, simply because they are highly geared (relying heavily on borrowing) and will therefore need to achieve a minimum rate of return in order to remain solvent.

An investor who is using a combination of debt and equity will at the very least require a rate of return from an investment which both services the debt rate and compensates for the opportunity cost of deploying the equity in the investment. That rate of return is sometimes referred to as the *weighted average cost of capital* and it is simply the combined interest rates of the debt and equity elements on a *pro rata* basis. For example, if the total cost of a significant commercial property investment were £10 million and the funds to acquire it comprised 80 per cent borrowing at an interest rate of 10 per cent and 20 per cent equity at an opportunity cost of 2 per cent, the weighted average cost of capital would be: $(80\% \times 10\%) + (20\% \times 2\%) = 8.4$ per cent.

The opportunity cost of equity of 2 per cent, which is subsumed within the overall rate of 8.4 per cent, would normally be benchmarked against a relatively riskless alternative investment such as the return on gilts or investment in a bond. A rational investor would therefore add a risk premium on top of the 2 per cent return on equity to compensate for putting the equity into something which is riskier than gilts or a bond. The logic is that the investor could already earn 2 per cent on the equity and would need an incentive in the form of a higher rate of return for redeploying it in something riskier. Property investment is riskier because the returns are less certain and because the investor has to arrange and service a significant loan against the predicted performance of the commercial property which is to be purchased. The investor might therefore expect at least an 8 per cent return on equity to compensate for the additional risks involved, and therefore the implied and subjective risk premium is the mark-up above 2 per cent, which is 6 per cent in this case.

One of the consequences of factoring in an allowance for risk is that the investor now has an equated yield (or minimum target rate of return) derived from the risk-adjusted cost of capital for the investment of $(80\% \times 10\%) + (20\% \times 8\%) = 9.6$ per cent. The investment could now be discounted at that rate to ascertain whether it met this minimum threshold. The £10 million purchase price for the investment is assumed to include purchase costs and reflects an initial yield of 7 per cent. Assuming the investment is to be held for 5 years until the first rent review and then disposed of and that the required exit yield is 7 per cent (that element is being held constant for the purposes of the example), the annual growth rate in the rent needed to achieve the equated yield could be calculated.

A number of methods could be used to calculate the growth rate but perhaps the most convenient is to structure an Excel® worksheet and its formulas so that the *Goal Seek* function can be used. Alternatively, iteration will arrive at the same result or the growth formula (see Chapter 5) could be used. If the formula approach is preferred, the key variables are: k which is the initial yield, n the rent review period and E the equated yield. These variables are known in this example and so the growth rate, G, becomes the variable to be identified as follows.

$$(1 + G)^n = \frac{\text{YP in perp. @ } k - \text{YP for } n \text{ years @ } E}{\text{YP in perp. @ } k \times \text{PV £1 in years @ } E}$$

$$(1 + G)^5 = \frac{14.2857 - 3.8298}{14.2857 \times 0.6323}$$

$$= 1.1575$$

$$(1 + G) = 1.1575^{1/5}$$

$$G = 0.02968 \text{ or } 2.97\% \text{ rounded up}$$

When that growth rate is applied to the cash flow below it generates an annual rent for capitalisation purposes in Year 5 of $(1 + 0.0297)^5 \times £700,000 = £810,311$. When that figure is capitalised at an exit yield of 7 per cent it produces £11,575,868 which is added to the final £700,000 of rent from that year to produce a total income of £12,275,868 (rounded up), shown in Year 5 below.

Year	Expenditure £	Income £	PV £1 @ 9.6%	DCF
0	10,000,000	0	1	−10,000,000
1		700,000	0.9124	638,680
2		700,000	0.8325	582,750
3		700,000	0.7596	531,720
4		700,000	0.6930	485,100
5		12,275,868	0.6323	7,762,031
			Net present value =	281

The NPV of £281 is inconsequential as it is difficult to achieve absolute zero. The point is that an annual growth rate of 2.97 per cent in the rent is required for the investor to achieve the minimum risk-adjusted return of 9.6 per cent.

13.5 Scenario testing and property investment

For the investor who requires a minimum rate of return of 9.6 per cent there remain risks that the rental growth rate and the exit yield do not behave as anticipated. This is perfectly possible as they are both factors which are subject to wider market forces and as such cannot be controlled by any single investor.

These variables are also being predicted 5 years ahead of when they will combine to determine the exit value of the investment. In the previous example the exit yield was assumed to be 7 per cent and the required rental growth rate calculated to be 2.97 per cent (now rounded up to 3 per cent) to justify a £10 million investment. It is important in these exercises not to double count for risk, so now let it be assumed that the investor's minimum required return is 9.6 per cent exclusive of an allowance for risk and that the investment is available for bids in the region of £10,000,000. In that scenario a prudent investor might model possible step changes around the assumed core values for the yield and the rental growth. The resulting array of 25 possible bids is shown in Table 13.2.

It is not clear from such an array which is the most prudent bid. If the investor is too risk-averse and assumes the most pessimistic combination of a 1 per cent rental growth rate and an exit yield of 7.5 per cent then the bid of £8.88 million would be the lowest within the array. That bid would not be competitive relative to an investor who had a slightly more optimistic outlook and who felt that a slightly higher rate of rental growth was realistic along with accepting a slightly tighter exit yield.

One way to strengthen conviction regarding the most prudent bid is to use the standard deviation, although the claim to science is tenuous given the reliance on judgement to frame the parameters and the need to import subjective probabilities.

To begin the exercise, the standard deviation around the expected core rental growth rate of 3 per cent could be calculated. In Table 13.3 subjective values have been used to replicate a distribution of probabilities. If such data existed in the market it would be preferable to use it. However, for this exercise a 40 per cent probability has been attributed to the core rental growth rate of 3 per cent with remaining probabilities spread symmetrically each side of that value. However if the decision-maker felt that a skewed pattern was more realistic then the probability spread should reflect that assumption.

The sum of the probability weighted growth rates in Table 13.3 is ΣVP. It could be thought of as the probability-adjusted expected growth rate, henceforth denoted as EV. Because Table 13.3 assumes a symmetrical pattern of probabilities the EV is the same as the expected growth rate at 3 per cent. However, given that the rental growth rate cannot be predicted with certainty, it

Table 13.2

		Exit yield				
		6.50%	6.75%	7%	7.25%	7.50%
Annual rental growth rate	1%	9,837,592	9,572,528	9,326,397	9,097,240	8,883,361
	2%	10,198,971	9,920,522	9,661,963	9,421,235	9,196,556
	3%	10,574,803	10,282,435	10,010,950	9,758,188	9,522,277
	4%	10,965,518	10,658,678	10,373,756	10,108,484	9,860,897
	5%	11,371,552	11,049,675	10,750,788	10,472,515	10,212,793

Table 13.3

Possible rental growth rates (V)	Subjective probabilities (P)	Weighted values (VP)	Deviation (D) from weighted value: V – (ΣVP)	Deviation² (D²)	Weighted probability (D²P)
1%	10%	0.1%	−2.0%	0.04%	0.004%
2%	20%	0.4%	−1.0%	0.01%	0.002%
3%	40%	1.2%	0.0%	0.00%	0.000%
4%	20%	0.8%	1.0%	0.01%	0.002%
5%	10%	0.5%	2.0%	0.04%	0.004%
Totals	100%	3.0%			0.012%

is necessary to go further by trying to identify a range within which it will almost certainly fall. This is known as the standard deviation and denoted by the Greek letter sigma (σ). The greater the standard deviation, the wider the possible spread of values and, from an investor's point of view, the greater the risk. The standard deviation is the square root of the *variance*, which is the total weighted probability in Table 13.3 of 0.012 per cent. The standard deviation is therefore:

$$\text{Standard deviation} = \sigma = \sqrt{0.012}\%$$
$$= 1.095\% \text{ (rounded)}$$

Statistically, there is a 68 per cent chance of the outcome being within 1 standard deviation either side of the predicted rental growth value of 3 per cent, i.e. between 1.905% and 4.095%. The degree of statistical certainty improves to 95 per cent when 2 standard deviations are included, i.e. EV between 0.81% and 5.19%. However, this range is quite considerable and of doubtful value to an investor in this context.

Perhaps not surprisingly, the risk-averse investor might focus upon the downside risk represented by one standard deviation below the EV so that the expected rental growth rate would be: 3% − 1.095% = 1.905%. If that value were adopted as a risk-adjusted growth rate then statistically there is an 84 per cent chance that the growth rate will be as good as if not better than that figure. The alternative perspective is that there is a 16 per cent chance that the rental growth rate will not be as good as 1.905 per cent.

A similar exercise can then be conducted for the exit yield as shown in Table 13.4 overleaf. The standard deviation arising from the variance of 0.000750 per cent in Table 13.4 is:

$$\text{Standard deviation} = \sigma = \sqrt{0.00075}\%$$
$$= 0.274\% \text{ (rounded)}$$

Given the investor's concern with risk the standard deviation in this case would be added to the core exit yield of 7 per cent to produce a risk-adjusted yield of 7.274 per cent. In this case there would statistically be an 84 per cent

Table 13.4

Possible exit yields (V)	Subjective probabilities (P)	Weighted values (VP)	Deviation (D) from weighted value: $V - (\Sigma VP)$	Deviation^2 (D^2)	Weighted probability ($D^2 P$)
6.50%	10%	0.7%	−0.5%	0.0025%	0.000250%
6.75%	20%	1.4%	−0.3%	0.0006%	0.000125%
7.00%	40%	2.8%	0.0%	0.0000%	0.000000%
7.25%	20%	1.5%	0.2%	0.0006%	0.000125%
7.50%	10%	0.8%	0.5%	0.0025%	0.000250%
Totals	100%	7.0%			0.000750%

chance that the yield would not extend beyond 7.274 per cent and therefore only a 16 per cent chance that it would.

The risk-adjusted yield is close to 7.25 per cent which was one of the step changes modelled in Table 13.4. When 7.25 per cent is cross-referenced with the risk-adjusted rental growth rate of 2 per cent (the nearest step change to 1.9 per cent in Table 13.2) a risk-tempered investment bid of around £9.4 million is suggested. In fact when the risk-adjusted yield and rental growth rate are run through the DCF below, the NPV (which is effectively the best bid on these terms) is £9,367,769. Purchasing the investment at this figure (or lower) does not imply that risk has entirely evaporated. However there is now a higher probability (but not a certainty) that the annual rental growth rate and exit yield are likely to support the achievement of the investor's overall target rate of return for the investment.

Year	Income £	PV £1 @ 9.6%	DCF
1	700,000	0.9124	638,680
2	700,000	0.8325	582,750
3	700,000	0.7596	531,720
4	700,000	0.6930	485,100
5	11,275,532	0.6323	7,129,519
		Net present value	9,367,769

13.6 Risk and property investment portfolios

Thus far the discussion has been about a single asset property investment where a risk premium plus a risk-free rate can be assembled to reflect the specific circumstances and then used as a discount rate against future income to arrive at a risk-adjusted capital value. As the perception of risk increases then so does the risk premium and the overall discount rate, with the effect that the capital value will progressively reduce. The outcome is reflected in market transactions so that, for example, a transaction reflecting a 10 per cent initial yield suggests an investment which is relatively more risky than a property investment with an initial yield of 5 per cent.

At a strategic level where property or even multi-asset portfolios are assembled, the way in which risk affects the overall portfolio becomes more of an issue than the way it affects specific elements in the portfolio. Markowitz (1959) was an early writer in this field who suggested that risk to a portfolio can be reduced by combining assets whose returns demonstrated less-than-perfect positive correlation. Essentially, the more diverse the collection of investments, the less risk-exposed the overall portfolio becomes.

One way to identify this desirable quality of diversity is to ascertain the *beta* value of an asset or asset class. The *beta* coefficient is an agreed measure of the sensitivity of financial performance relative to the market as a whole. It was originally used to define the riskiness of investing in particular company shares relative to the riskiness of investing more broadly across the market. For example, if a company's shares had a *beta* of 1.5 and the overall equities market fell by 1 per cent, the share price of the company could be expected to fall by 1.5 per cent. Conversely, if the market rose by 1 per cent the specific company's shares might be expected to rise by 1.5 per cent. The company's shares were therefore more volatile than the market generally.

The *beta* value essentially adjusts the mean risk for the relative riskiness of the specific shares under consideration. The *beta*s of ordinary shares on the Stock Market are distributed across a narrow range from 0.5 to 1.5, and a *beta* value at the top end of this range confirms above-average volatility.

The implications for property portfolio managers are that they should try to select from investment properties which have some overall performance potential, but are unlikely to perform in exactly the same way. For example, if there was a good spread of *beta* values for prime city-centre offices, high street shops, regional distribution warehouses and even residential properties, this would be a good reason for including a representation of these types of property in a portfolio. The diversity of financial performance would reduce risk to a property portfolio as well as to a multi-asset portfolio, in contrast to a portfolio containing only one type of asset.

Research undertaken for the Investment Property Forum (2012: 7) confirmed that, even in the difficult economic environment which followed the 2008 financial crisis when most investment assets lost value, property continued to play an important diversifying role in multi-asset portfolios. A similar conclusion was reached in the government-commissioned Montague report (Department for Communities and Local Government, 2012: 11) which explored ways to overcome barriers to institutional investment in the private residential sector:

> There is potential for diversification – returns from UK residential investment offer a different profile to commercial property or equities, and therefore offer existing portfolios good diversification opportunities.

There are, however, limits to what diversification can achieve in terms of risk reduction to a property portfolio. At a strategic level, there are two main categories of risk – *unsystematic* and *systematic risks* – and diversification can only make a beneficial impact on the former. Unsystematic risk is also known as 'non-market risk' because it relates to factors which are particular to a property or type of property and it is measured as a percentage return per annum. Where the percentage is relatively high, there is felt to be a higher specific risk. Through diversifying a portfolio, unsystematic risk can be reduced significantly. Systematic risk, however, relates to fluctuations in the property market generally and it cannot be diversified away. Portfolio managers cannot do very much about reducing systematic or market risk (such as shocks induced by the 2008/09 Credit Crunch) but they can at least try to identify assets whose financial performance is not correlated. Assembling a diverse property portfolio will significantly reduce unsystematic risk but it will not abolish property investment risk entirely as the Credit Crunch aptly demonstrated.

13.7 Statistical techniques, risk and portfolios

Section 13.5 discussed the role of the standard deviation in determining a risk-adjusted bid for a single investment. The standard deviation could also act as a surrogate for the degree of volatility and, in that guise, it can be used to assist in risk diversification in a property portfolio, as illustrated by Example 13.2.

Example 13.2

An investor is faced with two investment opportunities which have the following characteristics.

Variable	Notation	Opportunity A	Opportunity B
Return %	x	6 to 14	2 to 18
Probability of each return		0.5	0.5
Expected return	$\bar{x}$	10	10

In addition, the two opportunities are inversely correlated; the return on A is likely to be high when B is low, and *vice versa*.

The variance is the sum of the differences between the return and the expected return squared, divided by the number of returns:

$$\sigma^2 = \frac{\sum(x - \bar{x})^2}{n}$$

The lower and upper limits of each return are equally likely, so the variance and standard deviation for each investment are:

Opportunity A

$$\sigma^2 = \frac{(6 - 10)^2 + (14 - 10)^2}{2}$$

$$= 16$$

$$\sigma = \sqrt{16} = 4$$

Opportunity B

$$\sigma^2 = \frac{(18 - 10)^2 + (2 - 10)^2}{2}$$

$$= 64$$

$$\sigma = \sqrt{64} = 8$$

The investor now has a better guide to the volatility of each opportunity:

Variable	Notation	Opportunity A	Opportunity B
Return %	x	6 to 14	2 to 18
Probability of each return		0.5	0.5
Expected return	$\bar{x}$	10	10
Variance %	σ^2	16	64
Standard deviation	σ	4	8

Both opportunities have the same expected return but differ in risk. Opportunity B has a greater variance than A and is therefore more risky. Rational decision-makers faced with two projects of the same return will take the one with less risk. However, if the investor was seeking diversification to reduce risk and was aware that the two investments were inversely correlated a decision to invest two-thirds of the funds in A and one-third in B would be more rational.

The expected return on the portfolio is the weighted average of the returns on the individual opportunities, using the fraction in each as weights:

$$ERp = \sum_{i=0}^{n} x^i(E_i)$$

where

ERp is the return on the portfolio
x_i is the proportion invested in opportunity i
E_i is the expected return on opportunity i.

The expected return on an investment split between opportunities A $(2/3)$ and B $(1/3)$ is:

$$ERp = \frac{2}{3}(10) + \frac{1}{3}(10)$$

The expected return in the split investment is the same as if either opportunity A or B had been acquired. However, the risk to the split investment is reduced because A and B are inversely correlated, so that when A produces its highest return B will be producing its lowest return and *vice versa*.

A high: $ERp = \dfrac{2}{3}(14) + \dfrac{1}{3}(2) = 10$

B high: $ERp = \dfrac{2}{3}(6) + \dfrac{1}{3}(18) = 10$

In this combined investment approach the unsystematic risk to the portfolio has been reduced to zero: $\sigma = 0$. The situation has arisen because the investment opportunities are perfectly inversely correlated (coefficient of correlation $= -1$) and the proportion of funds invested in each was determined on this basis.

Unfortunately for those seeking to diversify the risk to property portfolios, it would be very difficult to find property investments that were inversely correlated. Perhaps the best that might be achieved in reality is to find different types of property with different *betas* (degree of volatility). Thus a balanced property portfolio might contain a spread of property assets across sectors (offices, retail, industrial, warehousing, leisure) drawn from different geographic markets. The scale of the portfolio will also help to dilute risk. With increasing size there is reduced risk exposure to underperforming elements within the portfolio as over-performance in other assets may compensate.

It is possible to explore the related concepts of correlation, diversification and scale of property portfolios but that discussion extends beyond the parameters of this book. Readers who are interested in those topics could refer to Isaac and O'Leary (2011: 275–84).

13.8 Risk, property development and sensitivity testing

It is well known that a relatively minor change in any of the large-value variables in a development appraisal (familiarly referred to as a residual valuation) can produce a change of greater magnitude in the resulting land value. Given the length of most development projects, changes to the monetary value of most of the variables are very likely. Inevitably, estimates made at the outset of a project will be at some variance with what ultimately transpires. As Loizou and French (2012: 199) comment, this type of uncertainty is an integral part of the development process:

> It is therefore important to know which variables have the largest effect on the change of outcomes and, thus, where the risk is the highest. In doing this it is then possible to try to decrease the risks that are seen to be too high.

Although Excel® spreadsheets allow an almost infinite number of 'what if?' scenarios to be explored, the appraiser has to set some practical parameters by selecting the 'big ticket items' where a relatively modest change in a variable can present a large risk. These variables include the estimated gross development value and the construction costs, but they could also encompass the developer's profit and the development timeline by modelling project delay. A simple sensitivity test could then be presented as a matrix of capital values arising from potential step changes in the selected variables, as illustrated below using the housing development residual valuation in Chapter 12. Although the appraisal has a simplified format in which, for example, interest is calculated in a basic manner, it is sufficient for the purposes of demonstrating the principles of sensitivity testing. The original calculation in Example 12.1 (p. 152), from which a site value of £360,284 is found, is shown opposite.

This can now be used to illustrate simple sensitivity testing, which involves changing one variable at a time to generate a new site value. The percentage change in the variable is then compared with the percentage change produced in the site value. If a percentage step change in the variable generates a larger percentage change in the site value, then the variable is sensitive. Consideration might then be given to measures which could control or limit potentially damaging variation in the particular variable. For example, it will be of no great concern to a developer if the building costs reduced and therefore no corrective

Calculation of site value from Example 12.1

Estimated development value of 4 houses @ £280,000 each		£1,120,000

Development costs
Construction costs,

4 houses @ £110,000 each	£440,000	
Professional fees @ 12% of building costs	£52,800	
Total borrowing	£492,800	
Interest on borrowing @ 10% over 6 months	£24,640	
Agent's sales fees @ 2% of value	£22,400	
Developer's profit @ 15% of value	£168,000	
Total costs therefore		£707,840
Amount available for site in 1 year (estimated value less total costs)		£412,160
PV £1 in 1 year @ 10%		0.9091
Present amount for site		£374,695
Less land acquisition costs @ 4%		£14,411
Site value today		£360,284

action is warranted. However, it would be an obvious concern if the building costs increased because of the damaging multiplier effect this can have in the calculation. It would therefore be legitimate in that scenario to consider measures of risk control or risk transfer (discussed later in the chapter).

Change in the GDV

In a development appraisal, change in the gross development value (GDV) will always be a candidate for sensitivity testing because it will ordinarily be the largest single monetary value in the calculation. It will also be highly susceptible to change because it is an estimate made at the outset of a project based upon market comparison at that time. Several years later when the project reaches completion, the market and therefore a scheme's GDV will almost certainly have changed. Because change in this variable is virtually inevitable and the developer cannot control the ebb and flow of the market, there is a stronger case for presenting the outcome of a development appraisal as an array of possible values rather than a single spot figure.

The residual below has incorporated a GDV which has been reduced by 10 per cent, arising from an assumed fall in the scheme's housing values. If this had been a commercial property development, a reduction in the GDV could be explored by both marginally increasing the yield (which reduces the YP multiplier) and reducing the rental value.

Gross development value of 4 houses @ £252,000 each		£1,008,000

Development costs

Construction costs of 4 houses @ £110,000 each	£440,000	
Professional fees @ 12%	£52,800	
Total borrowing	£492,800	
Interest on borrowing @ 10% over 6 months	£24,640	
Agent's sales fees @ 2% of value	£20,160	
Developer's profit @ 15% of value	£151,200	
Total costs therefore		£688,800
Amount available for site in 1 year		£319,200
PV £1 in 1 year @ 10%		0.9091
Present amount for site		£290,185
Less site acquisition costs @ 4%		£11,161
Site value today		£279,024

The key figures from the original valuation have been incorporated into the summary table below showing the full range of ± 5 and ± 10 per cent changes in the GDV and the rounded-up percentage change in the site value in each case.

	GDV + 10% £1,232,000	GDV + 5% £1,176,000	No change £1,120,000	GDV − 5% £1,064,000	GDV − 10% £1,008,000
Monetary effect	Increase of £81,259 to £441,543	Increase of £40,629 to £400,913	Unchanged site value is £360,284	Reduction of £40,630 to £319,654	Reduction of £81,260 to £279,024
Percentage change	22.6%	+ 11.3%	0%	−11.3%	−22.6%

The developer's focus will understandably be on the downside risk. In this scenario, if the GDV fell by 10 per cent from the initial estimate, the site value would reduce by 22.6 per cent, illustrating the sensitivity of this variable. If the developer had already purchased the site for its core value of £360,284 then £81,260 would be lost from the scheme, assuming that all other variables remained unchanged. The loss would be deducted from the developer's profit margin which would be almost halved in that case. This is one reason why developers try to secure off-plan sales or pre-lets in commercial schemes.

An alternative means for reducing risk is to negotiate a deferred payments scheme under which the site is valued and paid for at the completion of development rather than at the outset. In that case, the landowner bears the risk of land values falling but could also gain from a higher land value if the market strengthens over the timeline of the development.

Change in the construction costs

The construction costs will usually be the single biggest cost item in a residual valuation and would therefore also feature in most sensitivity testing exercises. Again, potential stepped changes can be explored with a focus on the impact of cost increases which pose risks for a developer. The same format is used below as in the GDV calculation: the construction costs are increased by 10 per cent and then the ±5 and ±10 per cent changes in the construction costs are tabulated.

Gross development value of 4 houses @ £280,000 each		£1,120,000
Development costs		
Construction costs of 4 houses @ £121,000 each	£484,000	
Professional fees @ 12%	£58,080	
Total borrowing		£542,080
Interest on borrowing @ 10% over 6 months	£27,104	
Agent's sales fees @ 2% of value	£22,400	
Developer's profit @ 15% of value	£168,000	
Total costs therefore		£759,584
Amount available for site in 1 year		£360,416
PV £1 in 1 year @ 10%		0.9091
Present amount for site		£327,654
Less land acquisition costs @ 4%		£12,602
Site value today		£315,052

	Construction costs + 10% £484,000	Construction costs + 5% £462,000	No change	Construction costs − 5% £418,000	Construction costs − 10% £396,000
Monetary effect	Decrease of £45,232 to £315,052	Decrease of £22,617 to £337,667	Unchanged site value is £360,284	Increase of £22,615 to £382,899	Increase of £45,230 to £405,514
Percentage change	−12.6%	−6.3%	0%	+6.3%	+12.6%

Although construction costs are still a sensitive variable with a 10 per cent change producing a 12.6 per cent change in the site value, this variable is less sensitive than the GDV.

In contrast to the GDV, the developer can control construction costs to some extent by adopting fixed-price contracting or through risk transfer when using design-and-build procurement contracts. It is doubtful that this type of cost-focused contracting practice is always consistent with quality and it is at odds with cultivating the synergies which can arise from partnering. However, if a contractor accepts a fixed price from the developer, this does not prevent the contractor from seeking to improve margins internally by reducing costs through effective project management. Contractors might also be able to benefit from their own supply chain relationships on materials, and they may have partnering arrangements with sub-contractors. In this way risk can be be diluted because it is effectively diffused as it cascades down the supply chain.

Change in interest rates and project duration

Although interest rates and project timelines are important, marginal changes in these variables will normally produce a far less pronounced change in the site value. Essentially interest rates and project timelines are less sensitive variables and quite dramatic changes in them are required in order to achieve the same sorts of swings in site value as for GDV or construction costs. For example, the core residual assumes an interest rate of 10 per cent. If this were to rise to 12 per cent, which is effectively a 20 per cent increase, the corresponding fall in site value would only be 3 per cent.

Project interest rates are also subject to some control as fixed-price loans can be negotiated with the acceptance of a slightly higher loan rate. Alternatively, cap-and-collar arrangements can be put in place to limit rate fluctuations, although there will be some costs involved in setting up these facilities with the lender. Essentially, if the developer suspects that a period of interest-rate volatility might be encountered, there could be some merit in paying more as a way of buying some additional security. In common with insurance premiums, the added security will come at a price.

Regarding project timelines, the prospect of delay is, of course, a risk for a developer. However, in this example, if the project timeline were to extend by 10 per cent (rounded up for practical purposes to two months) the effect of the over-run would only generate a reduction of £9,200 (2.5 per cent) in the site value. It would take an over-run of one year (which is a 100 per cent increase in this variable) to make a material difference (a reduction of 14.5 per cent in the site value, equivalent to a loss of £52,354).

13.9 Property development and scenario testing

The sensitivity testing explored above involved changing one variable at a time while keeping all other variables unchanged to gauge the sensitivity of the particular variable. This type of exercise provokes consideration of whether risk attenuation is possible or necessary. Scenario testing develops on sensitivity testing by exploring simultaneous changes to combinations of sensitive variables. The magnitude of change in the result can then be considered by the developer. Scenario testing usually involves the modelling of optimistic and pessimistic scenarios either side of the core valuation. A developer will probably be most interested in whether a scheme can remain viable if the pessimistic scenario were to manifest itself.

Judgement has to be exercised by an appraiser when calibrating the changes in the variables to reflect optimistic and pessimistic scenarios. Example 13.3 considers a pessimistic scenario of the housing development example previously considered.

Example 13.3

The appraiser has formed a view that in the worst case scenario the value of housing in the scheme could fall by up to 10 per cent over the development period. This judgment is reflected by reducing the GDV by 10 per cent. The appraiser then decides that, although the construction costs could increase, the uplift was unlikely to exceed 10 per cent and so that variable has been increased by that margin.

Assuming a variable rate loan, the appraiser decides that the worst that could happen to this variable over the development period is that it could rise from 10 to 12 per cent. Finally, if there were to be a delay to what is a very modest scheme, the appraiser concludes that it is unlikely to exceed 2 months so that period has been added to the development timeline.

Gross development value of 4 houses @ £252,000 each		£1,008,000
Development costs		
Construction costs of		
4 houses @ £121,000 each	£484,000	
Professional fees @ 12%	£58,080	
Total borrowing	£542,080	
Interest on borrowing @ 12% over 7 months	£37,946	
Agent's sales fees @ 2% of value	£20,160	
Developer's profit @ 15% of value	£151,200	
Total costs therefore		£751,386
Amount available for site in 14 months' time		£256,614
PV £1 in 14 months @ 12%		0.8762
Present amount for site		£224,846
Less land acquisition costs @ 2%		£4,409
Site value today		£220,437

If the site value were available to purchase at its pessimistic scenario value of £220,437, it would have fallen below the £250,000 threshold above which 3 per cent stamp duty applies at the time of writing (2013). It would therefore attract the 1 per cent stamp duty rate which, when added to solicitor's fees of around 1 per cent, would cause the total site acquisition costs at the end of the valuation to become 2 per cent. This figure is shown in Example 13.3 to illustrate the principle. This would be a small, and not very significant, saving for the developer, who was chasing a modestly-valued site. However, the issue would not apply if the site had already been purchased for its original core value of £360,284 and the value of the scheme subsequently fell by around £140,000. The originally envisaged profit margin of £168,000 would therefore fall to around £28,000 if the pessimistic scenario were to become reality.

Although the manifestation of the pessimistic scenario would obviously be very disappointing for the developer, the scheme would still be viable and all bills would have been paid. If the developer had been able to enter a deferred land purchase arrangement, the site would be purchased for £220,437 (61 per cent of its original value) and the developer would then be looking at a revised profit margin of £151,200.

For some developments, a pessimistic scenario test would result in a negative site value, signifying considerable risk. Schemes which can withstand a pessimistic scenario test and still return a plausible land value with some profit could be thought of as robust, offering some comfort to the developer.

13.10 Property development and probability

Discussions on sensitivity analysis and scenario testing inevitably bring into question the credibility of presenting the output from a development appraisal as a single value when an array of possible outcomes might be more informative. However, when presented with an array of outcomes, a client could reasonably ask an appraiser which was most likely to occur. Byrne (1996: 29–42) was one of the first to explore the use of probability in a property appraisal context. As with scenario modelling, the appraiser has to make subjective judgements when assigning probabilities to the variables to reflect the likelihood that they will achieve particular values. This would be true even if a wealth of data on market transactions were available for analysis.

In the simple housing scheme considered in Example 13.3, the GDV was varied by ± 5 and ± 10 per cent around the core site value to produce an array of five different site values:

	GDV + 10%	GDV + 5%	Unchanged	GDV – 5%	GDV – 10%
Housing site value	£441,543	£400,913	£360,284	£319,654	£279,024

Essentially, as the housing sales values were assumed to increase, the scheme became more successful and more could be devoted to bidding for the site. In contrast, if the housing market was felt to be entering a difficult period in which sales values would be depressed, then the scheme would be less successful and less would be available to bid for the site.

Similar relationships could be explored for a commercial development where the rents and yields become the variables which can be adjusted to reflect optimistic or pessimistic scenarios.

Given the range of values above, the appraiser might consider contextual information to form judgements on where the most likely outcome might lie within the spectrum. The backdrop for this type of judgement call might, for example, be that the housing market had gradually weakened over preceding months, the economy locally and nationally had begun to weaken and new investment and infrastructure was postponed. In that context, the appraiser could reasonably conclude that there was only a remote possibility that the GDV would rise by 10 per cent and so might then ascribe only a 5 per cent probability to that eventuality, as shown in Table 13.5. The appraiser might then consider that, given the contextual information, even a 5 per cent rise in the GDV was unlikely and so might ascribe only a 10 per cent probability to that outcome. The appraiser might then ascribe a 40 per cent probability to the core or unchanged site value with the balance of probabilities ascribed to the lower site values.

Of course this is a pessimistic framing of the probabilities and if there was contextual evidence of growth conditions then the probabilities might be skewed to reflect the possibility of rising values.

The sum of the probability weighted site values taken from Table 13.5 is $\Sigma VP = £346,063$. It could be thought of as the probability adjusted site value, which henceforth will be denoted as EV. In the context of a simple appraisal, that could be a legitimate place for the appraiser to stop because it is the most likely value within the array of possible site values taking into account relevant contextual information. For practical purposes, EV could represent the developer's maximum bid for the site.

Given that the site value cannot be predicted with absolute certainty, it is possible to go further by considering the standard deviation, as for investment decisions. Essentially, the larger the standard deviation, the more widely the potential site values are likely to be spread and the greater the risk from a developer's perspective. The standard deviation can be calculated from the

Table 13.5

Possible site values (V)	Subjective probabilities (P)	Weighted values (VP)	Deviation (D) from weighted value: $V - (\Sigma VP)$	Deviation^2 (D^2)	Weighted probability (D^{2}P)
£441,543	5%	£22,077	£95,480	£9,116,430,400	£455,821,520
£400,913	10%	£40,091	£54,850	£3,008,522,500	£300,852,250
£360,284	40%	£144,114	£14,221	£202,236,841	£80,894,736
£319,654	35%	£111,879	−£26,409	£697,435,281	£244,102,348
£279,024	10%	£27,902	−£67,039	£4,494,227,521	£449,422,752
Totals	100%	£346,063			£1,531,093,606

variance, which is the sum of the weighted probabilities in Table 13.5 of £1,531,093,606, by taking its square root of the variance:

$$\text{Standard deviation} = \sigma = \sqrt{£1,531,093,606}$$
$$= £39,129$$

Statistically there is a 68 per cent chance of the outcome being within one standard deviation either side of the EV of £346,063 and a 95 per cent chance of it being within a range of two standard deviations either side of the EV. Thus, there is a 68 per cent statistical chance that the site value will ultimately be £346,063 ± £39,129 or, to put in another way, there is a 68 per cent chance that the site value will lie somewhere between £306,934 and £385,192.

In common with the property investment scenario in Example 13.1, the risk-averse developer might focus upon the downside risk represented by one standard deviation below the EV, which would represent a site value of £306,934. If the site could be acquired for that value then there would be an 84 per cent statistical chance that the scheme would perform to at least that expectation. To put it another way, the developer had an 84 per cent chance of realising or bettering the originally-envisaged profit margin. A pessimist would probably say that there was still a 16 per cent chance that the developer would not reach that target.

13.11 Simulation

Probability-based modelling can be taken further with Monte Carlo simulations which can be run on a PC using software packages such as @RISK® and Crystal Ball®. As for the statistical exercises above, software-supported modelling still requires the operator to set the probable parameters for variables. The software then works within those parameters to conduct thousands of iterations using random numbers which generates a distribution for the selected variable around its central tendency. The distribution of the possible outcomes provides a measure of risk for the project. The standard deviation will emerge from the process so that there is both a numerical value and a graphic representation of the distribution which can be in bell shape or triangular graphic form.

French (2011: 320) feels that there is potential in harnessing the graphic output from simulation models and then embedding it into the valuation process, as this could add an interpretive dimension which might be particularly useful when markets are unstable. Thus a client would receive a central tendency valuation figure with a graphic showing the distribution around that central tendency to illustrate the degree of uncertainty in the valuation.

As for the standard deviation considered earlier, a tight distribution profile would suggest reduced possibility for variance from the central tendency while a wide spread would suggest increased risk. French acknowledges that, although computer-based simulation models imply a degree of sophistication, there will be no material effect on where the central tendency lies as that has already been imputed by the operator when setting the operating parameters. Even with software packages, there is no escaping the need for experience and judgement in risk-appraisal exercises.

There is justifiable scepticism regarding black box methods for risk evaluation in property or indeed wider financial settings because, despite the widespread availability of these models, nobody saw the Credit Crunch coming. Loizou and French (2012: 205–6) have summarised some of the criticisms associated with Monte Carlo simulations in property. Perhaps predictably, they identify the use of historical trends and data when parameters are set by operators because users are inevitably affected by and rely upon what has already happened in a particular market. Historic trends, however, might not be applicable to the contemporary and future risks posed to a project.

Loizou and French also suggest that this type of mathematical modelling is incapable of capturing the dynamics of the development process, wherein each stage is a sub-process with its own internal interactions and risks, some of which will inevitably spill over and have consequences for subsequent stages in the development process.

Software models, like their more traditional statistical counterparts, also have a tendency to lock the attention of the appraiser and client into the parameters which have been pre-set, when what a project may actually require is some 'outside of the box' thinking. On the plus side, Loizou and French note that this form of modelling can stimulate more objectivity and project learning. Identified risks can be ranked and then at least some consideration can be given to what might be done to mitigate or transfer the significant risks identified. This type of modelling is therefore as much about stimulating insights and enhancing project familiarisation as it is about producing quantitative outputs.

13.12 Summary

Given an uncertain future, any business decision involves taking some risks and, as a sub-set of business activity, property investment and property development are no different in that respect. Whether in a property or wider financial context, as the perception of risk increases then there is an expectation that the reward will increase commensurately. For this reason the rate of return expected from a high-cost speculative property development will need to be significant because it is an inherently risky venture. There are risks of one sort or another which surface along the timeline of a development and some of these risks are linked to market fluctuations which are uncontrollable.

In comparison, the risk associated with property investment is normally lower and thus the rates of return could be expected to be lower by comparison. However, even investment in established long-term property assets will still involve some risks of depreciation, illiquidity and market volatility. For that reason judgements have to be formed on what an appropriate risk premium should be, so that it can be added to a risk-free rate to arrive at an overall interest rate for the particular type of asset.

Although risks which affect the financial performance of property can be identified and discussed in a qualitative way, it is not straightforward to translate what might be perfectly defensible observations into a calibrated risk scale. This was illustrated by the *Sportelli* Lands Tribunal case, which as late as 2006 was exploring how a defensible risk rate could be compiled for (in that case) prime central London residential investment properties. The case is a reminder (which extends beyond residential property) that determining the risk rate which should apply in a particular set of circumstances is fundamentally an art requiring experienced individuals to form supportable judgements.

The cross-over between understanding what the risks are and then applying an appropriate rate of interest to reflect them is not easily reduced to a set of tables or a scientific formula. This perhaps explains why the concept of the all risks yield, which reflects market behaviour towards different assets in different locations, has remained such a durable concept when logically it should have become obsolete.

Identifying an appropriate risk rate and then using it to identify the value of, particularly, investment property is one legitimate way of dealing with risk, although not the only one. Given that property investment is usually a long-term activity and that developments will normally extend over several years, another way to confront risk is to explore change in the key variables within an appraisal. This can be done on a stepped basis linked to probability weightings. The standard deviation could also be used to bring at least a patina of statistical respectability to the exercise, and this could be extended with the use of random numbers in simulation modelling using software packages. Regardless of which technique is preferred, there remains the inevitable need for judgements to be made to set the parameters for analysis.

Because risk evaluation exercises remain more of an art than a science, then perhaps the real value of these exercises lies not in their output *per se* but in the way that they enhance project learning. The use of techniques such as sensitivity analysis may therefore improve the decision-maker's knowledge and intuitive feel about a project and this should improve the quality of the decision reached in the end. Confronting and trying to evaluate risk helps the investor or developer to frame realistic expectations about what a development or investment might actually achieve.

Given that there is a suite of optional risk evaluation techniques, it is easy to become drawn into double-counting for risk, for example by adopting a risk-adjusted discount rate and then modelling worst case scenarios. Although that type of 'belt and braces' approach would certainly screen out a lot of the financial risk, it would probably also leave a developer or investor with an uncompetitive bid for an asset, whether that be an income-producing investment or a development site. Thus, to be too obsessive about risk courts the danger of being uncompetitive and, by default, ineffective.

References

Baum, A. and Crosby, N. (2008) *Property Investment Appraisal*, 3rd edn (Oxford: Blackwell).

Byrne, P. (1996) *Risk, Uncertainty and Decision-making in Property Development*, 2nd edn (London: Taylor & Francis).

Department for Communities and Local Government (2012) *Review of the Barriers to Institutional Investment in Private Rented Homes (Montague Report)* (London: Department for Communities and Local Government).

French, N. (2011) 'Valuing in the downturn: understanding uncertainty', *Journal of Property Investment & Finance*, 29(3), 428–47.

Investment Property Forum (2012) *Real Estate's Role in the Mixed-Asset Portfolio: A Re-examination* (London: Investment Property Forum).

Isaac, D. and O'Leary, J. (2011) *Property Investment*, 2nd edn (Basingstoke: Palgrave Macmillan).

Lands Tribunal (2006) *Leasehold Enfranchisement Appeal Decision regarding Sportelli and others* (LRA/50/2005) (London: Lands Tribunal). Available in e-format at: www.landstribunal.gov.uk.

Loizou, P. and French, N. (2012) 'Risk and Uncertainty in Development: A Critical Evaluation of Using Monte Carlo Simulation Method as a Decision Tool in Real Estate Development Projects', *Journal of Property Investment & Finance*, 30(2), 198–210.

Markowitz, H. (1959) *Portfolio Selection – Efficient Diversification of Investments* (New Haven, CT: Yale University Press).

Saunders, O. (2011) *Valuation Calculations: 101 Worked Examples*, 2nd edn (Coventry: Royal Institution of Chartered Surveyors).

Self-assessment questions

1 In relation to a commercial property investment portfolio what are the implications of *systematic* and *non-systematic* risk.

2 What role might the standard deviation play for those involved in property development or property investment?

3 What is the significance of *beta* for those involved in strategic investment decisions?

4 What does the concept of *risk premium* mean for somebody involved in property investment?

5 What are some of the benefits and disadvantages of using software packages such as Crystal Ball® and @RISK® to appraise risk in a property context?

Outline answers can be found towards the back of the book.

14

Gearing and Financing Options

14.1 Introduction
14.2 Gearing
14.3 Ground leasing and rent sharing
14.4 The business tenant's perspective

14.5 Summary
References
Self-assessment questions

> **Aims**
> Having considered risk and development appraisals in previous chapters, this chapter will look at some of the funding options available to the different parties in the event that they might wish to take a longer-term stake in a completed development.

Key terms

>> **Gearing** – refers to the balance between debt (borrowing) and equity (developer or investor's own funds) used to finance a project. High gearing implies a high proportion of borrowing relative to equity, so that if a scheme underperforms a developer is faced with meeting repayments from diminished income. However, when a scheme performs well, high gearing increases the returns to equity stakeholders.

>> **Slicing** – splits ownership of a development between the parties where a landowner, funder and developer all retain a longer-term stake in a development. The slices can be arranged horizontally where the parties owning the lower slices receive a fixed return out of the scheme's annual income. Typically that begins with the landlord who receives a ground rent. A side-by-side slicing arrangement exposes the parties to the scheme's performance. If it did better than expected they would all share in that uplift on a *pro rata* basis, but if the scheme underperformed they would all be affected proportionately.

14.1 Introduction

In Chapter 12 a conventional model of the development process was explored in the context of discussion on the residual valuation model. That discussion assumed that the landowner had accepted an agreed price to sell the land and would then have no further involvement in the project. The developer would then implement the project, culminating in the letting of the completed building and selling it to a corporate property investor. The sale would enable the developer to realise a profit and to pay off the debt accumulated in the execution of the project. The developer is seen as an entrepreneur who adds value to a site before selling it and thereafter has no long-term involvement. The corporate property investor is then assumed to play a traditional property asset management role, dealing with issues such as rent reviews and re-lettings. The business tenants who generate the rental income which props up the viability of a scheme are also assumed to be passive recipients of occupational leases. The model encapsulates the traditional development process, but it also compartmentalises and stereotypes the parties as if they always 'played to type' in a development context.

This chapter will explore some variations in the conventional model where, for example, the developer might want to own the development outright or the landowner might want to retain some ongoing interest in the scheme. When the ambitions of the stakeholders change, there are financial implications and this chapter will examine some of the options which then arise.

14.2 Gearing

Example 12.2 contained a residual valuation and cash flow linked to a scenario in which an office unit was to be developed on a business park. At the culmination of the project, the developer was assumed to have let the building before selling the freehold to a property investor. The money from the sale would then be used to repay the accumulated project debt of £4,341,352 to the bank and to realise the profit of £818,478. A summary of the figures which arose from the scenario is as follows.

Construction costs	£2,457,600	Sale income	£5,159,830
Professional fees	£307,200	Less costs	£4,341,352
Contingencies	£138,240	*Profit*	£818,478
Local authority fees	£118,180		
Letting and legal fees	£49,109	Annual rental income	£409,240
Site value plus costs	£1,032,891	Total costs	£4,341,352
Interest	£238,132	*Annual return on costs*	9.43%
Total costs	£4,341,352		

The development model in the scenario is a conventional if somewhat stereotypical characterisation of the developer as an entrepreneur, who creates value in a project, realises that value in a sale and then uses the proceeds to begin the next project. However, having let the building, and assuming that there was no pre-sale agreement with a property investor, the developer could decide to retain the property by refinancing the project debt. In that scenario the developer effectively postpones taking the profit as a lump sum and instead takes some proportion of the annual rental income produced by the property, which was estimated to be £409,240.

Refinancing the debt and retaining the property might appeal to a developer for a number of reasons. For example, the market might be at a point where it was unwise to start another speculative project and where the corporate strategy might favour consolidation rather than additional risk-taking. Retaining the project for an interim period might also make sense where a property was thought to have growth prospects, so that a sale five years later to coincide with a rent review might realise considerably more capital than an immediate sale.

If the retain-and-refinance model were adopted, it is highly likely that the developer would be able to borrow at a lower interest rate than was possible for the development stage. This is because the risk profile has changed from a speculative development project, where the interest rate on costs was 9 per cent, to a refinancing loan against a completed and tenanted project which is producing a significant annual income. Given the added security of an actual income rather than an anticipated one, the reduced risk might see lenders offering a loan to refinance debt at a 7.5 per cent interest rate.

When a developer is considering a refinancing package, a decision has to be made on the proportion which might be borrowed and the proportion to be contributed from internal funds. This is the relationship between debt and equity which is commonly referred to as gearing. Where there is a high proportion of debt (borrowing) relative to equity (internal funds) the project is said to be highly geared.

Table 14.1 shows some of the gearing options for the project. For presentational purposes, the project costs to be refinanced have been rounded to £4,350,000 and the annual rental income to £410,000. It has been assumed that the 7.5 per cent refinancing rate applies to a fixed-rate, interest-only loan, so that ultimately the development would need to be sold in order to pay off the capital borrowed. It is also assumed that the developer has sufficient equity to invest in the project at the varying levels shown in Table 14.1.

Although both ends of the spectrum are shown, where either all of the project debt is refinanced by borrowing or is entirely paid off using equity, those

Table 14.1

Funding source	Proportionate stake	Share of total costs £	Annual return £	Annual rate of return
Debt (lender)	0%	0	0	0.0%
Equity (developer)	100%	4,350,000	410,000	9.4%
Debt (lender)	20%	870,000	65,250	7.5%
Equity (developer)	80%	3,480,000	344,750	9.9%
Debt (lender)	50%	2,175,000	163,125	7.5%
Equity (developer)	50%	2,175,000	246,875	11.4%
Debt (lender)	80%	3,480,000	261,000	7.5%
Equity (developer)	20%	870,000	149,000	17.1%
Debt (lender)	100%	4,350,000	326,250	7.5%
Equity (developer)	0%	—	83,750	

scenarios are less likely than some intermediate combination of debt and equity. From the developer's point of view the best return of just over 17 per cent is achieved where 80 per cent of the debt is refinanced using borrowing with the remaining 20 per cent funded from equity.

The gearing relationship for the 80/20 split can also be represented algebraically as follows:

$$R_p = (0.2)R_e + (0.8)R_d$$

in which R_p is the return from the project, R_e is the return to equity and R_d is the return on debt payable to the lender. Numerical values for the relative proportions of debt and equity have been inserted, along with the return to the project which is 9.43 per cent.

$$9.43\% = (0.2)R_e + (0.8)7.5\%$$

$$R_e = \frac{9.43\% - 6\%}{0.2} = 17.1\%$$

This illustrates the benefits of high gearing in that the returns to equity can be enhanced if the investment performs as expected. Thus, even if the developer had £4,350,000 of equity available to eradicate the project debt and so become the freeholder entitled to the annual rental income of £410,000 (a 9.4 per cent return), there would still be a case to use borrowing. This is because the same equity could be split five ways and the 20 per cent share used as leverage to acquire five similar properties supported by 80 per cent borrowing in each case. Thus for the same equity outlay, a 17.1 per cent return could be earned, which would be £743,850 compared to £410,000. Of course it would be difficult to find 5 identical properties but the principle remains that gearing will normally be a consideration for the property developer-cum-investor. Depending on the tax status of the borrower, there may also be other advantages because borrowing qualifies for tax relief in some situations.

There are, however, risks associated with high gearing. Because so much has been borrowed, the investment has to perform as well as or better than envisaged in order to pay the interest on borrowing. An underperforming investment would leave the borrower facing large interest repayments, which would obviously present difficulties if there was insufficient income.

14.3 Ground leasing and rent sharing

The business park example involves a site with a present net value of £818,069 which for practical purposes can be rounded down to £818,000. This represents what the landowner could expect to receive for selling the site to the developer at the outset and which represents approximately 16 per cent of the scheme's gross development value (GDV). If it were difficult to generate momentum around a scheme, such as in a regeneration context, an alternative approach might see the landowner enter a contract with the developer in which the land receipt was deferred. This would enable development to progress but, for the landowner to agree to wait for payment and thereby accept additional risk, the benchmark for the land value might be increased to 19 or 20 per cent of the scheme's GDV.

This arrangement might suit the developer as there would be no interest payments on the land over the development period which would compensate for the increased proportionate return to the landowner.

Deferring the land receipt can take a number of different permutations and the term 'claw-back agreement' is sometimes used in that context. However, sooner or later the landowner receives a capital payment and thereafter has no further involvement in the development.

There are situations where the landowner may wish to retain a longer-term involvement in a development by granting a long lease, which enables development to take place, in return for an annual ground rent. The motives for doing this vary, but might involve an organisation's need for relatively risk-free annual income, which can be protected from inflation with the inclusion of rent reviews in the ground lease. Alternatively, the landlord who has granted the long lease can exert a degree of control over how a scheme is developed and how it is subsequently managed.

The ground rent model is common in town centres where either the local authority or a financial institution owns the land and grants a long lease to a developer to build a shopping centre. The developer in that scenario is accepting the development and letting risk in return for a share of the rental income arising from the occupational leases in the shopping centre. The landlord's ground rent is the first deduction from the income and the balance goes to the developer, although there is usually a third party in the guise of a funding organisation. The latter will probably have funded the development costs and will also require a share of the scheme's income proportionate to the investment made. Although this type of arrangement is not common for business park schemes the figures arising from the example can be used to illustrate the principle.

Development costs excluding land and profit

Construction costs	£2,457,600
Professional fees	£307,200
Contingencies	£138,240
Local authority fees	£118,180
Letting and legal fees	£49,109
Interest	£238,132
Total costs	£3,308,461

The landowner might decide to retain ownership of the land but to enable development by granting a long lease to a developer. The landowner's ground rent might then be assessed at 6 per cent of the capital value of the land which is £818,000 and produces an annual ground rent of £49,080. This represents approximately 12 per cent of the annual rental income from the scheme and, in order to protect that income from inflation, it is likely that the landowner would require rent review clauses in the ground lease. As Dubben points out (2008: 373), where a ground rent is higher than 10 per cent of a scheme's income, financial institutions may be reluctant to become involved. If this type of objection were raised, the landowner might be persuaded to accept a premium of 2 per cent capitalised at 6 per cent, so that the ground rent could then be capped at 10 per cent of the annual income. However, this example adopts the simplifying assumption that, although the ground rent is consuming 12 per cent of the scheme's income, it is not so high as to cause a difficulty for the parties and remains at £49,080.

The landlord is, of course, perfectly entitled to sell the freehold to another party because the terms of the long lease granted to the developer are unaffected. The value of the freehold in that event would be the capitalised value of the income at close to 6 per cent, i.e. YP in perp. $1/0.06 \times £49,080$, which is £818,000.

The developer who had borrowed the remaining development costs of £3,308,461 from the bank would need to refinance those costs at the end of the development at a lower rate of interest and might therefore approach a financial institution for a long-term loan at say 7 per cent. This would commit the developer to annual payments of £231,592 which would come out of the annual rental income from the scheme of £410,000. When both loan repayments and ground rent have been deducted from the income the balance remaining for the developer would be £129,328. This is a horizontal slicing arrangement in which the top slice income to the developer is the most risky and conversely the ground rent is deemed to be at least risk (see Figure 14.1).

The middle slice income to the fund is assumed to be a fixed return on borrowing and so, as the scheme matures and when there are rent reviews, the principal beneficiary is the developer, followed by the landowner. The return on debt financing remains unchanged. However, if the development has good growth prospects it is unlikely that the fund would passively settle for providing debt on a fixed-rate basis. There might then be negotiation around a side-by-side slicing arrangement, so that the fund gained some exposure to the income buoyancy of the scheme. Essentially in that guise the fund becomes an equity partner, sharing in the potential uplift but also sharing in the risk that there might be no growth. Thus, the slicing arrangements that are brokered in any particular setting will be a reflection of the characteristics of the scheme and the appetite for equity-sharing, and therefore risk exposure, on the part of the stakeholders involved. For those readers who wish to explore the specialised topic of slicing in more depth, a number of permutations are discussed in Dubben and Williams (2009: 151–65) who also outline the sale and leaseback arrangements which are needed to bind the partners together in these situations.

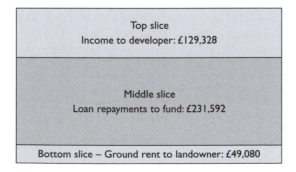

Figure 14.1

14.4 The business tenant's perspective

The occupier of the office building is assumed to have signed a full repairing and insuring lease for 15 years with five-year rent reviews and break clauses at Years 5 and 10. The initial annual rent of £410,000 (rounded up) is a significant annual cost for the business and there could be doubts about whether this scale of annual expenditure was sustainable.

There have been high-profile cases where hotel operators and healthcare companies have committed to long leases on premises only to find that the market for their services has become very competitive and the income generated by the business is insufficient to meet the rental obligations. Essentially those companies have committed to annual rental repayments which simply cannot be sustained and the survival of the company then rests upon whether the corporate landlords will agree to a rent reduction. In many cases landlords have little headroom to be flexible as they have often refinanced in the markets on the assumption that the income from the properties will not fall. This type of situation raises fundamental facilities management questions for a company on whether buying the property outright might be a better option than leasing it.

In the scenario the leasing option does provide some flexibility in that break clauses could be exercised if the corporate strategy changes in the future and requires the company to downsize or relocate. Subject to a few conditions, business tenancies can also be renewed if the full term of 15 years were reached and the company wished to remain in occupation. However, a substantial annual rent is being paid and rent reviews will probably see this increased every five years to stay in touch with inflation.

Our example property was sold to a property investor for £5,159,830 which, for the purposes of the exercise, can be rounded up £5,160,000. To become an owner-occupier of the property the business tenant could raise that sum using a commercial mortgage for say 80 per cent of the value while contributing the remaining 20 per cent as equity. This assumes that the tenant has a good corporate credit rating and has the equity which, at 20 per cent of the value of the property, will be £1,032,000. When interest rates are low this becomes a credible option for a business to consider.

The amortisation schedule in Table 14.2 shows the opening balance of the mortgage at £4,128,000, which is 80 per cent of the value of the property. The term of the loan is assumed to be 15 years on a capital-and interest-repayment basis at a fixed rate of 5 per cent, necessitating annual repayments by the business of £397,701. The repayments are therefore lower than the annual rent of £410,000 and, importantly, the repayments will remain the same for the whole term in comparison to the rent which will almost certainly increase at rent review.

Of course there is no need to construct a mortgage amortisation schedule and it is only shown in Table 14.2 to demonstrate how the repayments gradually erode the capital and interest outstanding on the loan each year. The same outcome can be achieved using the *Annuity £1 will purchase* formula which was first encountered in Chapter 1. The formula can be used for calculating

Table 14.2

Year	Balance £	Payment £	Interest £	Capital £	End Balance £
1	4,128,000	397,701	206,400	191,301	3,936,699
2	3,936,699	397,701	196,835	200,866	3,735,833
3	3,735,833	397,701	186,792	210,909	3,524,924
4	3,524,924	397,701	176,246	221,455	3,303,469
5	3,303,469	397,701	165,173	232,528	3,070,941
6	3,070,941	397,701	153,547	244,154	2,826,788
7	2,826,788	397,701	141,339	256,362	2,570,426
8	2,570,426	397,701	128,521	269,180	2,301,246
9	2,301,246	397,701	115,062	282,639	2,018,608
10	2,018,608	397,701	100,930	296,771	1,721,837
11	1,721,837	397,701	86,092	311,609	1,410,228
12	1,410,228	397,701	70,511	327,190	1,083,038
13	1,083,038	397,701	54,152	343,549	739,489
14	739,489	397,701	36,974	360,726	378,763
15	378,763	397,701	18,938	378,763	0

mortgage repayments for any given interest rate, term and size of loan and it has been used below to demonstrate that the figures in Table 14.2 are correct.

$$\text{Annuity £1 will purchase} = \frac{i}{1 - PV}$$

Inserting the values from the example produces:

$$\frac{0.05}{1 - \left(\frac{1}{1.05^{15}}\right)} = 0.096342$$

Multiplying by the capital borrowed gives the annual repayments required:

$$0.096342 \times £4,128,000 = £397,701$$

The web sites operated by banks and building societies have e-versions based upon the same principles which enable customers to input their loan variables in order to see the scale of repayments which would be required.

Purchasing the property using a commercial mortgage could, therefore, be advantageous for the business tenant, although more would need to be known about the company's characteristics. In particular, some assessment of the company's business plan would be needed: its appetite for owning its properties, its capacity to meet the scale of repayments required and whether it had the equity needed at the outset.

14.5 Summary

Funding the development of properties or acquiring them for investment purposes will normally involve considerable costs and there is always the question of how much should be borrowed and how much should be funded using equity. Even where a developer or funding organisation has all of the money required, there is often a good business case for borrowing and for spreading equity across a range of projects rather than concentrating it on one. Sensible gearing increases the returns to equity and it is a practice used by established and successful developers and property investors.

The property development process is often depicted as a linear process with a strict division of labour in which stakeholders enter and exit when their particular role is completed. Thus, the developer is seen as the risk-taking entrepreneur who purchases a site from a landowner, develops it with the help of the bank, then lets and/or sells the completed project to pay off costs and recover a capital profit. Although this model continues to have validity, it can be taken too literally, obscuring the fact that the parties have other options which they sometimes exercise.

This chapter looked at a few of the alternatives which the parties have, such as participating in a project over a longer period which changes the underlying funding dynamics. For example, a developer might forgo a capital profit at the end of a project in return for a share of the project's income. Part of that income could be used by the developer to gradually pay off the project costs with the objective of becoming the outright owner. Alternatively the developer might use part of the income to refinance the costs on an interest-only basis to buy time, before selling the property at a later date when market values might be more favourable.

Business tenants are also depicted as passive takers of occupational leases, although, given the scale of annual rents on some commercial properties, there is some justification for exploring whether purchasing a property using a commercial mortgage might be a better option. This type of issue lies within the domain of effective facilities management.

References

Dubben, N. (2008) 'Development properties', in R. Hayward (ed.) *Valuation: Principles into Practice*, 6th edn (London: EG Books).

Dubben, N. and Williams, B. (2009) *Partnerships in Urban Property Development* (Oxford: Wiley-Blackwell).

Self-assessment questions

1 A developer has just completed a major commercial project which is now earning £500,000 per annum, but the accumulated debt from the scheme is £5 million. The developer wants to retain a stake in the project and has identified a refinancing package which will necessitate the injection of 15 per cent equity and a commercial loan at 7 per cent for the balance of 85 per cent. What is the return on the equity stake in this gearing scenario?

2 From a developer's perspective what are the key advantages and disadvantages associated with using debt financing to the extent outlined in Question 1?

3 The development of the business park unit discussed in the chapter accumulated costs of £4,350,000 exclusive of the developer's profit. Using the *Annuity £1 will purchase* formula, identify whether it would be viable for the developer to take out a commercial mortgage over 10 years to refinance 80 per cent of the costs with the remaining 20 per cent being equity. Repayments on the mortgage loan would pay down the capital and interest at a fixed rate of 6 per cent and would be funded from the annual rental income produced by the scheme of £410,000.

4 A developer has recently completed a commercial development where the land is held on a long lease in return for an annual ground rent of £75,000. Because the scheme appears to have growth potential, the developer would prefer not to sell the now-tenanted project which is producing a net annual income of £800,000. However, the bank is still owed £6,910,000 of construction and related costs. Given that commercial loans are available in the market at 6 per cent, what advice might be given to the developer?

5 In a development partnership what is the essential difference between vertical and horizontal slicing?

Outline answers can be found towards the back of the book.

15

Evolving Agendas

Aims

This chapter considers some change agendas which have created opportunities to develop and apply some of the principles outlined in the book in contexts where they may be used to ascertain the business case for clients' projects. The aim is not to try to provide the answers as in any case some of the answers are unknown, but to provoke constructive thought about where some of these challenging agendas are leading.

Key terms

>> **Sustainability** – an approach that 'meets the needs of the present without compromising the ability of future generations to meet their own needs' (Brundtland Commission, 1987). This is just one definition but, whichever is preferred, a sustainable action is essentially one which reflects prudent stewardship of resources, so that future options are not compromised. Sustainability in the built environment is often linked to reducing carbon emissions from buildings as a way of mitigating climate change and thus energy efficiency and renewable energy technologies come into view. While these connections are valid, there are also social and economic dimensions to sustainability which tend to attract less attention in a built environment context.

>> **Green buildings** – are buildings which through development or retro-fitting have attracted a sustainability certification such as a BREEAM or a Green Star rating. These voluntary certifications can be achieved to varying standards such as Pass, Good and Excellent dependent upon the scores awarded independently against weighted sustainability criteria. The challenge for valuers is to determine whether a value differential arises between comparable green and non-green buildings. It is then for a developer to decide whether the value gap justifies the additional spend required to achieve green status.

15.1 Introduction

Since the last edition of this book in 1999 there have been unprecedented changes in a number of arenas which affect the property industry or, if the more globalised description is preferred, *the real estate sector*. For example, sustainability is increasingly conditioning government policy ambitions and it is beginning to affect markets and the behaviour of participants in those markets.

Climate change is making itself felt in a number of ways. Focusing just on the sub-category of flooding it is obvious to those who work in property and the closely related fields of property law, funding and insurance that standardised solutions and a 'business as usual' response is unlikely to be a satisfactory. Even the vocabulary is changing, and there are now research agendas on future-proofing cities so that they are more able to deal with whatever climate change may bring.

Changes of this nature and scale inevitably present some uncomfortable challenges to the legitimacy of established practices and procedures. In turn, these pose some difficult questions, but also opportunities, for those who work in or are planning careers in the property sector. It is not possible to deal systematically with all of the changes which have emerged in recent years, so this chapter will concentrate on some of the changes relating to *development viability* and *sustainability and property value*. In both cases the discussion will hint at where opportunities might lie for applying financially-related property expertise in order to provide clear and reliable advice for clients regarding their project ambitions.

15.2 Development viability

One of the consequences of the more constrained economic climate which followed the global financial crisis in 2008 was that developments which had previously been financially viable were no longer so. As late as 2013 the UK government was willing to consider evidence from developers who wanted to unpick planning gain commitments that they made in Section 106 agreements which had been signed during more buoyant periods. The rationale was that the agreement to fund infrastructure and affordable housing from the development process could no longer be met during a depressed market and this was holding back otherwise viable developments. In these situations, there is a requirement for impartial evidence on development viability to ascertain what a development can or cannot carry in terms of Section 106 commitments.

Even the situation on value capture is changing, as local authorities have begun to adopt the Community Infrastructure Levy (CIL) as a more systematic way to part-fund infrastructure. The CIL framework does not expect the development process to meet all of the costs of infrastructure, and there will remain some reliance upon the tax-payer, along with contributions from the budgets of infrastructure providers. Where a local authority decides to use CIL, the contributions previously sought under Section 106 agreements will be scaled back so that those agreements are left to focus upon affordable housing (in housing schemes) and to secure site-specific impact mitigation where that may be needed.

Research by Monk and Burgess (2012: 5) confirms that local authorities are keen to adopt the CIL, as it is seen as a fair and transparent process. However some local authorities reported that they were not confident about setting the CIL charging schedule at the right level, so that it did not deter development but at the same time was capable of capturing reasonable contributions from the development process.

Dartford Borough Council (2012), for example, decided to set a zero rate for all retail developments in some parts of the district. For other commercial developments, such as offices and industrial which contain at least $100m^2$ of floorspace, there will be a flat rate CIL charge across the borough of £25 per m^2 of development. For housing there is a differential CIL rate depending on whether the site is in the north of the borough, where a CIL charge of £100 per dwelling will be levied, or in the south, where a rate of £200 per dwelling will be levied. The judgements on framing area-specific and graduated CIL charging schedules like Dartford's rely on credible infrastructure cost and property valuation advice and this will be needed more widely as charging schedules are adopted nationally.

The RICS (2012) confirms that it is legitimate for local authorities to seek affordable housing and contributions for infrastructure in compliance with local policy. However, it also provides a reminder that these are costs which a development has to bear. As was explored in Chapter 12, developments have a finite value and if the development costs escalate beyond a certain point, the residual sum available will be insufficient to release a site. Valuation advice will therefore be needed to ensure that the costs are not so disproportionate as to remove the developer's profit incentive or the landowner's incentive to supply a site. Checks would also have to be made to ensure that the value side of the equation was sufficiently robust to meet cost commitments. There could be situations in which an appraisal identifies the need for additional enabling development to meet the cost commitments. Viability modelling and scenario testing can therefore play a constructive role in informing the scale and composition of development proposals in specific settings and market conditions.

Because of their knowledge of development appraisal, valuers are seen as the specialists who can shed light on a development's viability and in marginal regeneration situations they can identify whether gap funding will be needed to support a project. Marginal schemes are often reliant upon mixed funding streams and valuers are well-placed to ascertain whether such projects are viable overall, which is a pre-requisite for banks to lend against such schemes.

For mixed-use developments of any scale or where housing is the only or major component, there will normally be a requirement for the inclusion of affordable housing. This element raises challenging valuation issues because even the term 'affordable housing' can mean different types of tenure, from social rented through to various forms of intermediate housing arrangements including shared ownership. In those situations there will need to be some awareness of what the affordable units are worth to a scheme which will reflect what they are worth to the housing association (or registered provider) who will acquire them. If the units are to be shared ownership then as Treanor (2009: 55–67) illustrates,

DCF (discussed in Chapter 3) has a role to play in modelling the future net rental income from the retained equity combined with future stair-casing receipts. The net present value arising, in combination with any grant, will need to match or exceed the development costs including the land.

Going beyond private-sector-led schemes, valuers also have roles to play where housing associations or social enterprises become the lead developers and where funders require reassurance that development loans can be repaid over project lifetimes. These roles require that a business case can be made, and again valuers are well placed to provide reliable advice.

15.3 Sustainability and property value

Sustainability is a well-established concept which in the context of property development and investment has been thoroughly discussed. Most students and practitioners in the built environment disciplines will be familiar with at least one of the definitions of sustainability in circulation. The most commonly-cited version derives from the 1987 Brundtland Commission report and defines sustainability as:

> development that meets the needs of the present without compromising the ability of future generations to meet their own needs.

Sustainable development is an important driver in various strands of government policy and, regarding the built environment, the policy emphasis has been to try to reduce carbon emissions from buildings as a way of mitigating the effects of climate change. This type of policy shows a laudable commitment to tackling the environmental strand of sustainability but of course there are also social and economic dimensions to this holistic concept. If it were to be accounted for, a truly sustainable action would be one which recorded a positive score across the so-called 'triple bottom line'.

The green building accreditation brands which have emerged globally – the Green Star label, Energy Star, LEED (Leadership in Energy and Environmental Design) and BREEAM (Building Research Establishment Environmental Assessment Method) – play a practical role in assessing the extent to which a building is sustainable. Thus the points system in BREEAM awards weights credit against criteria such as Management, Health and Well Being, Energy, Transport, Waste, Land Use and Ecology. These green building labels have now been operating for a sufficient period of time (BREEAM since 1999) for a stock of certified buildings to have accumulated, either as new developments or as retro-fitted refurbished buildings. The issue is whether the minority of certified buildings can yet be distinguished from the larger stock of non-certified counterparts in value terms and what, if any, the margin should be.

Exploring this conundrum, Lorenz and Lützkendorf (2011: 651) identify three possible approaches. The first approach is to add a lump sum to the final valuation to reflect the presence of a sustainability certification. The second approach is to apply a correction factor to reflect the probability of a superior investment performance signified by a sustainability certification. The third approach, which Lorenz and Lützkendorf advocate, is to adjust single valuation input parameters, such as the rent and yield, to reflect a sustainability certification. This explicit approach has merit in that a valuer would have to justify the margin of adjustment relative to market norms, which are largely determined by buildings which do not possess a sustainability accreditation.

To illustrate the principles of Lorenz and Lützkendorf's favoured option, suppose there were two soon-to–be-completed commercial buildings: *A* and *B* which are to be sold to property investors. A valuer has been asked to value both on the assumption that they would be held by an investor until the first rent review and then sold. The annual incomes of £70,000 are assumed to grow at 3 per cent per annum over the holding period and will then be reviewed. Table 15.1 shows the DCFs for both schemes. The reviewed rent is assumed to be capitalised at 8 per cent to reflect a sales receipt of £1,014,365 in Year 6, as shown in the DCF. The only material difference between the buildings is that building *A* has a green certification, such as a BREEAM Excellent accreditation, while building *B* is a standard building with no sustainability credentials.

The valuer might decide that there was insufficient market evidence to justify a distinction between buildings *A* and *B* on rental or yield terms, or indeed in the rental growth rate. Those variables would be held in common, as shown in the net income column of Table 15.1. Despite the absence of clear market evidence, the valuer may still feel less confident about the prospects for the uncertified building *B* in comparison to sustainable building *A*. Instinctively the valuer feels that building *B* presents more risk and on that basis might decide to adjust the discount rate to reflect that perception.

Adjusting the discount rate gives rise to a value differential of £41,597 between the two NPVs shown in Table 15.1. The differential stems from the valuer's awareness of building *A*'s BREEAM status and the 1 per cent adjustment in the discount rate for building *B* reflects the valuer's perception that it represents a relatively higher risk. The margin of adjustment to the discount rate is a judgement made by a valuer. The process has a lot in common with the implicit adjustments made to the all risks yield in the traditional valuation process to reflect risk variation. In the absence of comparable market

Table 15.1 Differential discount rates to value a green (*A*) and a non-green building (*B*)

Year	Net income £ for A & B	PV £1 @ 8%	DCF for A @ 8%	PV £1 @ 9%	DCF for B @ 9%
1	70,000	0.9259	64,813	0.9174	64,218
2	70,000	0.8573	60,011	0.8417	58,919
3	70,000	0.7938	55,566	0.7722	54,054
4	70,000	0.7350	51,450	0.7084	49,588
5	70,000	0.6806	47,642	0.6499	45,493
6	1,014,365	0.6302	639,253	0.5963	604,866
		NPV for *A* = 918,735		NPV for *B* = 877,138	

evidence, this type of 'adjustment for sustainability' faces the same 'black box' criticisms as those levelled at the all risks yield method discussed in Chapter 2.

The alternative to adjusting the discount rate is to explicitly adjust the rent, its growth rate and the exit yield, which in combination are driving value in this scenario. The discount rates would then be the same to prevent double counting for sustainability. This approach appears logical, transparent and defensible in a context where there is some market evidence of a value premium for buildings with a sustainability certificate. For example, a valuer might decide that there was some evidence to justify increasing the annual rent (by 3 per cent) to reflect building A's sustainability credentials as shown in the DCF in Table 15.2.

The valuer might also decide that the sales prospects in 5 years' time for a building which did not possess any sustainability credentials would be difficult when compared to sustainably accredited counterparts. A valuer might therefore decide to slacken the exit yield to 8.5 per cent for building B to reflect a 'brown discount'. The valuer might also feel that for uncertified buildings the annual rental growth rate might be more modest, at say 2 per cent per annum in contrast to 3 per cent for buildings with a sustainability certification.

In combination, these adjustments would reduce the sale receipts in Year 6 for uncertified building B, and this would create a value differential of £93,809 (the difference between the NPV outcomes in Table 15.2). The value gap is larger in this approach because sustainably certified building A has been attributed a value uplift while uncertified building B has been devalued because it is felt that it will depreciate in the face of competition from sustainably certified properties.

From a developer's perspective, the value differential should match or exceed the additional cost which would have to be spent on building A to achieve a BREEAM Excellent certification, otherwise there would be no financial incentive to do so. This is, of course, a simplified hypothetical model (see further comments below) but it illustrates the principle that if a value gap could be consistently demonstrated across a market, then it would provide the incentive to bring forward more sustainable buildings. However, if property investors, who constitute a large proportion of end purchasers in the supply

Table 15.2 A value comparison between a green (A) and a non-green building (B)

Year	Net income £ for A	PV £1 @ 8%	DCF for A @ 8%	Net income £ for B	PV £1 @ 8%	DCF for B @ 8%
1	72,100	0.9259	66,757	70,000	0.9259	64,813
2	72,100	0.8573	61,811	70,000	0.8573	60,011
3	72,100	0.7938	57,233	70,000	0.7938	55,566
4	72,100	0.7350	52,994	70,000	0.7350	51,450
5	72,100	0.6806	49,071	70,000	0.6806	47,642
6	1,044,796	0.6302	658,430	909,243	0.6302	573,005
		NPV for A = 946,296			NPV for B = 852,487	

chain, remain unconvinced that there is a value gap, then they are unlikely to pay the value premium which developers need to produce more sustainable buildings.

If a value gap does exist then it will rely upon adjustments to key variables by a valuer in the context of market evidence and this, unfortunately, is where difficulties are encountered. Researchers have found some evidence in the United States and more recently in London (Chegut *et al.*, 2012: 6) that there is a green premium for sustainably certified commercial buildings relative to their uncertified counterparts. However Warren-Myers (2012: 130) points out that, while these studies provide strategic information which is of academic interest, there are inconsistencies and the studies are often too specialised or hybrid to be of much use to practising valuers.

Warren-Myers (2012: 130) has detected a mis-match between normatively-driven research projects, which have a tendency to delve into case studies, hypothetical scenarios and hybrid statistical exercises, and valuation practice based in market reality. Not surprisingly, therefore, research findings, such as they are, have failed to jump the gap to influence practice. Having reviewed research studies extending back over a decade Warren-Myers (2012: 121) feels that:

> The impact sustainability has on value remains elusive and time does not seem to have provided answers to the question.

Warren-Myers goes on to ponder whether one of the barriers to recognising the value of sustainability certification may be the valuers themselves, whose understanding of sustainability may be fragile and who may have inertial ways of working which are counterproductive to this agenda. The valuation toolkit is also a suspect, because it may currently lack the repertoire required to adequately reflect what might be very subtle effects of sustainability accreditations in value terms. Warren-Myers (2012: 138) ultimately rejects these candidates as the prime suspect, but suggests that there is a need for unbiased, i.e. non-normative, research. Against that backdrop, valuers might better be able to exercise their heuristic skills to detect whether, in the markets in which they practise, there is indeed a value premium associated with a sustainability certification. Thus, rather than continue the search for a universal solution to what has become known as the *metrics problem*, Warren-Myers (2012: 138) seems to suggest that a more local gradualist approach may be better.

> As the market changes and develops, valuers need to develop their opinions and understanding concurrently with the market.

This position is not dissimilar to that reached by the RICS (2009) in its advice to valuers on how to deal with the challenge of reflecting a commercial building's sustainability characteristics in a valuation. Similarly the RICS (2011: 3–4) asks valuers in the residential property market to stay abreast of changes in the sustainability agenda so that they remain well placed to reflect the presence or absence of sustainability characteristics in the properties which they value. The RICS confirms that it is a valuer's duty to reflect in a valuation the characteristics which combine to create value, acknowledging that sustainability is just one (and perhaps a minor one) of those characteristics.

While the concept of sustainability is supported by just about every stakeholder involved in the built environment, this does not always or necessarily translate into willingness-to-pay for a sustainably accredited building above a non-certified building. The RICS (2009: 5) explains this reality as follows.

> Although sustainability principles may be embedded in the policies of property owners and occupiers, translating them to their property decisions has been difficult. An important contributory reason for this is that not all aspects of sustainability translate easily or demonstrably into market value, yet they nevertheless exist. However, currently little is known about their impacts on value and it is important, therefore, that claims of relationships that cannot be evidenced are considered cautiously.

Given the difficulties of precisely calibrating the effects of sustainability certification on value, the RICS (2009: 16–19) urges valuers to remain vigilant on this issue. Thus a valuer might consider how a sustainability certification might signal reduced energy costs for owner-occupiers or tenants and how that might be valued in the particular market. The valuer might also consider whether a sustainable building was more likely to secure tenants of better covenant for a longer lease, thus reducing the prospects of voids and strengthening the prospects of rental growth. The valuer might then consider how those possibilities would be perceived in the investment market.

Although there may still be a shortage of data in a form that valuers can use to support a value premium between sustainably certified and non-certified buildings, this has not prevented some large corporate property investors and developers from producing sustainably accredited buildings. For example British Land is a leading Real Estate Investment Trust (REIT) in the UK which has adopted a key performance indicator committing the company to produce all of its office developments to BREEAM Excellent standard (British Land, 2012: 26).

British Land is not alone among its peer group of REITs in adopting this type of policy and there is tangible evidence in the form of completed and certified buildings that these policies are being adhered to. The degree of commitment to developing sustainably accredited buildings reveals an, as yet, unquantifiable belief in their investment durability. That belief is buoyed up to some extent by the increasing adoption of corporate social responsibility policies by many large companies, who include sustainability among their search criteria when they source premises.

Although there is at present limited market evidence to justify the additional cost involved in procuring a sustainable building, there is some momentum in the commercial property supply chain. Although the momentum is less developed in the residential property market it is likely that a combination of regulation and policy targets will see more sustainable properties developed in the coming years. As the RICS states (2011: 3), it is likely that the market will become increasingly sensitised to the presence of sustainability features in buildings.

15.4 Summary

This chapter has tried to provoke thought about how change can pose challenges but also opportunities for those who have financial expertise related to property and who are able to master and apply the techniques set out in this book. Two very prominent agendas for change were explored in this chapter: the viability of development and the relationship between value and sustainability.

Regarding development viability, valuers have traditionally enjoyed an overview role in assessing the balance between value and costs. A development is viable if a developer is left with sufficient reward relative to the risks and a landowner is presented with sufficient incentive to provide the land. The need for this appraisal independence and expertise was heightened in a difficult post-Credit Crunch global environment where, for example, a number of Eurozone countries required significant financial support to keep them solvent. It is important to make the business case for a scheme where viability is found, but it is equally important to risk unpopularity by explaining that a scheme is not viable because nobody benefits from embarking upon a high-risk venture which soon fails. Independence and ethical values are as important as the ability to use the valuation toolkit.

Sustainability has been debated as a policy driver since the 1980s and in the built environment that has largely translated into trying to limit the carbon emissions from buildings. The rationale is that this can mitigate the effects of climate change. Cynics would argue that it is already too late to do very much about climate change because the atmosphere has already absorbed several centuries of significant CO_2 production arising from industrialisation and population growth. To make a real impact on climate change there would have to be drastic action on a global scale, such as a virtual cessation in the use of fossil fuels. Given that this is most unlikely to happen for political and practical reasons, the production of more sustainable buildings becomes relatively insignificant and may only amount to fiddling while Rome burns.

However, trying to demonstrate an economic rationale for procuring green buildings may play an important role in avoiding defeatism and trying to show that something constructive can be done. It also makes sense in terms of future-proofing, which accepts the inevitability of climate change but tries to do something practical about the consequences by designing for that eventuality.

Valuers have a role in trying to demonstrate a value premium for sustainable buildings as this will provide a helpful signal in the building supply chain. However the property market does not readily or consistently divulge this hoped-for relationship and thus there are no easy-to-apply formulas to determine the green building premium. Practitioners are, therefore, encouraged by researchers and their professional bodies to progressively strengthen their awareness of sustainability features and to try at a practical level to interpret what these might mean in value terms.

References

British Land Company plc (2012) *Annual Report and Accounts, 2012* (London: British Land Company plc).

Brundtland Commission (1987) *World Commission on Environment and Development: Our Common Future* (Oxford: Oxford University Press).

Chegut, A., Eichholtz, P. and Kok, N. (2012) *Supply, Demand and the Value of Green Buildings, RICS Research Report* (London: Royal Institution of Chartered Surveyors).

Dartford Borough Council (2012) *Dartford Community Infrastructure Levy – Draft Charging Schedule* (Dartford: Dartford Borough Council).

Lorenz, D. and Lützkendorf, T. (2011) 'Sustainability and property valuation: systematisation of existing approaches and recommendations for future action', *Journal of Property Investment and Finance*, 29(6), pp. 644–76.

Monk, S. and Burgess, G. (2012) *Capturing Planning Gain – The Transition from Section 106 to the Community Infrastructure Levy* (London: Royal Institution of Chartered Surveyors).

RICS (2009) *Sustainability and Commercial Property Valuation, Valuation Information Paper No. 13* (Coventry: Royal Institution of Chartered Surveyors).

RICS (2011) *Sustainability and Residential Property Valuation, RICS Information Paper* (Coventry: Royal Institution of Chartered Surveyors).

RICS (2012) *Financial Viability in Planning, RICS Guidance Note* (Coventry: Royal Institution of Chartered Surveyors).

Treanor, D. (2009) *Housing Investment Appraisal*, 2nd edn (London: National Housing Federation).

Warren-Myers, G. (2012) 'The value of sustainability in real estate: a review from a valuation perspective', *Journal of Property Investment and Finance*, 30(2), pp. 115–44.

Outline Answers to Self-assessment Questions

Chapter 2

1 Simple definitions of the following types of yield could be as follows.

- The **initial yield** represents the percentage return on a property investment in the first year. For example, if the net income on a retail warehouse were £60,000 in the first year of ownership and the investor had paid £1,200,000 for the property then the initial yield is 5 per cent.
- The **running yield** is the percentage return from a property investment identified from a re-appraisal at any intermediate point after the first year of ownership by an investor. For example, an investor who had originally paid £1,000,000 for a property several years ago might now own an asset which is producing a net annual rental income of £55,000 for which the capital value had appreciated over the preceding year by £15,000. That year, therefore, the combined return to the investor was £70,000 reflecting a 7 per cent return to the investor on the capital originally invested. This is the running yield for that year.
- The **reversionary yield** applies where an investment property is reversionary, i.e. there is an upcoming event such as a rent review or lease renewal which is likely to result in the rent increasing. However, because the event is in the future, the reversionary yield cannot be calculated from the data arising from the transaction. The reversionary yield is derived from a synthesis of market yields which have arisen from transactions on similar properties, tempered by the specific risks attributable to the subject property.
- The **equivalent yield** is the single discount rate which, when applied to the term and reversionary income from an investment property, produces its true capital value. For example, using the traditional term and reversion valuation technique, a valuer might adopt a yield of 6.5 per cent to capitalise the term income arising from an investment property and a yield of 8 per cent to capitalise the reversionary income. The overall capital value arising from the valuation might be £500,000. If all the circumstances were known, the equivalent yield could be calculated by iteration or formula. The equivalent yield is the weighted average annual rate of return which in this example might be 7.5 per cent in order to produce a capital value of £500,000.

  The equivalent yield is also the investment's *Internal Rate of Return* and it provides a useful comparison with the rates of return on other investments.

2 The basic principles underpinning the traditional approach to valuing leasehold interests begin with the premise that leasehold interests will inevitably be worth less than their freehold counterparts. This is because leaseholds are wasting assets and are less versatile than freeholds in terms of disposal or redevelopment. For this reason the yields used to value leasehold interests are adjusted upwards relative to their rack-rented freehold counterparts. The adjustment of the yield upwards has the effect of reducing the YP for *n* years multiplier used to generate the capital value for the term of the lease.

The income to be capitalised is the profit rent, which exists where the rent being paid by the tenant is lower than the market rent. An annual allowance is also deducted from the profit rent to represent a payment into an annual sinking fund, which accumulates at a low-risk rate of interest to replace the original capital invested. The annual allowance has to be grossed up, so that the effects of annual taxation do not prevent the sinking fund from compounding sufficiently to replace the original capital.

3 The criticism which is often levelled at the traditional method of valuing reversionary investment properties is that the process of calibrating yields in order to capitalise the term and reversionary rents appears arbitrary. The method is said to implicitly reflect the risks perceived to affect the different incomes, but there appears to be a lack of science in the way that marginal percentage adjustments to a yield actually represent differential risks. The reversion is also capitalised using current market rents even though the reversion may be several years later when in all probability the market rent will be quite different.

4 One of the defences for using the traditional investment method is that it is used by qualified and experienced valuers and so a consistent tone of values emerges within property markets. The method does not become involved in forecasting and that may have merit in that the values produced are based on known data rather than forecasts that might be unrealistic.

5 A traditional term and reversion valuation of the freehold high street shop currently producing a net annual income of £50,000 might look as shown below. As for all of these types of exercise, the figures rest upon a set of assumptions. Readers may well have legitimately adopted different assumptions to arrive at different results, as not all of the facts regarding a property can be ascertained from a summary scenario.

The answer below suggests that the valuer has considered the 7 per cent all risks yield arising from comparable market-rented properties and has decided that, because the reversion to a market rent for the subject property was three years into the future, it was less certain. Thus the perception of additional risk is reflected in the selection of a yield of 8 per cent to capitalise the reversionary income. The valuer might however have felt that the term rent was more certain, because the tenant was enjoying a lower-than-market rent and so a 7 per cent yield has been selected to capitalise that tranche of income. The yield adjustment implicitly reflects the valuer's perception that the term income has additional security.

The adoption of a 7 per cent yield to capitalise the term income and an 8 per cent yield to capitalise the reversion would produce an equivalent yield of 7.98 per cent (rounded up). Although not required by the question, that figure would confirm that a reversionary property is a marginally more risky prospect than currently market-rented properties which have an all risks yield of 7 per cent.

Term		
Net rent received	£50,000	
YP 3 years @ 7%	2.6243	
		£131,215
Reversion		
Net market rent	£62,000	
YP in perp. def. 3 years @ 8%	9.9229	
		£615,220
Capital value		£746,435

Chapter 3

1   Your friend may be harbouring a common misapprehension regarding the significance of the NPV arising from this type of exercise. The positive sum of £10,000 is not the profit but a marginal addition to an annual rate of return reflected by the discount rate. Thus this scheme is promising to return all of the original capital invested in the house purchase plus the equivalent of an annual rate of return of 11 per cent plus a 'bonus' of £10,000 on top.

The margin of £10,000 is not however sufficiently substantial to preclude further investigation of the characteristics of the property, the area and the various risks involved. This applies particularly to the forecasts of rental growth and capital value over 10 years which must inevitably feature in such an exercise. Alternative investment opportunities would also need to be considered in relation to the friend's particular investment needs. The buy-to-let idea might still be abandoned, but not because it only promises a £10,000 profit over 10 years, as that is a misunderstanding of the DCF appraisal and its outcome.

2   If your colleague wants to discount the scheme on a true quarterly equivalent discount rate then 5.5 per cent is incorrect and the formula $((1 + i)^n) - 1$ could be used to convert the annual rate of 22 per cent as follows: $(1.22^{0.25}) - 1 = 0.051$ (rounded) which is 5.1 per cent. This is only a marginal change but it might have a significant effect for a high-value scheme.

On the second issue it would be double counting to maintain the annual discount rate at 22 per cent, which already embodies an allowance for risk, and to include an explicit profit allowance in the last quarter of the DCF. Very few schemes could carry both requirements and remain viable. If an explicit allowance for a profit linked to the scheme's GDV is to remain in the appraisal, then the discount rate should be adjusted downwards by removing the allowance for risk from it.

3   Although other factors pertaining to the characteristics of the two projects might come into play, strictly on the test of which project meets the target rate of return the completed DCFs reveal that Project B with a positive NPV would be chosen.

Project A

Year	Expenditure £	Income £	Net cash flow £	PV £1 @ 9%	DCF
0	250,000	0	−250,000	1	−250,000
1	0	60,000	60,000	0.9174	55,044
2	0	65,000	65,000	0.8417	54,711
3	0	70,000	70,000	0.7722	54,054
4	0	65,000	65,000	0.7084	46,046
5	0	60,000	60,000	0.6499	38,994
			Net Present Value £=		−1,152

Project B

Year	Expenditure £	Income £	Net cash flow £	PV £1 @ 9%	DCF
0	250,000	0	−250,000	1	−250,000
1	0	65,000	65,000	0.9174	59,631
2	0	65,000	65,000	0.8417	54,711
3	0	65,000	65,000	0.7722	50,193
4	0	65,000	65,000	0.7084	46,046
5	0	65,000	65,000	0.6499	42,244
				Net Present Value £=	2,824

4 The completed DCF reveals that the development opportunity did not meet the target rate of 20 per cent, as the NPV is negative at −£75,175. The developer might be able to reduce the offer on the land by around £75,000 or reduce the costs by a similar amount or some combination of both, so that the scheme met the target rate. If that were not possible then the IRR could be calculated (see Question 5) to ascertain what the scheme was actually earning and how far that differed from the target rate.

Year	Expenditure £	Income £	Net cash flow £	PV £1 @ 20%	DCF
0	1,500,000	0	−1,500,000	1	−1,500,000
1	700,000	0	−700,000	0.8333	−583,310
2	1,150,000	0	−1,150,000	0.6944	−798,560
3	150,000	5,000,000	4,850,000	0.5787	2,806,695
				Net Present Value £ =	−75,175

5 In order to calculate the IRR of the development scheme, a lower target rate of 16 per cent has been used in the DCF to generate a positive NPV which enables the interpolation formula to be used. The lower target rate of 16 per cent becomes R_1 in the formula and the existing 20 per cent target rate used in Question 4 becomes R_2.

Year	Expenditure £	Income £	Net cash flow £	PV £1 @ 16%	DCF
0	1,500,000	0	−1,500,000	1	−1,500,000
1	700,000	0	−700,000	0.8621	−603,470
2	1,150,000	0	−1,150,000	0.7432	−854,680
3	150,000	5,000,000	4,850,000	0.6407	3,107,395
				Net Present Value £=	149,245

$$R_1 + \left[(R_2 - R_1) \times \frac{\text{NPV @ } R_1}{\text{NPV @ } R_1 - \text{NPV @ } R_2}\right] =$$
$$16\% + [(20\% - 16\%) \times \frac{149,245}{149,245 - -75,175}] = 18.66\%$$

Alternatively the IRR function in Excel® could be used by referencing the cells containing the net cash flow figures. A guess of, say, 17 per cent should then be inserted to enable the IRR function to iterate to find the correct answer. The answer in Excel® will be slightly different from that produced long-hand by the formula because of rounding in the calculation. Whichever method is used, the developer would have to take a view on whether 18.7 per cent was sufficiently close to the desired 20 per cent return, although sometimes corporate policy rules out consideration of any opportunities which fall below the target rate.

Chapter 4

1 In theory an interest rate which is used to assess the worth of an investment using DCF, is made up from three elements:

- A time preference element which is supposed to reward the investor for deferring consumption and is calibrated with reference to the return on a risk-free investment such as index-linked gilts.
- A risk premium which is supposed to compensate for the risks borne by the investor and which arise out of the specific type of investment. This is not easy to calibrate but theoretically investment in property is thought to be less risky than investment in equities and so the risk premium for property will usually be lower than in the financial markets. Judgement would then need to take place regarding the type of risks posed to the particular type of property, such as degree of market volatility, illiquidity, obsolescence and depreciation. If there is any market evidence then it will be helpful in this process.
- An allowance for inflation or growth. This can be determined by examining time series data on RPI (or exceptionally CPI) from the past.

2 Differences might arise between an investment valuation of an asset and a market valuation because the former is undertaken from the perspective of a specific entity (or client). For example, the entity might be heavily leveraged and the operational focus might then be upon what an investment has to earn so that at the very least there is a margin above the WACC. Of course, the expectation will normally be higher than that. Essentially the bar is raised for the leveraged purchaser who can afford to pay less for an asset relative to its income stream in comparison to an investor who is relying less on borrowed money. In this context market value is more likely to be closer to the level of the equity-only bidder than the leveraged bidder.

3 Transposing the risk premium from the equities market to a property situation has been considered by the Lands Tribunal who felt that, although it was interesting contextual information, it was not determinate in a property context. Although these observations arise from a Lands Tribunal case which considered a particular property type (high value residential property in central London) the wider ramifications are that the risk premium could vary depending on the type of property. This is because, while factors such as market volatility are risks which both share owners and property owners face, there are a number of risk factors which are specific to property and which include illiquidity, depreciation and obsolescence.

Despite these risks property investors still own an interest in something which is tangible and assuming a relatively unencumbered freehold and conducive planning, a property could be re-used in a number of different ways or ultimately redeveloped. The same is not true of shares whose value can plummet or in the worst case scenario evaporate to zero value.

4 The aspirant buy-to-let investor's weighted average cost of capital is simply $(0.25 \times 0.02) + (0.75 \times 0.05)$, which is 4.25 per cent.

5 The buy-to-let investor could combine the weighted average cost of capital from Question 4, which is 4.25 per cent, with the risk premium for the property type, which is 4.5 per cent plus an additional allowance of 2.5 per cent for inflation, to arrive at a target rate of 11.25 per cent. Another name for that figure is the equated yield, which is discussed in Chapter 5. The investment may or may not reach those lofty heights but at first base it must at least achieve 4.25 per cent as otherwise it is not even covering the cost of capital.

Chapter 5

1 One way to identify the rental growth rate required of the office building on the business park is to use the formula:

$$(1 + G)^n = \frac{\text{YP in perp. @ } I - \text{YP for } n \text{ years @ } E}{\text{YP in perp. @ } I \times \text{PV £1 in } n \text{ years @ } E}$$

where:

    I The initial yield in the scenario: £260,000/£4,000,000 = 6.5 per cent.
    E The investor's target rate of return which is 8.5 per cent.
    G The annual growth rate for the rent which is to be determined.
    n The rent review period in years, which is 5.

Calibrating the variables in the formula therefore produces:

$$(1 + G)^5 = \frac{\text{YP in perp. @ 6.5\% } - \text{YP for 5 years @ 8.5\%}}{\text{YP in perp. @ 6.5\% } \times \text{PV £1 in 5 years @ 8.5\%}}$$

This reduces as follows to identify the annual rental growth rate: *G* which would be required for the target rate of 8.5 per cent to be achieved.

$$(1 + G)^5 = \frac{15.3846 - 3.9406}{15.3846 \times 0.6650}$$
$$= 1.1186$$
$$(1 + G) = 1.1186^{1/5}$$
$$G = 0.0227 \text{ or } 2.27 \text{ (rounded up)}$$

2 Excel®'s *Goal Seek* function could be used to verify the answer in Question 1 or a short-cut DCF could be used. The growth rate of 2.27 per cent identified in Question 1 has been used to inflate the rent on review to £290,881 (i.e. $(1 + 0.0227)^5$ × £260,000 (rounded up)). The NPV result should then be close to zero.

Years	Cash flow	YP 5 years @ 8.5%	YP in perp. @ 6.5%	PV £1 in 5 years @ 8.5%	DCF
0	−£4,000,000				−£4,000,000
1–5	£260,000	3.9406			£1,024,556
5 into perp.	£290,881		15.3846	0.6650	£2,975,933
				NPV =	£489

The NPV of £489 arises because of presentational rounding up. If un-rounded numbers are used in a spreadsheet the outcome is very close to zero. Essentially the check using DCF has confirmed that the identified growth rate of 2.27 per cent is correct.

3 Legitimate criticisms of the process using equated yield analysis to identify the required rate of rental growth are as follows:

- The process is exploring rental growth but this is arguably not a consistent approach as it is only exploring change in one variable. The process is conveniently ignoring any countervailing forces such as building obsolescence which might hold back the rate of growth.
- The rather delicate calculation process could lead to some detachment from the real world, where wider social and economic forces will inevitably affect assumptions made now about what rents might be in, say, 5 years' time.

4 A competent analyst would look beyond the rental growth figure arising from the calculation, recognising that it should only be one part of a broader decision-making process. Other issues which might be looked at include:

- General economic indicators such as growth in GDP, inflation, unemployment rates and borrowing rates.
- Time-series data on the specific property type being evaluated to see if the envisaged growth rate looks credible against what has been achieved in the past.
- Structural issues which impinge upon the business sector to which the tenant belongs. For example if the tenant were in the financial services sector, some investigation would be valid, for example, to determine whether that sector was growing or stable or downsizing and what the prospects for the sector were in the particular locality.
- Property and location-specific factors such as whether new and more sustainable properties were in the development pipeline and would provide quantitative and qualitative competition for the subject property.
- The scenario involves an office unit on a business park, and so some investigation of change in market comparables might be undertaken. The void rate on the business park might also be compared with sector-wide norms and some investigation might be made into the prospects for re-letting second-hand property, should that be required.

5 Equated yield analysis is a delicate process which may be applicable where an evaluation of the worth of an investment property is being undertaken for a specific investor who understands the strengths and weaknesses associated with a forecasted approach. Equated yield analysis is perhaps more consistent with sophisticated in-depth investment analysis for corporate clients who have specific target rates of return for their assets. The process is more in-depth and qualitatively different from that undertaken for a market valuation.

Chapter 6

1 Regarding the industrial unit let to a reliable tenant on a long FRI lease with five-year rent reviews, the incremental rent is the difference between the annual rent passing on the unit, which is £48,000, and the market rent of £62,000, which is £14,000. The hardcore calculation might start by attributing a 7 per cent yield to the hardcore income as it is perceived to be secure and warranting a 1 per cent mark-down on the

market-rented comparable. Given these variables, the calculation to identify the yield needed to capitalise the incremental rent might look as follows.

Market rent	£62,000	
YP in perp. @ 8%	12.5	
		£775,000
Hardcore rent	£48,000	
YP in perp. @ 7%	14.2857	
		£685,714
Capital value of increment		£89,286

Yield on increment therefore $\dfrac{£14,000}{£89,286} = 15.7\%$

The hardcore valuation would then appear as follows:

Hardcore rent	£48,000	
YP in perp. @ 7%	14.2857	
		£685,714
Incremental rent	£14,000	
YP in perp. @ 15.7%		
deferred 2 years	4.7581	
		£66,613
Capital value		£752,327

A comparison could then be made against a notional market-rented equivalent which was currently generating an annual rent of £62,000 and which was capitalised using the all risks yield of 8 per cent. That comparable property would therefore have a capital value of around £775,000, which is logical given that it should be more valuable than its reversionary counterpart which is valued at £752,327.

2 The literature which explores the hardcore valuation method invariably compares it with that of the term and reversion technique and the latter is often invoked as a way to check the outcome of a hardcore valuation. Given that very large sums of money can be at stake, it is always advisable to use an alternative method, if one exists, as a means for checking accuracy and credibility.

Perhaps another reason for undertaking a check using an alternative method is that quite alarming yield differences can emerge within the hardcore method, differences which a valuer would not arrive at intuitively. In Question 1 it is 7 per cent for the hardcore income and 15.7 per cent for the incremental income. The margin of difference does create a sense of unease about whether these particular figures really reflect the differential risk between the hardcore and incremental incomes.

If a term and reversion valuation were used to provide a second opinion for the scenario in Question 1 then it might look as shown overleaf. Readers can decide for themselves whether the outcome of £751,219 builds confidence around the capital value identified by the hardcore method in the answer to Question 1.

Term
Net annual rent   £48,000
YP for 2 years @ 7%   1.8080

Value of the term   £86,784

Reversion
Reversion to market rent   £62,000
YP in perp. @ 8% deferred 2 years   10.7167

Value of the reversion   £664,435

Capital value   £751,219

3   The office unit on a business park which is currently achieving an annual rental income
    of £95,000 is over-rented and the incremental rent of £20,000 is likely to disappear in
    two years' time with a reversion to a market rent of £75,000. Given that market-rented
    properties are exchanging in the investment market to reflect a yield of 7.5 per cent a
    hardcore method valuation might look as follows:

Term rent   £95,000
YP in perp. @ 8.5%   11.7647

                                                                £1,117,647
Reversion to market rent   £75,000
YP in perp. @ 7.5%   13.3333

                                                                 £999,998

Capital value of increment   £117,649

Yield on increment therefore: $\dfrac{£20,000}{£117,649} = 17.0\%$

Hardcore net annual rent   £75,000
YP in perp. @ 7.5%   13.3333

                                                                 £999,998
Incremental annual rent   £20,000
YP for 2 years @ 17.0%   1.5852

                                                                  £31,704

Capital value   £1,031,702

4   Some of the key criticisms associated with the hardcore technique are:

- It lacks transparency and consistency in the yield calibration which is supposed to
  reflect the differential risks posed to income slices.
- The valuation of hardcore income in perpetuity is inconsistent with the probability
  that during recessionary periods commercial investment properties may well exhibit
  intermittent income streams due to voids.
- The method is capable of over-valuing the hardcore income through the use of a
  lower-than-market yield and therefore higher YP multiplier. Despite its alleged
  security, it is questionable whether a lower-than-market rent should in fact be
  capitalised as if it were more valuable than a market rent.
- The method seems to have a dependent and subsidiary relationship with the term
  and reversion approach.

- Current market rents are applied to situations which may be several years into the future regardless of the possibility of growth or the effects of inflation.
- Creates artificial horizontal divisions in the income which, if it is defaulted upon, is lost entirely.

5 Some of the key strengths associated with the hardcore technique are that the method:

- Can evaluate over-rented properties as well as those subject to stepped and turnover rents. It is argued by some that this puts the landlord in more of a risk-sharing and stakeholder role alongside the tenant, and that this is thought to be a more healthy relationship.
- Is flexible and confronts valuers and other stakeholders with the risk implications likely to arise at different stages for investment properties.

Chapter 7

1 A term and reversion calculation to identify the capital value of a retail warehouse let at an annual rent of £70,000 and with 3 years until review might look as follows. A valuer might have assessed the term at 6.5 per cent yield to reflect its greater certainty relative to the reversionary income which is benchmarked against market-rented properties and for which a yield of 7.5 per cent might apply.

Term		
Rent passing	£70,000	
YP 3 years @ 6.5%	2.6485	
		£185,395
Reversion		
Market rent	£80,000	
YP in perp. @ 7.5% deferred 3 years	10.7328	
		£858,624
Capital value		£1,044,019

2 The equivalent yield for the above property would lie somewhere between 6.5 and 7.5 per cent and so the DCF calculation to identify the rate precisely would adopt these two figures as the trial rates. The result is likely to be close to 7.5 per cent as more of the value is tied up in the reversion (valued at 7.5 per cent) than the term (valued at 6.5 per cent).

Years	Cash flow	YP 3 years @ 6.5%	YP in perp. @ 6.5%	PV £1 in 3 years @ 6.5%	DCF
1–3	£70,000	2.6485			£185,395
3 into perp.	£80,000		15.38	0.8278	£1,018,830
					£1,204,225
				Less capital value	£1,044,019
				NPV =	£160,206

Years	Cash flow	YP 3 years @ 7.5%	YP in perp. @ 7.5%	PV £1 in 3 years @ 7.5%	DCF
1–3	£70,000	2.6005			£182,035
3 into perp.	£80,000		13.3333	0.8050	£858,665
					£1,040,700
				Less capital value	£1,044,019
				NPV	–£3,319

$$IRR = 6.5\% + \left[(7.5\% - 6.5\%) \times \frac{160,206}{£160,206 - -£3,319}\right] = 7.48\% \text{ rounded up}$$

A check using Excel®'s *Goal Seek* function confirms that the IRR which is also the equivalent yield is 7.48 per cent.

3 Statements (b) and (c) are correct but statements (a) (d) and (e) are incorrect as they are flawed in one way or another.

4 The fundamental difference between the equivalent yield and the equated yield is that the latter explicitly factors in growth while the former deals with known current values. There might be some merit in using current and known values and ignoring forecasts of growth as these could lead to an over-valuation of an asset. In a recessionary context rents can fall as well as rise and thus using the equivalent yield could be thought of as playing it safe.

5 The interest-only yield on gilts reveals part of the investment performance by confirming the relationship between what was paid to acquire the gilts in contrast to the annual interest paid to the investor. Thus if gilts with a face value of £100 and a premium of 5 per cent were 4 years from maturity and were purchased on the market for £120 the interest-only yield would be: $5/120 = 4.16$ per cent.

The interest-only yield might appear to be a reasonable indicator of return but it does not consider the probability that the market price will gradually converge towards par, i.e. the face value of £100. Although one year later the investor will have received an income equivalent to 4.16 per cent (which is £5) the market price of the gilts may have reduced to, say £117 and so £3 was lost on the capital value, leaving a net income that year of only £2 against an outlay of £120. The overall rate of return for that year was therefore only: $2/120 = 1.67$ per cent. The convergence towards face value of £100 will continue, so the other important piece of information needed to assess the performance of this type of investment is the gross redemption yield.

Chapter 8

1 Regarding the landlord with the target rate of return of 10 per cent who is going to let a high street shop to a tenant on a 15-year lease with three-year rent reviews, Rose's formula below generates an equivalent rent of £63,590. That rent would create parity with comparable properties leased at £65,000 per annum on five-year rent reviews.

$$K = \frac{A - B}{A - 1} \times \frac{C - 1}{C - D}$$
$$= \frac{(1 + 0.1)^3 - (1 + 0.025)^3}{(1 + 0.1)^3 - 1} \times \frac{(1 + 0.1)^5 - 1}{(1 + 0.1)^5 - (1 + 0.025)^5}$$

$$K = \frac{1.331 - 1.0769}{0.331} \times \frac{0.6105}{1.6105 - 1.1314} = 0.7677 \times 1.2743 = 0.9783$$

The equivalent rent = $0.9783 \times £65,000 = £63,590$ (rounded)

The DCF below was produced in Excel®, where *Goal Seek* was used to identify the equivalent rent on a three-year cycle, and provides a check for the accuracy of the answer using Rose's formula. The equivalent rent of £63,588 in Year 1 suggests that the calculation was correct as a £2 difference at this scale is due to rounding.

Year	Rent £ on 5-year reviews	Equivalent rent £ on 3-year reviews	PV £1 @ 10%	DCF £ on 5-year reviews	DCF £ on 3-year reviews
1	65,000	63,588	0.9091	59,092	57,808
2	65,000	63,588	0.8264	53,716	52,549
3	65,000	63,588	0.7513	48,835	47,774
4	65,000	68,477	0.6830	44,395	46,770
5	65,000	68,477	0.6209	40,359	42,517
6	73,542	68,477	0.5645	41,514	38,655
7	73,542	73,742	0.5132	37,742	37,844
8	73,542	73,742	0.4665	34,307	34,401
9	73,542	73,742	0.4241	31,189	31,274
10	73,542	79,412	0.3855	28,350	30,613
11	83,206	79,412	0.3505	29,164	27,834
12	83,206	79,412	0.3186	26,509	25,301
13	83,206	85,518	0.2897	24,105	24,775
14	83,206	85,518	0.2633	21,908	22,517
15	83,206	85,518	0.2394	19,920	20,473
			NPV =	541,105	541,105

2 Regarding advice to the manufacturing firm which occupies an industrial unit under a 30-year lease granted 15 years ago and where there is an upcoming rent review, the likely rent can be arrived at using a number of different methods. One method is to use the rental growth formula outlined in Chapter 5 and then to insert the identified growth rate into Rose's formula to find the equivalent rent which is likely to apply for the 15 years remaining on the lease. The growth rate formula is applied as follows.

$$(1 + G)^n = \frac{\text{YP in perp. @ } I - \text{YP for } n \text{ years @ } E}{\text{YP in perp. @ } I \times \text{PV £1 in } n \text{ years @ } E}$$

where:

  I initial yield or capitalisation rate.
  E investor's target rate of return and which is also the equated yield.
  G annual growth rate for the rent which is to be determined.
  n rent review period in years, for the comparable which is 5.

Calibrating the variables in line with the scenario produces:

$$(1+G)^5 = \frac{\text{YP in perp. @ 8\% } - \text{YP for 5 years @ 10\%}}{\text{YP in perp. @ 8\% } \times \text{PV £1 in 5 years @ 10\%}}$$

This progressively reduces as follows to finally identify the annual rental growth rate, G, which would be required for the target rate of 9 per cent to be achieved.

$$(1+G)^5 = \frac{12.5 - 3.7908}{12.5 \times 0.6209} = 1.1221$$

$$(1+G) = 1.1221^{1/5}$$

$$G = 0.0233 \text{ or } 2.33\%$$

Once the rental growth rate has been identified using the formula above, it could be compared with any records over the medium to longer term to assess whether such a growth rate was a realistic prospect. Assuming it did reflect the low but steady rate of growth for industrial units on this industrial estate, that variable could be used in Rose's formula to identify the equivalent rent which is likely to apply for the remaining 15 years of the lease as follows.

$$K = \frac{A - B}{A - 1} \times \frac{C - 1}{C - D}$$

$$= \frac{(1+0.1)^{15} - (1+0.0233)^{15}}{(1+0.1)^{15} - 1} \times \frac{(1+0.1)^5 - 1}{(1+0.1)^5 - (1+0.0233)^5}$$

$$= \frac{4.1772 - 1.4127}{3.1772} \times \frac{0.6105}{1.6105 - 1.1221} = 0.8701 \times 1.25$$

$$K = 1.0876$$

The equivalent rent would then be the product of $1.0876 \times £50,000 = £54,380$.

The DCF below was produced in Excel® using *Goal Seek* to identify the equivalent rent for the remaining 15 years and provide a check on the accuracy of the answer found using Rose's formula. The equivalent rent of £54,377 below suggests that the calculation was correct.

Year	Rent £ on 5-year reviews	Equivalent rent £ over 15 years	PV £1 @ 10%	DCF £ on 5-year reviews	DCF £ on 15-year equivalent rent
1	50,000	54,377	0.9091	45,455	49,434
2	50,000	54,377	0.8264	41,320	44,937
3	50,000	54,377	0.7513	37,565	40,853
4	50,000	54,377	0.6830	34,150	37,139
5	50,000	54,377	0.6209	31,045	33,763
6	56,103	54,377	0.5645	31,670	30,696
7	56,103	54,377	0.5132	28,792	27,906
8	56,103	54,377	0.4665	26,172	25,367
9	56,103	54,377	0.4241	23,793	23,061
10	56,103	54,377	0.3855	21,628	20,962

11	62,951	54,377	0.3505	22,064	19,059
12	62,951	54,377	0.3186	20,056	17,325
13	62,951	54,377	0.2897	18,237	15,753
14	62,951	54,377	0.2633	16,575	14,317
15	62,951	54,377	0.2394	15,070	13,018
			NPV =	413,592	413,590

3 The retailer who is paying an annual rent of £45,000 for a shop when the market rent is £60,000 possesses a saleable profit rent of £15,000 for the four years remaining on the lease. Assuming an assignment of the lease, the retailer might well receive a premium in the vicinity of £48,596 from the assignee, to reflect the capitalisation of the profit rent for four years at 9 per cent. The calculation is as follows.

Estimated annual market rent	£60,000
Annual rent for the remaining 4 years of the lease	£45,000
Profit rent	£15,000
YP 4 years @ 9%	3.2397
Premium payable for profit rent	£48,596

Although not required by the question, the accuracy of the above calculation could be checked using DCF. The DCF confirms that the likely premium payable for the profit rent would be in the vicinity of £48,596.

Year	Annual profit rent £ for 4 years	PV £1 @ 9%	DCF £
1	15,000	0.9174	13,761
2	15,000	0.8417	12,626
3	15,000	0.7722	11,583
4	15,000	0.7084	10,626
		NPV =	48,596

4 Concerning the suite of recently refurbished prime city centre offices which could achieve a market rent of £85,000 per annum, the effects of a £65,000 premium on entry would be to reduce the annual rent for the first term to £68,720 as shown below.

Present value of the first 5-year term without premium		
YP 5 years @ 8%	3.9927	
Annual market rent	£85,000	
Capital value		£339,380
Deduct premium		£65,000
		£274,380
Decapitalise by YP 5 years @ 8%		3.9927
Annual rent reflecting premium		£68,720

Some might prefer to use DCF as shown below to demonstrate that the premium and rent reduction scenario leaves the parties in the same position mathematically as a scenario where no premium was paid. However the payment of a premium has secured an up-front commitment from the tenant and this has reduced the risk to the lessor. This was made possible by market conditions which have tipped the balance of power towards the landlord and away from the tenant in this scenario.

Year	Market rent £ without premium	£65,000 premium paid on entry	PV £1 @ 8%	DCF without premium £	DCF with premium £
0	0	65,000	1		65,000
1	85,000	68,720	0.9259	78,702	63,628
2	85,000	68,720	0.8573	72,871	58,914
3	85,000	68,720	0.7938	67,473	54,550
4	85,000	68,720	0.7350	62,475	50,509
5	85,000	68,720	0.6806	57,851	46,771
			NPV =	339,372	339,371

5 The calculation to identify the equivalent rent for the industrial unit which is to be leased for 20 years at a headline annual rent of £65,000 but where the first two years are rent-free is shown below.

Headline annual rent		£65,000
YP 3 years @ 8%	2.5771	
Deferred 2 years @ 8%	0.8573	
	2.2093	
Capital value of the term		£143,605
Decapitalise by YP 5 years @ 8%		3.9927
Equivalent annual rent		£35,967

A DCF constructed in Excel® could be used to check the answer as follows. The *Goal Seek* function can be used to find the equivalent rent which will balance the NPV for the term which is £35,969.

Year	Headline rent and rent-free period £	Equivalent rent £	PV £1 @ 8%	DCF £ on headline rent	DCF £ on equivalent rent
1	0	35,969	0.9259	0	33,304
2	0	35,969	0.8573	0	30,837
3	65,000	35,969	0.7938	51,597	28,552
4	65,000	35,969	0.7350	47,775	26,437
5	65,000	35,969	0.6806	44,239	24,481
			NPV =	143,611	143,611

Chapter 9

1 The appropriate formula for identifying the interest-only element which arises over 3 years on a loan of £500,000 at an annual interest rate of 8 per cent is:

$$((1 + i)^n) - 1$$

which, when applied to the figures in the question, produces:

$$(1.08^3) - 1 = 0.2597$$

The interest element is then the outcome of $0.2597 \times £500,000 = £129,850$

2 The quarterly equivalent rate of an annual rate of 9 per cent could be calculated as follows:

$$((1 + i)^{0.25}) - 1 = (1.09^{0.25}) - 1 = 2.18\% \text{ (rounded up)}$$

3 The appropriate formula for this question is:

$$\text{YP in advance 5 years @ 6\%} = 1 + \text{YP in arrears } (5 - 1) \text{ years @ 6\%}$$
$$= 1 + \text{YP in arrears 4 years @ 6\%}$$
$$= 1 + 3.4651 = 4.4651$$

When the multiplier 4.4651 is applied to the annual income of £25,000 the present value of the income on an in advance basis is found to be £111,628.

4 The above calculation could be undertaken on a quarterly in advance basis by first converting the annual rate of 6 per cent into its true quarterly equivalent rate as follows:

$$((1 + i)^{0.25}) - 1 = (1.06^{0.25}) - 1 = 1.47\% \text{ rounded up.}$$

There would be a total of 20 quarters over a five-year period, so the formula would appear as follows:

$$\text{YP in advance 20 'years' @ 1.47\%} = 1 + \text{YP in arrears } (20 - 1) \text{ 'years' @ 1.47\%}$$
$$= 1 + \text{YP in arrears 19 'years' @ 1.47\%}$$
$$= 1 + 16.4726 = 17.4726$$

When the multiplier 17.4726 is applied to the quarterly income of £6,250 the present value of the income on a quarterly in advance basis is found to be £109,204 (rounded up).

5 The present capital value of the annual income of £80,000 over 5 years on an annual in arrears basis at 7 per cent can be calculated using the conventional YP for n years' formula as follows:

$$\frac{1 - (1 + i)^{-n}}{i}$$

In the scenario the YP (in arrears) formula generates a multiplier of 4.1002 which when applied to the annual income of £80,000 produces a present capital value of £328,016.

To begin the quarterly in advance comparison, the first step would be to convert the annual rate of 7 per cent into its true quarterly equivalent rate:

$$((1 + i)^{0.25}) - 1 = (1.07^{0.25}) - 1 = 1.71\% \text{ rounded up.}$$

There would be 20 quarters over a five-year period, so the formula would appear as follows:

$$\text{YP in advance 20 'years' @ } 1.71\% = 1 + \text{YP in arrears } (20 - 1) \text{ 'years' @ } 1.71\%$$
$$= 1 + \text{YP in arrears 19 'years' @ } 1.71\%$$
$$= 1 + 16.1060 = 17.1060$$

When the multiplier 17.1060 is applied to the quarterly income of £20,000 the present value of the income on a quarterly in advance basis is found to be £342,120 (rounded up). This exceeds the figure of £328,016 generated by the annual in arrears method by £14,104.

Chapter 10

1 The illustration and calculation using the hardcore method to identify the capital value of the over-rented retail warehouse would appear as follows. Variations on the assumptions are, of course, possible and will influence the out-turn figure.

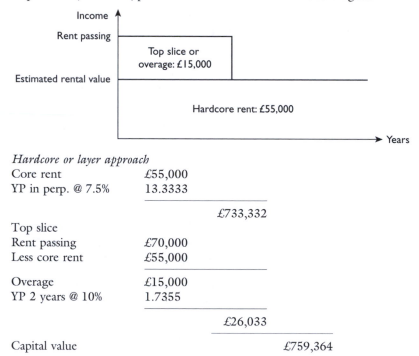

Hardcore or layer approach

Core rent	£55,000	
YP in perp. @ 7.5%	13.3333	
		£733,332
Top slice		
Rent passing	£70,000	
Less core rent	£55,000	
Overage	£15,000	
YP 2 years @ 10%	1.7355	
		£26,033
Capital value		£759,364

2 The diagram and calculation opposite reflect the use of the term and reversion technique to re-calculate the capital value arising from the over-rented retail warehouse scenario in Question 1. The capital value arising from the use of this technique is almost £32,000 lower than that produced by the hardcore method.

The reason for the discrepancy is mainly because of the application of a relatively high capitalisation rate of 10 per cent (and therefore a relatively low YP multiplier) to the whole of the term rent rather than just a slice of it as in the hardcore method. There is also a suspicion that the hardcore method involves some double counting, as it is placing quite a high value on the core income (implying growth) and adding the capitalised overage, part of which overlaps with the growth expected in the core income.

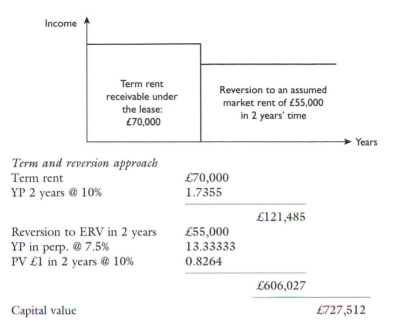

Term and reversion approach

Term rent	£70,000	
YP 2 years @ 10%	1.7355	
		£121,485
Reversion to ERV in 2 years	£55,000	
YP in perp. @ 7.5%	13.33333	
PV £1 in 2 years @ 10%	0.8264	
		£606,027
Capital value		£727,512

3 The calculation of the growth rate required is simply the application of the compound interest formula $(1 + i)^n$ in which the growth rate i can be found by iteration or by using Excel®'s *Goal Seek* function. In this case the annual rate would need to be 12.82 per cent over the two years before the next rent review. The calculation would then be: $1.1282^2 \times £55,000 = £70,004$.

   An annual growth rate in rents of 12.82 per cent is considerable and although double-digit rental growth might occasionally occur during a 'bounce back' year following a recession, it would be unsustainable in the longer term. In the scenario such a growth rate appears to be unrealistic given that trading on the retail park has been difficult and rents have fallen over the preceding three years.

4 The short-cut DCF calculation which has included the assumed annual growth rate of 3.5 per cent in the market rent for the retail warehouse is shown below with the counterpart diagram. The calculation is simply $1.035^2 \times £55,000 = £58,916$ which for practical purposes can be rounded down to £58,900.

   It is assumed that there is no upwards-only rent review clause in the lease to prevent the rent from falling to market levels. The leverage provided by the tenant's break clause option means that the landlord will probably have to accept that the rent will fall back to market levels.

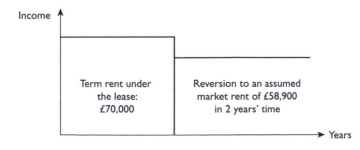

Short-cut DCF

Term rent	£70,000	
YP 2 years @ 10%	1.7355	
		£121,485
Reversion to ERV in 2 years	£58,900	
YP in perp. @ 7.5%	13.33333	
PV £1 in 2 years @ 10%	0.8264	
		£648,998
Capital value		£770,483

5 The DCF below is produced from the perspective of the property investor who has a target rate of return of 10 per cent and who is interested in acquiring the retail warehouse discussed above. The GPV of £728,545 signifies the value of the asset inclusive of acquisition costs. The purchase would initially secure two years of rental income at £70,000 per annum up until the first rent review.

Because the property is over-rented the expectation is that the rent will then fall to £58,917 because there is no upwards-only rent review clause and the tenant has a break clause option. The reviewed rental value arises from the market rent of £55,000 growing at the investor's expectation of 3.5 per cent per annum over the two years until the first rent review: $1.035^2 \times £55,000 = £58,917$. In reality, that figure would probably be rounded down to £58,900 but the full figure has been included in the DCF so that the calculation can be understood.

The capital value on disposal in Year 7, which is £823,247, reflects an expected exit yield of 8.5 per cent, which has been used to capitalise the reviewed rent at that stage. This would be £69,976 and is the product of $1.035^5 \times £58,917$ (allowing for rounding).

Year	Lease rent £	Sale value £	PV £1 @ 10%	DCF £
1	70,000		0.9091	63,637
2	70,000		0.8264	57,848
3	58,917		0.7513	44,264
4	58,917		0.6830	40,240
5	58,917		0.6209	36,582
6	58,917		0.5645	33,259
7	58,917	823,247	0.5132	452,726
			GPV =	728,556

Chapter 11

1 Although there is only three years' difference between a lease with 79 years unexpired and one with 82 years unexpired, the critical distinction from a lease extension or enfranchisement perspective is the 80-year boundary. Under the Leasehold Reform, Housing and Urban Development Act 1993 (and subsequent amendments) the marriage value is deemed to be nil for the purposes of premium calculation where a lease has 80 years or more unexpired. This is likely to have a significant effect on the premium which a leaseholder will have to pay to a landlord for either a lease extension

or enfranchisement. For this reason professionals involved in the process advise leaseholders to take action before the 80-year boundary is reached.

2 Before contacting legal and valuation enfranchisement experts, the leaseholder could check to see if basic eligibility criteria were satisfied. For example, if there were shops or other commercial uses on the ground floor of the block the leaseholder could work out whether those uses were occupying anything close to 25 per cent of the floorspace in the block. If there were only 3 storeys and the ground floor was occupied by commercial uses such as shops, it is unlikely that leaseholders in the block would be eligible for enfranchisement (but they could still seek lease extensions). However, if there were six storeys with retail on the ground floor and flats on all other floors, the 25 per cent threshold would not have been exceeded and on that criterion enfranchisement would still be a possibility.

The leaseholder could find out who the landlord was and whether they were exempt from the legislation by virtue of charitable status. He or she could also find out whether at least 50 per cent of the leaseholders in the block were interested in taking action and whether they were qualifying tenants. In order to qualify, tenants would need to own their leases outright and not be, for example, shared ownership tenants who had not acquired 100 per cent ownership of their leases. Their leases, when originally granted, would have to have been at least 21 years in length. There are other qualifying criteria, but a rudimentary check could be made by going to the Leasehold Advisory Service web site at www.lease-advice.org which has a number of guides on the process.

3 Large sums of money may be at stake in leasehold extensions and enfranchisement cases and that fact alone can create adversarial tension. Although a number of factual issues can be agreed between the parties, disagreements can arise regarding the calibration of some of the variables used in the calculation of the premium to be paid to the landlord. Where the lease has fewer than 80 years remaining, the marriage value comes into the equation and this necessitates consideration of the deferment rate which is applied to the reversionary value of the property.

Although the *Sportelli* case provided indicative deferment rates for the reversion of leasehold flats and houses, it has been acknowledged that the risks to properties in other parts of the UK might be different. The subsequent *Zuckerman* LVT decision confirmed that, if sufficient and convincing evidence was compiled by one or other of the parties, then there might be grounds to vary the application of the standard deferment rates. Typically the representatives of tenants might try to find evidence to support a higher deferment rate, which would have the effect of lowering the premium payable to the landlord. Conversely representatives acting for the landlord might try to find evidence to support the adoption of a lower deferment rate which would have the effect of increasing the premium.

4 In the context of a lease extension or enfranchisement where a lease has less than 80 years remaining it is necessary to consider the relative value held in a residential lease and the counterpart freehold at the valuation date. This is because relativity will be one factor which will influence the calculation of the premium which the leaseholder(s) will ultimately have to pay to the landlord.

Where a case is in dispute, the LVTs will prefer to rely upon direct market comparison to assess the value split between the lease and the freehold. However, because these proceedings are specialised, it is sometimes difficult to identify relevant comparable market evidence to support a particular relativity percentage. In those situations, thin market evidence might play a secondary role and more reliance will be placed on graphs of relativity. The recognised graphs in circulation have effectively pooled market evidence from wide catchment areas over a number of years. Because the data sets and plotted graphs are all slightly different, it is not unusual to see an averaging process of those deemed to be most relevant to the case.

5   When the leaseholders in a block of flats have acted collectively and used the legislation to enfranchise their freehold they may then grant themselves 999-year leases. The leaseholders as a collective (some may form into Right to Enfranchise Companies) inherit the responsibilities which the landlord previously had and which include managing the maintenance of the common areas within a block. The leaseholders might decide to contract out that work to managing agents, but essentially the leaseholders now have control over those activities which the landlord once did.

Chapter 12

1   The residual valuation method remains a useful appraisal tool but it has some weaknesses which include:

- The calibration of costs and values relies upon market data which reflects where the property market has been rather than where it is going. There is thus an in-built contradiction in using historic data for a project which may be realised in two or three years' time when circumstances will almost certainly have changed.
- Interest charges are calculated as if project costs were accumulating on a straight-line basis when in fact costs under different budget headings arise on different patterns. For example the major costs will usually be construction costs and those tend to start slowly before accelerating towards the back end of the project in an S-curve pattern. The residual method cannot deal with this subtlety and will thus tend to over-calculate interest charges leaving less for the site.
- A residual is not particularly good at capturing the fine grain of costs and values as they arise over the timeline of a development. In that respect it could be thought of as a blunt instrument which is only capable of providing a guide on the value of a site.

2   The steps which could be taken to strengthen the reliability of the outcome from a residual appraisal include:

- Linking the appraisal to a period by period cash flow which enables more precision over the timing and scale of costs and values in a project.
- Conducting a sensitivity test (discussed in Chapter 13) and presenting the results in terms of an array of possible outcomes rather than a single point figure.

3   The correct figures have now been inserted in the shaded boxes below.

Amount available for site in 1 year's time (estimated value less total costs)	£475,000
PV £1 in 1.75 years @ 10%	0.8464
Present amount for site	£402,040
Less site acquisition costs @ 4%	£15,463
Site value today	£386,577

The figures derive from:

- The present value of £1 in 1.75 years is $1/(1.1^{1.75}) = 0.8464$
- $0.8464 \times £475,000 = £402,040$
- Acquisition costs at 4% = £402,040 − (£402,040/1.04) = £15,463
- £402,040 − £15,463 = £386,577

4 The completed monthly cash flow would look as follows and the deficit by the end of month 6 would be £153,573.

Annual borrowing rate:	9%		Monthly equiv. rate:	0.721%

Month	1	2	3	4	5	6
Mthly costs	20,000	22,000	24,000	26,000	28,000	30,000
Balance b. f.	0	20,144	42,448	66,927	93,597	122,474
Tot. mth. exp.	20,000	42,144	66,448	92,927	121,597	152,474
Sales income	0	0	0	0	0	0
Outstand. bal.	−20,000	−42,144	−66,448	−92,927	−121,597	−152,474
Int. on bal.	−144	−304	−479	−670	−877	−1,099
Cumul. bal.	−20,144	−42,448	−66,927	−93,597	−122,474	−153,573

5 The quarterly cash flow has been completed below and it reveals that the present value of the developer's profit: £308,436 is superior to the return to the landowner: £250,000.

Annual borrowing rate:	10%		Quarterly equiv. rate:	2.411%
Annual deposit rate:	2%		Quarterly equiv. rate:	0.496%

Quarter	1	2	3	4	5	6
Qterly costs	250,000	60,000	80,000	120,000	140,000	160,000
Balance b. f.	0	256,028	323,647	413,379	546,239	−64,077
Tot. qt. exp.	250,000	316,028	403,647	533,379	686,239	95,923
Sales income	0	0	0	0	750,000	450,000
Out. balance	−250,000	−316,028	−403,647	−533,379	63,761	354,077
Int. on bal.	−6,028	−7,619	−9,732	−12,860	316	1,756
Cumul. bal.	−256,028	−323,647	−413,379	−546,239	64,077	355,833

Profit arising in 1.5 years	355,833
PV £1 in 1.5 years @ 10%	0.8668
Present value of profit	308,436

Chapter 13

1 In relation to a commercial property portfolio, *systematic risk* arises from movements of the market as a whole. Market fluctuations will result from the interplay of a number of factors, such as the setting of interest rates by the central bank or regional, national or global economic shocks. It is difficult to take action to reduce this aspect of risk.

However *non-systematic risk* has more to do with the type of property and it can to some extent be reduced by the scale of the portfolio and by choosing assets which are dissimilar in their economic performance. Diversification can be achieved by selecting assets which are not perfectly correlated and this will have the effect of reducing non-systematic risk.

2 The standard deviation is a statistical term which describes the degree of dispersal within a distribution around its central tendency. If the standard deviation is a relatively small value in comparison to the central or mean value, then this implies a narrow distribution and reduced risk. Where the standard deviation is a relatively large value in comparison to the central tendency then the distribution is widely spread and this implies added risk.

   Those involved in modelling outcomes in property development or investment might choose to use the standard deviation, particularly if they wish to make a risk-adjusted bid to acquire an asset or site.

   For example, if an appraisal suggests that a site has a value of £5 million, but that the standard deviation about this central value is calculated to be £300,000 a bid of £4.7 million might be made. That bid reflects a position one standard deviation below the core value, within which 34 per cent of the possible values would be found. When the 50 per cent of values lying above the central tendency are added there is statistically an 84 per cent chance that the scheme will correspond to a site value of £4.7 million or better. There would however remain a 16 per cent chance that it will underperform.

   The risk has not been entirely removed but perhaps at a practical level a more sober site bid has been calculated. As for all risk evaluation exercises, the reliability of the output will only be as good as the judgements made by the operator when setting parameters for the exercise.

3 The concept of *beta* derives from financial market analysis where company performance relative to the market (often reflected in an index such as the FTSE 100) is measured. Thus, if the market index rose over a trading period by 5 per cent and a company had a *beta* of 1.5 then it would be expected that the company's share price would rise by 1.5×5 per cent $= 7.5$ per cent. The company is, however, volatile relative to the market, so if the market index fell by 5 per cent then of course it would be expected that the company's share price would fall by around 7.5 per cent. Those involved in strategic investment decisions would be familiar with the concept of *beta* and they would probably try to introduce some diversification in a portfolio by selecting assets with varying *beta* values. There would be significant risks in the event of a downturn if, for example, all of a portfolio's assets were volatile with *beta* values of around 1.5.

4 A *risk premium* in a property investment context reflects the additional interest rate which would need to be added to the risk-free rate available in the markets. The latter is usually measured as the return on index-linked gilts, as index linking removes the corrosive effect of inflation. The risk-free rate will tend to move in harmony with the base rate set by the central bank and it is a rate which is unlikely to excite most investors. The risk premium theoretically compensates investors for the additional risk of investing in assets such as property.

   Although the risk premium will increase as the perception of risk increases, it is not always a straightforward task to determine precisely what an appropriate risk premium should be in any particular set of circumstances. The *Sportelli* case discussed in the chapter arrived at a risk premium for prime central London houses of 4.5 per cent. That rate was added to the risk-free rate at that time of 0.25 per cent to arrive at an overall deferment (or discount) rate of 4.75 per cent. However that rate was only settled upon after the synthesis of contributions made by a number of financial experts and valuers who differed on what the risk premium should be and on the methodology that should be used to determine it.

5 There are some obvious benefits of using software packages such as Crystal Ball® and @RISK® for analysts whose role it is to explore risk to property projects. These packages can rapidly generate distributions around the central tendency of chosen variables in an appraisal using random numbers. Risk-averse positions for key variables can be identified and then inserted into an appraisal to generate a risk-adjusted value or site bid. The modelling exercise will strengthen understanding of a project's characteristics so that, even if the output is ultimately rejected, the analyst will have an improved feel for the risks posed to the project. The final decision is likely to be a better one than if no risk assessment had taken place.

There are of course some disadvantages when using computer supported scenario modelling which users should remain aware of. Once the operator has chosen the variables to explore change in and decided on the parameters, other possibilities tend to become locked out. These initial framing judgements will inevitably come from experience of what has happened in similar situations in the past, although the risks going forward might be entirely different. Modelling at this degree of sophistication can also become an end in itself which has a tendency to induce a blinkered perspective which prevents seeing beyond the parameters set. There is also the problem of snow-blindness in that the weight of data makes it increasingly difficult to detect fundamental errors or poor judgement calls which ultimately invalidate the output.

Chapter 14

1 The gearing formula in the chapter has been used below to identify the return on the developer's equity in the scenario in which the development is earning £500,000 per annum but has accumulated costs of £5 million which need to be re-financed. The calculation shows that the return to equity is considerable at 27 per cent.

$$R_p = (0.15)R_e + (0.85)R_d$$
$$10\% = (0.15)R_e + (0.85)7\%$$
$$R_e = \frac{10\% - 5.95\%}{0.15} = 27\%$$

2 The principal advantage of using debt financing, as shown in Question 1, is that equity can be spread further to earn more for the developer or investor. Thus if the developer had £5 million to invest in the above scheme, the rate of return would be a respectable 10 per cent. However as can be seen in Question 1, by spreading the same equity across several schemes and using that as leverage to support borrowing, a return closer to 27 per cent is possible. Debt financing also limits the return to the funder, because if the scheme does better than expected the funder cannot benefit from the improved performance given that the return on the debt is fixed at 7 per cent of what was loaned.

The principal disadvantages of using debt funding on this scale include the increased risk for the borrower, as the scheme (or schemes) has to preform to meet repayments. An underperforming scheme can reduce or entirely eradicate the returns to equity, as the first call on income will be to service the debt. In the above example 85 per cent of £5 million is being borrowed at 7 per cent so annual repayments will be £297,500. This lies comfortably within the annual income from the scheme, although there is always the latent risk that the tenant could default (for example, by going into liquidation) resulting in the income evaporating entirely. The interest rate is also single-digit and assumed to be fixed. However, where a developer is highly leveraged against floating double-digit interest rates, there could be problems if the rate rises in situations where the margin between income and repayments was already slender.

3   The Annuity £1 will purchase formula below could be used to ascertain whether it would be viable for the developer to use a 10-year commercial mortgage to pay off the development costs using the rental income from the scheme to become its outright owner.

$$\frac{i}{1 - PV}$$

Inserting the values from the question into the formula produces:

$$\frac{0.06}{1 - \left(\dfrac{1}{1.06^{10}}\right)} = 0.135868$$

0.136868 × £3,697,500 (the capital borrowed)

= £502,372 (annual repayments required)

Although not required by the question, the amortisation schedule below proves that it would require annual repayments of £502,372 to pay off the loan over 10 years. Valuation tables could also be consulted to check the answer.

Period	Balance £	Payment £	Interest £	Capital £	End Balance £
1	3,697,500	502,372	221,850	280,522	3,416,978
2	3,416,978	502,372	205,019	297,353	3,119,625
3	3,119,625	502,372	187,178	315,194	2,804,431
4	2,804,431	502,372	168,266	334,106	2,470,325
5	2,470,325	502,372	148,219	354,152	2,116,173
6	2,116,173	502,372	126,970	375,401	1,740,771
7	1,740,771	502,372	104,446	397,925	1,342,846
8	1,342,846	502,372	80,571	421,801	921,045
9	921,045	502,372	55,263	447,109	473,936
10	473,936	502,372	28,436	473,936	0

It would appear that the developer's desire to purchase the development over 10 years using this option is over-ambitious, given that the annual income of £410,000 is well below what would be needed to service the annual loan repayments of £502,372. The developer has also forgone a capital profit in this scenario and has injected a 15 per cent equity stake which is £652,500.

However, if the term of the loan were extended to, say, 15 years then the situation changes as annual payments would then be £380,706 and are within the annual income of £410,000. The difference between the two figures only leaves a modest annual income and the developer would really need other projects to justify the scale of equity input and risk exposure to this particular scheme. There is also a question of whether the developer is predisposed to a 15-year involvement, as longer-term commitments like this are really a characteristic of corporate property investors.

4   Regarding the developer's ambition to retain an interest in the scheme which is producing an annual income of £800,000 there are a number of options, which include refinancing the outstanding costs with an interest-only loan at 6 per cent. This

would enable the developer to hold the property up to the first rent review and then to sell it to capture the capital growth at that point. Meanwhile, the refinanced debt would attract annual interest payments at 6 per cent of £6,910,000 which is £414,600. Adding the ground rent of £75,000 the total outgoing would be £489,600 leaving a return of £310,000 from the scheme's net income of £800,000.

There are of course other alternatives, such as using a commercial mortgage to buy the project outright with, say, a loan at 80 per cent of the debt (£5,528,000). This assumes the developer has the 20 per cent equity to contribute. Assuming a capital and interest repayment loan at a fixed rate of 6 per cent, the buy-out option could be achieved in 11 years with annual payments of just over £700,000 leaving a sufficient balance to pay the ground rent of £75,000. However, there would be little remaining for the developer until the first rent review, which might change the situation. In the meantime, the developer would need alternative income sources.

5   In a horizontal slicing arrangement priority is given to the landowner and funder who generally have first call on the income from a scheme proportionate to their stake. These stakeholders therefore benefit from less risk exposure but at the same time they cannot benefit from the buoyancy of a scheme, so that if it does better than expected then that enhanced performance is captured by the developer who generally takes the riskier top slice.

In a side-by-side or vertical slicing arrangement the parties are all exposed to the buoyancy of the scheme, so if it does better than expected they can all share in that relative to their proportionate stake. Conversely because they are all risk-exposed (and in that sense they are all equity stakeholders) if the scheme underperforms they all suffer proportionately. For these reasons the slicing arrangements for major schemes like shopping centres are carefully negotiated and may end up containing elements of horizontal and vertical slicing.

Bibliography

Armatys, J., Askham, P. and Green, M. (2009) *Principles of Valuation* (London: EG Books).

Banfield, A. (2009) *Valuation on Quarterly in Advance Basis and True Equivalent Yield* (Reading: College of Estate Management).

Baum, A. and Crosby, N. (2008) *Property Investment Appraisal*, 3rd edn (Oxford: Blackwell).

Baum, A., Mackmin, D. and Nunnington, N. (2011) *The Income Approach to Property Valuation*, 6th edn (Oxford: EG Books).

Blackledge, M. (2009) *Introducing Property Valuation* (Abingdon: Routledge).

British Land Company plc (2012) *Annual Report and Accounts, 2012* (London: British Land Company plc).

Brundtland Commission (1987) *World Commission on Environment and Development: Our Common Future* (Oxford: Oxford University Press).

Byrne, P. (1996) *Risk, Uncertainty and Decision-making in Property Development*, 2nd edn (London: Taylor & Francis).

Chan, N. and Harker, N. (2012) 'Dual Rate Taxed Valuation: A More Rational Approach', *Journal of Property Investment and Finance*, 30(2), pp. 105–14.

Chegut, A., Eichholtz, P. and Kok, N. (2012) *Supply, Demand and the Value of Green Buildings*, *RICS Research Report* (London: Royal Institution of Chartered Surveyors).

Dartford Borough Council (2012) *Dartford Community Infrastructure Levy – Draft Charging Schedule* (Dartford: Dartford Borough Council).

Davidson, A. (2013) *Parry's Valuation and Investment Tables*, 13th edn (London: Estates Gazette).

Department for Communities and Local Government (2012) *National Planning Policy Framework* (London: Department for Communities and Local Government).

Department for Communities and Local Government (2012) *Review of the Barriers to Institutional Investment in Private Rented Homes (Montague report)* (London: Department for Communities and Local Government).

Dubben, N. (2008) 'Development Properties', in R. Hayward (ed.) *Valuation: Principles into Practice*, 6th edn (London: EG Books).

Dubben, N. and Williams, B. (2009) *Partnerships in Urban Property Development* (Oxford: Wiley-Blackwell).

Enever, N., Isaac, D. and Daley, M. (2010) *The Valuation of Property Investments*, 7th edn (London: Estates Gazette).

Fraser, W.D. (2004) *Cash-Flow Appraisal for Property Investment* (Basingstoke: Palgrave Macmillan).

French, N. (2011) 'Valuing in the Downturn: Understanding Uncertainty', *Journal of Property Investment & Finance*, 29(3), 428–47.

GENECON LLP and Partners (2011) *Understanding High Street Performance* (London: Department for Business, Innovation and Skills).

Havard, T. (2004) *Investment Property Valuation Today* (London: Estates Gazette).

Hubbard, C.C. (2008) 'Leasehold Enfranchisement', in R. Hayward (ed.) *Valuation: Principles into Practice*, 6th edn (London: EG Books).

Investment Property Databank Ltd (2012) *IPD UK Annual Property Index* (to 31.12.11) (London: IPD).

Investment Property Forum (2012) *Real Estate's Role in the Mixed-Asset Portfolio: A Re-examination* (London: Investment Property Forum).

Isaac, D. and O'Leary, J. (2011) *Property Investment*, 2nd edn (Basingstoke: Palgrave Macmillan).

Isaac, D. and O'Leary, J. (2012) *Property Valuation Principles*, 2nd edn (Basingstoke: Palgrave Macmillan).

Jayne, M.R. (2008) 'Rating', in R. Hayward (ed.), *Valuation: Principles into Practice*, 6th edn (London: EG Books).

Jones Lang LaSalle (2002) *The Glossary of Property Terms*, 2nd edn (London: Estates Gazette).

Lands Tribunal (2006) *Leasehold Enfranchisement Appeal Decision Regarding Sportelli and Others* (LRA/50/2005) (London: Lands Tribunal).

Leasehold Valuation Tribunal of the Midland Rent Assessment Panel (2008) *Zuckerman and Others* v. *Trustees of the Calthorpe Estate, Lease Extension Decision Regarding Properties at Carpenter Road, Edgbaston (BIR/00CN/OLR/2008/0013-0032)* (Birmingham: Midland Rent Assessment Panel).

London Borough of Camden (2010) *Local Development Framework – Camden Development Policies 2010–2025* (London: Camden Council).

Loizou, P. and French, N. (2012) 'Risk and Uncertainty in Development: A Critical Evaluation of using Monte Carlo Simulation Method as a Decision Tool in Real Estate Development Projects', *Journal of Property Investment & Finance*, 30(2), 198–210.

Lorenz, D. and Lützkendorf, T. (2011) 'Sustainability and Property Valuation: Systematisation of Existing Approaches and Recommendations for Future Action', *Journal of Property Investment and Finance*, 29(6), 644–76.

Markowitz, H. (1959) *Portfolio Selection – Efficient Diversification of Investments* (New Haven, CT: Yale University Press).

Marshall, P. (1989) *Donaldson's Investment Tables* (London: Donaldson's).

Monk, S. and Burgess, G. (2012) *Capturing Planning Gain – The Transition from Section 106 to the Community Infrastructure Levy* (London: Royal Institution of Chartered Surveyors).

Office for National Statistics (2012) *Statistical Bulletin: Consumer Price Indices, June 2012* (London: Office for National Statistics).

Parsons, G. (2005) *EG Property Handbook* (London: EG Books).

Portas, M. (2011) *The Portas Review: An Independent Review into the Future of our High Streets* (London: Department for Business, Innovation and Skills).

RICS (2008) *Valuation of Development Land – Valuation Information Paper 12* (Coventry: Royal Institution of Chartered Surveyors).

RICS (2009) *Leasehold Reform: Graphs of Relativity, RICS Research Report* (London: Royal Institution of Chartered Surveyors)

RICS (2009) *Sustainability and Commercial Property Valuation, Valuation Information Paper No. 13* (Coventry: Royal Institution of Chartered Surveyors).

RICS (2010) *Discounted Cash Flow for Commercial Property Investments* (London: Royal Institution of Chartered Surveyors).

RICS (2010) *Valuation of Land for Affordable Housing – RICS Guidance Note* (Coventry: Royal Institution of Chartered Surveyors).

RICS (2011) *Leasehold Reform in England and Wales: Guidance Note*, 2nd edn (London: Royal Institution of Chartered Surveyors).

RICS (2011) *Sustainability and Residential Property Valuation, RICS Information Paper* (Coventry: Royal Institution of Chartered Surveyors).

RICS (2012) *Comparable Evidence in Property Valuation – Information Paper* (Coventry: Royal Institution of Chartered Surveyors).

RICS (2012) *Financial Viability in Planning – RICS Guidance Note* (Coventry: Royal Institution of Chartered Surveyors).

RICS (2012) *RICS Valuation – Professional Standards* (Coventry: Royal Institution of Chartered Surveyors).

Rose, J. (1979) *Tables of the Constant Rent* (Oxford: The Technical Press).

Saunders, O. (2011) *Valuation Calculations: 101 Worked Examples*, 2nd edn (Coventry: Royal Institution of Chartered Surveyors).

Scarrett, D. (2008) *Property Valuation: The Five Methods*, 2nd edn (Abingdon: Routledge).

Shapiro, E., Mackmin, D. and Sams, G. (2012) *Modern Methods of Valuation*, 11th edn (London: Estates Gazette)

Treanor, D. (2009) *Housing Investment Appraisal*, 2nd edn (London: National Housing Federation).

Warren-Myers, G. (2012) 'The Value of Sustainability in Real Estate: A Review from a Valuation Perspective', *Journal of Property Investment and Finance*, 30(2), 115–44.

Wiggins, K. (2000) *Discounted Cash Flow: The Principles and the Practice* (Reading: College of Estate Management).

Wyatt, J. (2011) 'Property Risk Premia and Deferment Rates', *Journal of Property Investment and Finance*, 29(3), 323–30.

Wyatt, P. (2007) *Property Valuation in an Economic Context* (Oxford: Blackwell).

Index

Printed and bound in Great Britain by
CPI Antony Rowe, Chippenham and Eastbourne